PROFITABLE PROPERTIES

AIRBNB INSIDER SECRETS

TO **FIND, OPTIMIZE, PRICE,** & **BOOK DIRECT** ANY SHORT-TERM RENTAL INVESTMENT FOR **YEAR-ROUND OCCUPANCY**

Rusteen, Daniel V.

Supercharge your short-term rental by visiting:
www.OptimizeMyBnb.com

Book website:
www.OptimizeMyBnb.com/Profitable-Properties

Daniel Rusteen is available for speaking engagements and conferences. To inquire about a possible appearance, please contact OptimizeMyBnb.com LLC at media@optimizemybnb.com.

First edition: April 2023

ISBN 978-0-9997155-7-4 (paperback)
ISBN 978-0-9997155-8-1 (hardcover)
Also available in digital and audio

Printed in the U.S.A

Interior Page Design: Ljiljana Pavkov
Editor: Michael Sanders
Cover Design: Syril Lagapa Pulido

CONTENTS

PROFITABLE PROPERTIES

XII. READER BONUS

Thank you for purchasing my second book all about short-term rental success! You're in for a real treat. If you purchased my first book *Optimize YOUR Bnb: The Definitive Guide To Ranking #1 in Airbnb Search (OMBNB)* then you read a similar message offering a bundle of free goodies. I want to keep that tradition alive. As a thank you for purchasing, I'd like to offer you a new bundle of free goodies.

1. In *Chapter 4.6 Amenities*, I talk at length about, well, amenities. I sell a list-format version of this chapter on my website for $125, and you can download it for free with the QR code below. You'll receive two versions, one for standard and one for luxury rentals, both organized by room and separated into required and optional amenities.

2. A Deal Sheet containing my preferred STR tools, all of which I personally use, is also claimable with the same QR code below. Most categories have only one recommendation. All come with a discount, and many of these partners have increased it for my readers. This comes out to over $1,000 in discounts from 14 companies. I refrain from mentioning most recommended tools by name, instead opting to reveal them in the bonus items, so that I can easily change or update any recommendation, as needed, in this ever-evolving industry.

3. *Featured Product Discounts* (explained below) worth $840 to my online store.

4. Plus, you will find eight additional free bonus items throughout the book in relevant sections, some of which include:

   • Profitability spreadsheet I used to analyze and buy *The Belmonte Penthouse*
   • Behind-the-scenes video

- Negative review response game with examples
- All photos from the book in color
- Booking Lead Time spreadsheet

Download your bonus items by scanning the QR code or clicking 'Claim Bonus' at www.OptimizeMyBnb.com/Profitable-Properties.

XI. QR CODES

Unlike *OMBNB,* I won't be slowing down your reading fun with a bunch of, often outdated, URLs that you have to manually type into your browser. Throughout *Profitable Properties*, you'll find QR codes which will bring you to bonus items, useful resources, or relevant videos. Using QR codes will allow me to easily update any URL so nothing is ever out-of-date.

Upon scanning a 'bonus item' QR code with your mobile phone, I will ask where you'd like me to send the bonus items. Once you share and confirm your email, all will be instantly delivered to your inbox. No need to scan various 'bonus item' QR codes as you will have access to everything upon the first request.

X. FEATURED PRODUCT DISCOUNTS

I have been in business helping hosts all over the world make more money since 2016. During that time, I have created products that provide an edge over the competition or, simply, make life easier. Throughout *Profitable Properties* I will mention all of these products and offer a special discount.

In total you will find seven *Featured Product Discounts* with discounts ranging from **5%** to **60%** which comes to more than **$840** in total.

IX. DISCLAIMER

All opinions and advice in this book are solely those of the author, provided "as-is", and do not reflect the opinion of Airbnb, Booking.com, VRBO, HomeAway, or any other company mentioned herein. The author has no relationship with Airbnb. This book is for educational purposes only. Care has been taken to ensure the information in this book is true and correct as of the time of publication. Any changes to the Airbnb platform made after the time of publication may impact the accuracy of the information contained herein. The author assumes no liability of any kind with respect to the completeness or accuracy of the contents. The author cannot be held liable by, or responsible to, any person or entity with respect to any loss or incidental or consequential damages caused by or alleged to have been caused directly or indirectly by the information contained herein. The author does not offer professional advice as it related to legal, accounting, or any other service.

VIII. FOREWORD BY BRIAN PAGE OF BNB FORMULA, #1 RENTAL ARBITRAGE COURSE

One of the perks of founding the world's leading short term rental educational company is that I get to meet many of the great thought leaders in our industry. Although I've known Danny for many years, it wasn't until this past year that I had the opportunity to introduce him to my clients and invite him to share his extensive knowledge with our community.

We co-hosted a live training call with the goal of optimizing listings for our members. After fixing the first three listings presented to him, I was astounded by his wealth of knowledge of how to increase the profitability and effectiveness of listings. His knowledge of short-term rentals (STRs) goes beyond simply updating pictures or tweaking titles. He has a gift for combining high level hospitality principles with industry leading tools in order to give hosts a market-leading advantage on the home sharing platforms.

His first book, Optimize YOUR Bnb, has become a classic in the industry. It's a book that is constantly recommended to my students who are either looking to improve their listings or determine which tools they'll need to automate their rapidly growing businesses.

Since Optimize YOUR Bnb was first published, there have been massive shifts in the STR industry.

There is much to be learned from how the top hotels and resorts run their properties. From quality control and hospitality principles to everyday operations, best practices can be applied by "citizen hoteliers" as they carve out their own small domains. Danny is one of the first people I have heard talk about these changes. He remains at the forefront of this rapidly evolving industry and has once again put together a practical and comprehensive guide to help hosts navigate these changes and ultimately find more success. My hope is that you will learn from and apply what you find in the following pages for a more profitable property. Enjoy!

Brian Page,
Founder of the BNB Formula,
#1 Rental Arbitrage Course

VII. ABOUT THE AUTHOR

It's December 2012, and I'm a 24-year-old unemployed Certified Public Accountant. I quit my job at a public accounting firm a week ago. It would be the last time I did that in a decade.

My life was about to change drastically beyond imagination with a 15-second conversation.

I'm making lunch one Saturday afternoon in my San Francisco 4-bedroom apartment when my roommate walks in....

"You ever heard of Airbed and Breakfast?"

"Nope, what is it?"

"They allow you to rent a room in somebody's home when you're traveling."

Bingo. This idea had legs, as we say in Silicon Valley.

It clicked. I don't know what exactly clicked, or why. But, the lightbulb lit up above my head.

At the time, I was thinking about it in terms of being the guest. That's how I liked to travel. I liked to do more authentic things, so staying with a local person seemed awesome.

One of my first Airbnb stays shortly thereafter would be with a single Korean mother in Seoul. She asked me to bring her a few English children books for her child, and I obliged.

I walked in a local park. I went to a local shopping mall and market.

I was the only non-Korean there.

I slept on a floor mat that night.

It was awesome.

Long story short, I pursued Airbnb for employment. After four months, two openings, and eighteen interviews they hired me, employee #700. A few short years later, the company had 7,500 employees.

I worked both in the accounting and marketing departments.

These experiences gave me a unique perspective on Airbnb—the company—and how it operates from two different departments.

After Airbnb, I started working for a local property management company eventually hiring out a team of 10 and managing 75 Airbnb listings.

A year later, I was ready to move on.

I started a property management company that focuses on Airbnb. I still run that company today, but now I do so fully remote and never manage more than five Airbnbs at a time. It's where I test out my latest strategies to see what works and what doesn't.

Through that experience I noticed a clear correlation between listing quality and search rank. Another light bulb went on, and I started testing out a digital product designed to help STR owners rank high in Airbnb search.

I called it an "Airbnb Listing Optimization" and sold the first version on July 26, 2016. I earned $5, and it took me 45 minutes.

That business is essentially what I do now except it has grown into a service encompassing a lot more, in fact most everything that touches every facet of your Airbnb operation with the one goal of helping you rank number one in Airbnb search. Today, I also charge a bit more than five bucks.

More than any other expert, I know Airbnb from the inside as an employee, as a property manager, as a Superhost, as a super guest, and as a vacation rental investor.

Super guest? In 2017, I started living in short-term rentals and Airbnbs on a permanent basis, and to date, I have spent more than 2,000 nights living this lifestyle. No other expert in the world can say that. It gives me a unique perspective as an active Airbnb guest. I know how to please guests, and I know how to evade problems, and I know how to navigate them when they do arise.

In 2018, I published my first ever book *Optimize YOUR Bnb: The Definitive Guide To Ranking #1 In Airbnb Search*. I didn't know what I was doing, but I did it anyway, and I'm glad I did.

In 2021, I purchased my own rental in Medellin, Colombia. I call it *The Belmonte Penthouse,* and it has been a phenomenal investment returning 27% last year and an even more phenomenal learning experience. If I thought I knew it all with my experience up until being an STR owner, wow, was I wrong! Being the property owner comes with its own distinct learnings, and I have learned so much since that purchase.

(In *Part 2: Vacation Rental Market Analysis*, I highlight that investment decision and apply it to an overall strategy that you can use for your next vacation rental investment.)

That brings us to today. I travel the world as a guest, I create content about my experiences, I hang out with my community via the course, and I occasionally drop into a live STR event.

I'm glad you've found me, and I hope you'll join me on this journey as it appears that I'm on it for life. Let's do this!

VI. SELF-PUBLISHED BOOK

I'm what you call an "indie" author. Indie authors self-publish their books. When you self-publish, you go through the book writing, production, and marketing parts on your own (feel sorry, very sorry for me! Kidding!). That is not a complaint. In fact, I had an offer from a publisher for this book due to the success of my last book. I turned it down.

I did so because I would have had less say resulting, in my opinion, in an inferior end product. A traditional publisher wants a more general book which can be purchased by the general public. That is not this book. Although this book is lengthy, it's as short as I could make it while containing everything I needed to communicate. With a traditional publisher, I would have had to reduce it substantially.

I've been writing consistently ever since I started a personal journal in 7th grade. In high school and college, I got poor grades in writing classes. A teacher once accused me of cheating because my writing on one particular assignment wasn't terrible. I suppose I'm not supposed to be an author, but I've always enjoyed the act of writing. It can be therapeutic and helps you organize your thoughts.

With that said, grammar and spellcheck are not my forte. Did you know that books from publishers typically use five different editors? Crazy, huh. Well, I hired one. If you count me, that's two. I apologize in advance for any grammatical errors (although I'm confident there are very few!), some of which made some readers very upset in the last book (I read all reviews, many of them various times). I encourage you to tell me privately of these errors when you find them so that I can correct them (I can correct them). Being an indie author also means that I'm not super famous. You can actually message me directly via social media or my website. Although annoying, I think of them the same way I think of learning a second language (which is the topic of my third book): am I communicating ideas clearly and being understood?

Finally, an indie book does not have a marketing team behind it. *OMBNB* did as well as it did because of you, the reader, 100%. The sales were due to word-of-mouth and thoughtful, lengthy reviews which Amazon, like Airbnb, highly covets. Thank you for talking about my book, for posting it to your Facebook groups and in forums. It's the only way this book will be successful. I really do read every review, and I look forward to reading yours soon.

I want to present the first, admittedly a bit corny, bonus. A week after I decided to write this book, I also decided to create a new website, release my first course, and intensely focus on growing my video content with two videos per day. Plus, some personal issues requiring a lot of time sprang up. Honestly, it was way too much. I had no life for a period of five

Bonus Item – "behind-the-scenes" video

SCAN ME

months which turned out to be the single busiest time in my entire life. In total, this book took me nearly one thousand hours for you to be reading it. If you'd like to watch the behind-the-scenes video of me writing this book in 17 different cities and six countries, please scan the QR code.

V. DIFFERENCES FROM *OPTIMIZE YOUR BNB*

In 2018, I published *Optimize YOUR Bnb: The Definitive Guide To Ranking #1 In Airbnb Search*. It became the best-seller with more than 50,000 copies sold across print, digital, and audio.

Back then, you could have posted a vacation rental listing in most markets around the world and seen success as there was little competition. Today, a large part of your success comes before you even put the rental online. That's why I've dedicated an entire section to locating not only profitable vacation rental markets anywhere in the world, but also on finding the right neighborhood and profitable property for ultimate success. This will be covered in *Part 2: Vacation Rental Market Analysis*.

Profitable Properties is for both new and existing short-term rental owners, as well as those interested in the industry. One of the biggest changes is that it's applicable more broadly than just to Airbnb. I signed up for Booking.com, VRBO, and a few other online travel agencies (OTAs) in preparation for this book. I am still a specialist in Airbnb, and, when a section only applies to that platform, I will say so.

In additional to using more platforms, I've also started not using any. This is called direct booking, and I have an entire section dedicated to it.

The direct booking option has gained in popularity among both hosts and guests and justly so. Airbnb is not going away, but they have created the market and the opportunity for change. Unlike the past, today, it is now easy to do many things yourself that once only the platforms provided. I am now a proponent for the majority of hosts getting a direct booking website. This is a big departure from my prior stance which argued for staying on one platform, usually Airbnb. In *Part 6: Direct Bookings,* I'll go over who might want to pursue this strategy, who it's not right for, and how to secure direct bookings as easily as possible.

I've noticed an intense interest and general confusion from the host community on all things pricing. The good news is that I consider myself highly qualified on this subject and have developed a refined, effective, and straightforward strategy for a variety of situations that I will present to you in *Part 5: Pricing.* All of your questions and then some will be answered.

In *Part 8: How To Rank #1 On Airbnb,* for the first time ever, I will reveal the Airbnb algorithm to you. This is specific to Airbnb, but one can imagine it is mostly relevant for all OTAs. I list the top 13 ranking factors, in order, based on my research and experience working at the company, as an employee, as a guest and property manager, Superhost, and optimizer of over a thousand listings in more than 100 countries. There are going to be surprises for you there, I'm sure of it.

But don't fret, it's not all brand-new information.

For example, photos were and still are very important. The only difference is that today, with an hour of study and a new smartphone, you don't need to hire a professional photographer. I discuss this topic in the longest chapter of the book: *Chapter 3.5 Photos.*

Unlike in *OMBNB,* I have decided not to include directly in the book the name of the various partners and tools that I recommend, use myself, and know will help your short-term rental business. Instead they will all appear in the Deal Sheet of the bonus items. The industry is growing fast, and many of the companies mentioned in the prior book either no longer exist, or I no longer recommend them. This will allow me to more easily keep it up-to-date and relevant.

If you never bought the first book, you may be wondering if you should. You should if Airbnb will play a major role in your business. That's because I wrote *OMBNB* for intermediate and advanced Airbnb hosts, only talked about the Airbnb platform, and referenced very specific things about that platform. You will find similar information in both books for foundational concepts like title, text, and photos, but if the information hasn't changed significantly, the information will remain only in *OMBNB*. If you decide to buy the first book, you can skip the following chapters: 8, 24, 26, 29, 37, 40.

IV. THE PROFITABLE PROPERTIES COURSE

Another huge difference is that I'm releasing, in conjunction with this book, my first online course. As an early purchaser of this book, you will be receiving a 50% discount code good for the first three months from the time of publication and claimable in the bonus items.

You can think of the course as an extension of this book with an interactive environment. For the first three months, I will be doing weekly live video calls with course members. I'm dedicated to helping you start off strong or level up your existing rental.

If you are looking to invest in a rental, but are not sure where, one module will be particularly interesting for you. I'll be documenting my search to find the most profitable markets around the world, starting with the USA, where I plan to purchase my next short-term rental this year. Let's do this together!

Scan the QR code to learn more.

The Profitable Properties "Optimized Business" Course

SCAN ME

III. TERMINOLOGY

Below is terminology that will appear throughout the book. Some concepts and definitions were created by me and are identified as such. These are followed by general terms for the vacation rental industry. You can skip this section for now and return as needed.

OptimizeMyBnb.com Terminology

50% Rule – Has to do with respecting the guests' attention (See *Chapter 1.9 The Vacation Rental Commandments*) and conversion. Hosts have the tendency to add too much text, too many check-out instructions and house rules, etc. In general, only include info that applies to 50% or more of guests.

For example, adding a house rule to not make excessive noise or that illegal drugs are not allowed violates the 50% rule. If one reservation in twenty makes too much noise or you suspect uses illegal drugs, I would argue you should not add this text as it doesn't apply to 95% of the reservations and will have little effect on the 5% of guest's behavior. By adding it, you are taking the guest's limited attention from things that are probably more important.

The exception is very important info which maybe even be need to be communicated more than once.

If you have to add something for legal reasons, then the Hierarchy concept (explained below) becomes relevant.

Flexibility Concept – Another way to think about occupancy. In an ideal situation, you have such a popular, successful listing that you can restrict your pool of FPGs (future potential guests) while charging the highest rates and maintaining high occupancy. This ideal situation would be considered an inflexible listing. An inflexible listing reduces your general risk (fewer bad guests thus less liability, damage, etc.) by only allowing the very best guests to book.

On the other hand, increasing your listing flexibility will increase your pool of FPGs, your probability of receiving a reservation, and thus your risk. To increase your listing's flexibility, you might lower your minimum nights, liberalize your cancellation policy, or make your space pet- or child-friendly.

During slow season you *might* want to make your listing more flexible due to an expected decrease in FPGs. But you may also do this during high season. It depends on your occupancy. If your occupancy drops, increase your listing flexibility.

The most powerful way to increase your listing's flexibility—but what we try to avoid—is by lowering the price.

FPG – Future Potential Guest; all potential vacation rental guests who have the ability to book your listing. When an FPG makes a reservation, they turn into a future guest. The term is a continuum. At one end, you have every human on the planet who takes a vacation and looks to make a reservation on a short-term rental platform like Airbnb. On the other end, you have a narrow selection of potential ideal guests who meet your criteria to book (already positively reviewed, 25+ years old, budget of $300 per night, no pet, etc.).

Hierarchy – When I reference the hierarchy whether it's for text, the digital guidebook, or photos, I'm referring to the relationship between the placement on the page and the likelihood the guest will see whatever you're trying to communicate. Most people read left to right (titles) and top to bottom so we want to put the most important information in the top/left and follow it, in order of importance, to the bottom/right. For example, if I was building out a summary text section, I would put the most important feature at the top, followed by the second most important, and so on.

Level 1, 2, 3 Host – I break out vacation rental owners into three levels. The levels refer to the total value or offer. It refers simultaneously to the host, the space, and the hospitality. Think of it as guest comfort.

- *Level 1.* Essentials are provided (bed, Wi-Fi, water, non-leaky roofs, etc.). It's a no-frills space. This does not mean it's a poorly reviewed listing even though these are more likely to receive low reviews due to mismanaged expectations.

- *Level 2.* The majority of hosts are here. This host is more conscious of the guest experience and thinking of their rental more as a business which requires investment and improvement. There are more non-essential amenities provided to increase the guest experience and spaces are better used.

- *Level 3.* The preeminent difference for this host is their mindset. They are thinking about potentialities (like what *might* the FPG want to be more comfortable). They know that every problem has a solution and one that both benefits the host and the guest. Providing numerous Surprise and Delight features (explained below) is a telltale sign of a Level 3 host.

New Listing Calendar Strategy (NLCS) – Please refer to *7.22 What Is The New Listing Calendar Strategy?* for a more detailed explanation.

One-of-a-Hundred – As a short-term rental owner, you have a hundred decisions to make. They're all individually important, but not one decision alone will make you a success. Instead, those hosts who consider and correctly act on the most decisions will experience the greatest success.

Optimized Airbnb – This is the service I'm most known for, the best seller on my website, and the first product ever offered. It consists of an overall look at your online listing and presence. It's meant to help you rank high, specifically in Airbnb search, by presenting your offer as clearly as possible to your ideal

FPGs while leveraging and incorporating as much as possible my most relevant and recent hacks of Airbnb. Optimized Airbnb comes in two options:

- *Super Host Listing Optimization (SHO)* – The most customized option where I examine both the front end and back end settings and implement the majority of changes on your behalf.

- *Advanced Host Listing Optimization (AHO)* – This option is semi-custom where I examine P2 (explained below) of your online listing and offer specific changes and recommendations for you to implement.

Optimized Business – The Profitable Properties course.

Optimized Host – My most premium service. Introduced as an overall look at your operation to both decrease your workload by automating where possible while improving the guest experience and increasing your income with an additional focus on pricing strategy. It comes with face-to-face time with me to ensure success.

Spaces – Unique portions of a property. For example, an open-design concept living/dining/kitchen is one room, but three or more spaces. If your outdoor area has a pool area, a BBQ area, and a cabana or hammocks, that would be three unique, individual spaces. I want you to start thinking in spaces, not rooms.

A 'space' is anywhere in the house that can be considered its own usable area. Each additional space increases the usefulness and perceived size of your rental. Many 'spaces' are easily added like a hammock or reading nook.

Surprise and Delight (S+D) – These are, generally, amenities that are not advertised publicly but revealed to the guest upon arrival to their surprise or delight. They are not advertised publicly because they're not things that will secure the booking, and we don't want to use the FPGs' limited attention on them, instead they are bonuses better revealed upon check-in. In *The Belmonte Penthouse*, one of my surprise and delight features are bubbles for the jacuzzi. A common surprise and delight feature is a welcome gift.

Troubleshooting – When I refer to troubleshooting your vacation rental, I'm referring to an individual rental and its associated online listing. All problems can be solved by taking this three-step approach. First, and easiest to do, ask yourself if your online listing is up-to-date, accurate, following this book's best practices, and converting highly. Second, examine your reviews. In *Chapter 3.10 How To Remove a Negative Review*, we will discuss why anything below a 4.95 represents opportunity for potential improvement. Third is pricing. If both the listing and reviews are in order, and you're still not happy with your occupancy, it means your price is too high. This could mean you are in slow season or a bad market.

The Belmonte Penthouse – My first vacation rental. A luxury apartment in Medellin, Colombia. I quadrupled the prior owner's income, and I will use this experience as an example throughout the book.

Industry Terminology

Booking/Reservation – When the FPG sends payment, they make a reservation, and become a future guest.

Booking Lead Time (BLT) – An important concept as it relates to pricing and occupancy. Each listing has a unique BLT which represents, in days, the amount of time in advance of check-in the reservation is completed. For example, a reservation that is confirmed today on January 1st with a check-in date of January 20th has a BLT of 20 days. The more important metric is the average BLT for your listing. We cover this in detail in *Part 5: Pricing*.

Demand – One side of the vacation rental marketplace, referring to the number of guests trying to book the available rentals in a market. I find that demand is often missing from host analysis. We will go over this in *Part 2: Vacation Rental Market Analysis*.

Dynamic Pricing Tool – Software that connects to your rental and changes the nightly rates on your listing based on seasonality, market factors, and specific listing data. Also referred to as Intelligent Pricing Tool. Not to be confused with Airbnb's Smart Pricing which is included on the Airbnb platform as a free service and generally underprices your rental.

Host – The term 'host' was made popular by the Online Travel Agency (OTA) Airbnb, and it describes someone who has available space to rent out on a short-term basis. Generally, I'm referring to the owner or operator of the vacation rental. This could be the property manager or co-host.

Listing – I'm talking about the online publication on an OTA. It could be a shared or private bedroom or an entire home. If I'm referring to the physical space or location, I will say rental, vacation rental, or short-term rental.

Medium-Term Rental (MTR) – Generally, these are multi-month reservations. Confusion comes from Airbnb offering a "long-term" discount to reservations of 28 nights or longer.

OTA – Online Travel Agency. It's the platform where FPGs and hosts meet. They are Airbnb, Booking, VRBO, Furnished Finder, etc.

P1, P2, P3 – Although the term was created by Airbnb, all OTAs follow the same website layout. P1, P2, and P3 refer to the three pages before the guest can reserve your listing. By understanding how the platform works from the guest perspective we can better optimize our online listing. P1 is the home page.

P2 is the search page with the map. It's where the OTA presents the FPG with many listing options. P3 is the listing page where the FPG make a reservation.

PMS – Property Management System. They help the host sync calendars, listing details, and more between OTAs. They also allow for automatic messages, automatic reviews, cleaner and maintenance coordination, building of direct booking websites, and more. They're an essential and affordable tool for all hosts whether they have one or many listings.

Rental Arbitrage – The process of taking on a lease as a renter and subleasing that space out to short-term rental guests. The difference between what the owner is charging the long-term renter and what the renter is earning as a short-term rental host is the arbitrage, or revenue.

STR – Short-term rental. Also used: vacation rental or property rental to mean the same thing. I prefer using STRs because it's more encompassing. To me, a vacation rental is exclusive to a vacation destination. STRs receive reservations from one night to about a month in length. This is different from traditional long-term renting to tenants on an annual basis.

Supply – One side of the vacation rental marketplace, referring to the number of rentals available for guests.

II. SHOULD YOU BECOME A SHORT-TERM RENTAL HOST?

Let's assume you've been thinking about starting your own short-term rental and have a lot of questions. I'm going to tell you the basics required to be a successful host. If it turns out you're not cut out to be one, then I hope to communicate that to you in this section and save you time, money, and headache.

Let's start with an anecdote. Here is my favorite review of *OMBNB*:

 DEB

 Talked us right out of having a B and B.
Reviewed in the United States on December 17, 2021
Verified Purchase

Lots of cautionary words.

There are an alarming number of bad or bare-minimum hosts. Deb probably would have been one of them.

I probably saved Deb a lot of wasted time, money, and headache.

I am not here to convince you to go buy a rental property and that this business is passive and easy money. Quite the opposite. While STRS are great money, they are not passive. If you go into it with that mindset (see *Chapter 1.4 The Right Mindset*) you will not be pleased.

This chapter will help you understand whether or not becoming a host will be a profitable idea for you.

You're probably already familiar with Airbnb, the most popular OTA.

Essentially, it's an online platform that connects buyers and sellers just like Amazon, Craigslist, and E-Bay.

The buyers, or FPGs, are people looking to rent space on a short-term basis. They do not have to be tourists. They can be your neighbor who has work being done on her house, is going through a divorce, or has parents coming to town.

Sellers, or hosts, are owners of vacation rentals and interested in renting on a short-term basis.

If this is all totally new to you, and you aspire to be a host, you should use an OTA like Airbnb to stay at least once as a guest. In fact, it is my best practice to stay as a guest twice per year, including in my own rental.

A Brief Summary of This Chapter

For this chapter, I am assuming you are either fully unfamiliar with renting or you have only rented on a long-term basis in the past. I am also assuming that *if* you decide to be a host, you want to be one of the best in your market which means you want to make the most money.

The following chapter is exhaustive. You will not know every-thing I'm talking about. You may feel overwhelmed. This chap-ter is not to convince you to be a host. It is to weed out those who are unfit.

This chapter will introduce a lot of new information to help you decide if renting your space on a short-term basis makes sense for you and your situation.

I will explain both the positives and the negatives.

Especially the negatives! There are plenty of passive Airbnb pushers.

There are issues you need to consider that are specific to short-term renting such as specific legalities, if it's allowed in your building or city, tax issues, security deposit issues, cleaning, visitor policy, emergency maintenance issues, parking, etc.

But in the end, it will all come down to these two questions:

1. How risk averse are you? Income is not consistent on a monthly basis, and many strangers will enter your home.
2. How hands-off do you want to be? Some people actually want to interact with the guests while others want to be totally hands-off. For the latter, in *Part 4: Elevate Your Hospitality*, I will discuss whether or not you want to hire a property management company and how to identify a good one.

A Closer Look at Short- vs. Long-Term Rentals

Monthly Income. The amount of income will be wildly dif-ferent from month to month. You will experience slow and busy seasons.

In slow seasons you might charge 50% of the nightly rate you would in busy seasons, and your occupancy could be equally as low. In slow seasons you *may* make less than you would on a traditional rental, but in busy months, you will make two to five times more than you would on a long-term rental.

Furnished Space and Amenities. STRs are furnished. You can go budget or luxury, but you must furnish as well as provide extras like an iron, bath towels, dish soap, slippers, black-out curtains, blender, etc. Some are optional, but this is a huge difference between long-term rentals and a potential competitive advantage for your future STR. Many hosts even purchase a Netflix subscription for their guests.

More Costs and Maintenance. That you have to spend money to make money is no truer than here. Along with the two to five times higher income comes more expenses. You will have linen expenses when the guest damages a towel. If you have a faulty water heater, it must be repaired or replaced. Consumables (paper towels, soap, etc.) need to be replenished. Surprise and delights need to be provided to increase guest satisfaction, amenities like bed lamps with USB plugs to charge your guests' phones.

Occupancy and Price Management. While occupancy is less of an issue for traditional, yearly rentals, it is a constant issue for short-term rentals. You need to consistently monitor your occupancy and adjust your pricing. The best practice is to connect to a dynamic pricing tool that will automatically update your calendar prices. When there are local events—concerts, graduations, big sports games, Homecoming—coming to town, you'll need to take that into account and adjust your nightly rate or minimum nightly stay. (On average, STR reservations are three or four nights.) The two to five times more you make doesn't come for free. Pricing mastery helped me quadruple the income on *The Belmonte Penthouse* from the prior owner.

More Like a Business. If you haven't guessed by the last few points, you will need to be entrepreneurial. If you are a host, you are a small business owner. You need to manage your income (nightly rates and occupancy) and expenses. You will need to develop processes, use specific management and automation tools, and solve sometimes unexpected problems and resolve difficult situations.

Advertising. Related to the above, you are now a marketer. You need to create and optimize a listing on an OTA and get familiar with the system to properly sell your space.

Customer Service. Your FPG needs to be able to reach you or your proxy 24/7. This includes at 2am on Saturday and may involve a locksmith. If you are doing things right, this should very rarely, if ever, happen. If the electricity goes out, you need to get that fixed ASAP. Same with the internet, hot water, heat, anything. When the guest leaves and forgets their favorite t-shirt (or sex toy...true story), you'll have to ship it to them.

Exploding Heads. When a guest calls you to tell you the internet doesn't work, and you get the internet company over there ASAP only for them to tell you that it just needed to be plugged in....

When the guest tells you the electronic door lock doesn't work so you rush over only to find out the guest typed the code incorrectly....

When the guest says the shower drain is clogged, and the plumber tells you that the drain was simply covered in hair, probably from one of the guests shaving in the shower....

These situations occur on a regular basis. You will have to know how to troubleshoot any and every guest problem. Is the power ON for the router? Tell me what access code you typed in? Can you check the drain for anything visible?

You can hire a property management company to field all the customer service calls, or you can figure things out for yourself. These issues will decrease as you learn how, what, and when to communicate information to your guest. All covered in this book.

Cleaning. You will be responsible for cleaning your rental after each reservation. The normal check-out time is 10-11am and the normal check-in time is 3pm. This gives you or your cleaners about five hours to clean. Typically, the guest pays the cleaning fee.

This is going to be one of the hardest things to figure out and is the most common guest complaint. Your cleanliness standard will rise significantly after being a host.

Here is my advice: Don't go budget on your cleaning team. They will do more than clean.

Online Reputation. You now have reviews to maintain. Each guest gets to review your space and their experience. There are no slum lords in vacation rentals. Or, at least, not for long.

Security Deposit and Claims. Using OTAs, this can be a long process and a headache. Typically, you have to submit a claim and accept the OTA judgement as final.

Once, I had a guest smash the side of the garage with their car. I took pictures noting the scratches in the exact height on the car, but ultimately got denied by Airbnb....

Direct bookings avoid this hassle.

Insurance. I once was the property manager for a $1,200 per night hillside mansion when a guest broke the expensive wooden dining table. Replacement cost was $5,000. Airbnb denied the judgement, at first. The host removed his property from the platform, and Airbnb sent over the $5,000. The host lost over $15,000 in missed rented nights.

It is for situations like these plus liability issues that you may want to add additional short-term rental insurance, either separately or on your homeowner's policy. The OTAs generally offer some type of insurance, but the coverage can be hit-or-miss.

Hospitality. You are now responsible for each guest stay in your city starting from when they land in the airport until they leave upon check-out. This is one of the many things that separates the excellent hosts from the mediocre ones who complain about low occupancy.

Refunds. Issues happen. When they do, you will offer a refund. Even when issues don't happen, the guest may request a refund. Now it becomes a business decision. Fight and potentially get a negative review. Or, send the refund? There are strategies to deal with these common situations.

Positives of Short-Term Renting

Less Wear and Tear. That's right. While long-term tenants probably use the kitchen on a regular basis and spend more time inside, a short-term renter is only in your city for a few days and is likely to eat out and spend a lot of time outside, potentially only using your bathroom and bedroom.

Higher Market Value. If you rent your home out on a short-term basis, you can sell it as a business for a higher price. Businesses sell based on the return-on-investment. Be sure you keep good records of your income and expenses. I see homes sell at a multiple as high as 10 times the yearly revenue.

Flexible Use of Property. Unlike long-term rentals, you can now block off your calendar when you want to use your space. And, it will likely be a beautiful space because you've paid extra special attention to the interior design, a place so lovely you will be proud to have friends and family from out of town stay there.

Curtailed Renter Rights. Many cities create stringent tenant rights which makes it near impossible and expensive to remove a long-term tenant.

With short-term rentals, however, something to be aware of is squatter rights. Sometimes if a malicious guest stays in the home for 30 days, they get automatic tenancy rights, can stop paying rent, and have you spend time (usually months) and money to legally evict them. This is an extremely rare situation, but something to be aware of. This can easily be avoided by listing for one day less than the term your local laws identify with the invoking of tenants' rights.

Income. As mentioned earlier, you will make a lot more money if you are a good host, and after this book, you will be.

The best hosts make up to five times more than they would with a traditional rental. In numbers, that means if you rented your space for $1,000 per month, or $12,000 per year with an annual contract, you could earn $5,000 per month, or $60,000 per year as an STR.

Meet People Across The Globe. This is more applicable to hosts who will rent out a room in their home, but you can also opt to meet your guests upon check-in or check-out.

When I was hosting the couch in my San Francisco apart-ment living room, I met hundreds of people from numerous countries. You feel like you're traveling in your own city!

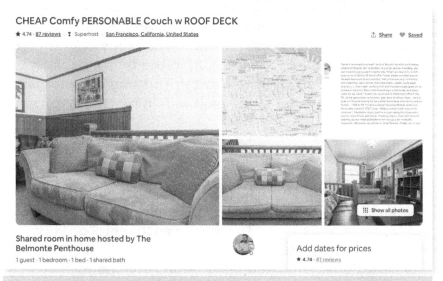

This is the more popular of two couches I rented via Airbnb while living with three housemates in North Beach, San Francisco. We met cool people and made good money.

Don't underestimate this. Meeting a single guest, making a single connection, could change your life in ways previously unknown, if you're open to it.

Negatives of Short-Term Renting

Guest Issues. You will have to deal with your guests as issues arise. If you set up correctly, you can optimize your home and processes so this aspect is limited. But in the beginning, especially, you will have to work out all these issues that are bound to arise.

That little wiggle you have to do to get the key to lock the door? Or a touchy faucet you need to position just right for hot water in the shower? All of these quirks turn into complaints and will need to be fixed.

When I was a guest in Colombia, the front gate needed to be yanked up and pulled out to open the front door, making a high-pitched noise. A great way to cause issues with the neighborhoods and create guest issues at the same time!

Emergency Situations. Occasionally (like once or twice per year) you will have an emergency situation with your guest that needs to be addressed. One of the houses I managed years ago had a minor explosion in the firepit causing the tempered glass above it to shatter. This was an emergency situation that needed to be dealt with in real time. You need to plan for this in advance.

Heavier Time Commitment. This is offset by the more money you will earn, but overall, and unless you have a bothersome long-term tenant, short-term renting does require more of your time. After all, you're now a small business owner, remember. My system allows you to manage each rental on your own with one hour per week.

I've mentioned this a few times already. I hope you're catching on. If not yet, you will after you read *Chapter 1.4 The Right Mindset*.

Increased Stress. You have more things to manage, like your calendar, the guest expectations, etc. This can cause a lot of added stress if you don't know how to manage it. There is a thing called Airbnb Burnout!

Legal Issues. Your city may have laws that make it impossible or unprofitable to rent on a short-term basis and/or you may have to pay more taxes. Please investigate this *before* investing by checking your municipality's website or visiting the town/city office.

Neighbor Relations. Unfortunately, it's common to not know your neighbor even if they share a wall with you.

If you don't know your neighbor, go over with an offering (wine, baked goods, anything), give it to them, and ask if you can meet them for a coffee this week. Do this regardless of whether or not you will be a host.

When you see them in the hallways of your apartment building or in front of their home, make an effort to say hello.

If you decide to be a host, you can and should tell your neighbors. If you're on good terms with them, you can even ask them to keep an eye on your home.

Some Increased Costs. Just a few of the additional costs might be installing digital locks, higher insurance premiums particularly for liability associated with the rental, and maintenance and security.

Thieves do research and know STR properties may be largely unoccupied and thus good targets unless outfitted with security systems.

To Be or Not To Be...a Host

Did I scare you? I hope not, but I want you to be confident in your ultimate success if you decide to become an STR owner.

Answer these questions to find out if you're ready:

- Are you okay making $2,500 one month and $10,000 the next?

- Do you have the ability to think like a business owner? Are you going to invest today (maintenance, amenities, etc.) for a return tomorrow (positive reviews)?

- Do you have the time, especially when you start, to more actively manage your rental, the guest requests, messaging, dealing with issues, monitoring your calendar and pricing, and carrying out repairs and maintenance, etc.?

Yes to all three? Then I think you'd be a good host. Let's take the next step!

I. HOW TO GET STARTED IN SHORT-TERM RENTALS

Being an STR host is not easy. Have I drilled that in enough? It's also not hard, but if you go in with the easy-money mindset made popular by many online gurus selling the idea of making money passively without owning any property (a magnificently sellable idea!) then you're in for subpar performance.

It's better to think of it as hard work and be pleasantly surprised *when* you do things right. Repeat after me: I want to do it right and be in the top 20% of earners for my market.

This chapter will:

- Help you decide what type of STR host you want to be

- Help you ready your space for your first guest arrival

- Introduce STR automation tools

Declutter and Organize

You need to get your *space*, your STR, ready. Some people seem to have a knack for this while others don't. To do this right, **start off with an empty home and add back only the essentials**. Then remove half of the essentials. There's always too much stuff.

Having too much 'stuff' inside your home only makes it feel smaller than it is. There are other tangible benefits to having a decluttered house, including fewer guests leaving things behind and fewer things to be broken.

Ask yourself when setting up your home: "Will the guest use this?" If the answer is no, remove it.

You are going to have amazing photos in your listing (we'll get to this), so you don't want the guest entering your home and having the feeling that the photos are much better than reality.

In fact, as a guest who sometimes stays with Airbnb Superhosts, I find one of the consistent differences is that their space is more refined, more pleasant to be in, and a key element to making it feel more like the guests' space is decluttering.

Many hosts decide to lock off a special area or closet that may have some personal belongings and can double as an extra linen/cleaning supplies closet. You can turn any closet into a private space with a door knob lock.

While we're talking about entire home rentals, I need to mention that it's a very bad idea to close off any bedrooms, especially the master bedroom. Some potential hosts ask me this, as they want to only rent for a portion of the year. Just know that if you do this, it will significantly hurt both your rates and occupancy.

Anything in your home that holds significant monetary or sentimental value needs to be removed, even from the private closet area. In *The Belmonte Penthouse*, the owner had a $10,000 painting in the living room. Nothing happened to it, thankfully, but that was a bad idea and unnecessary.

Create a Flawless Check-in Process

You'll need to figure out a way for your guests to enter your home, easily and consistently for every reservation, at any time of day or night. Use a digital lock, coded lock box, or hire someone to meet the guest at the property.

Short-term rental hosts need to control what's within their control because some things are not. The check-in process is within your control.

When I'm in Medellin, often I personally greet each guest upon arrival. If you do this, be sensitive to a travel-weary guest who may just want to shower and hit the sack—rather than wait through your meet-and-greet.

Though I lack direct experience with them, there are other services which you can use to deliver or store keys. Search '[your city] Airbnb key delivery service'.

Remember to always have a backup option. I like having a backup lockbox some-

Video - My live check-in process at *The Belmonte Penthouse*

SCAN ME

where nearby for emergencies. This could also be used by the cleaners, maintenance workers, or emergency personnel.

Purchase a Full Set of Amenities and Consumables

You'll want to purchase and replenish essential items that your guest will need plus some extras that can make the guest experience richer and smoother. An example of extras is con-sumables, everything from orange juice, bottled water, snacks and coffee in the kitchen to fresh bath amenities like bubble bath, moisturizer, and tissues.

You, your cleaner, emergency contact, or property manage-ment company will take care of this.

If you live on-site, it makes sense for you to do this, at least in the beginning.

If not, then I recommend you either have the cleaners do this (you'll have to pay extra) or stock three months of con-sumables in the house for the cleaners to replenish as part of their job. The cleaners will tell you when the supply closet gets to 20% for any item at which point you will add more to the supply closet.

A frequent question and one that you may encounter is how much consumables you should provide. Some hosts provide more than enough, others provide a starter pack. It depends on your offer and what your guests expect.

Personally, I provide more than enough for a standard reservation, but I don't promise to restock during a month-long reservation.

POP QUIZ

You're getting your space ready for your first guest. What type of towels do you provide?

Take a minute to think about your answer.

This decision, though it's a small one, will be a great indicator of how you approach a whole range of things in the future.

If you think a towel doesn't matter and get a cheap one, you will probably not anticipate guest needs, both ordinary and extraordinary and prepare for them, which is something that successful hosts think about in order to make their guests' trip as seamless and pleasant as possible.

If you imagined the guest, post-shower, wrapping themselves in a plush, generously-sized quality cotton towel with a grateful sigh after their long day of uncomfortable travel, (and how that will affect your review *today* which will affect your success *tomorrow*), then you're on the right track!

Indeed, a towel is something the guest has a lot of interaction with! It's not uncommon for the guest to take a shower upon check-in, every day they stay, and before check-out. I suggest you get the nicest, fluffiest, most pleasant feeling towels you can afford. Towels are an underleveraged amenity and low hanging fruit.

In Chapter 4.6, we'll talk more about all the amenities you should be providing by room.

Hire a Cleaning Team

I recommend you clean (and manage) your space for as long as possible, even if that means just for one full reservation. If not, it's like enrolling your kid in a school system where you have no idea what goes on behind the scenes and crossing your fingers as to what that system will produce of your child.

Most hosts decide to hire a cleaning team or a property manager. The difficult part is *finding* and *choosing* the right person or team. I cover these important topics in *Chapter 4.5 Cleaning Process* and *Chapter 4.10 How To Choose a Good Property Manager*, respectively.

Don't go budget on your cleaning team. Instead, opt for the premium option. They'll do more than just clean for you. I've said that twice for a reason.

High-Quality Photos

This is the last step after you ready your house and before you put it online. You can hire a professional photographer or take your own photos. Each option has its own benefits.

If there is one area that will define your online success, it is the photos. *Chapter 3.5 Photos* is the longest in the book for good reason.

Create Your Host Profile and Optimized Airbnb Listing

Create your online host profile and fill it out completely. We'll cover this in *Chapter 7.12 Does My Hosting Profile Matter?*

Part 3: Build and Optimize Your Listing will go into detail about your online listing.

After you create your online listing, do NOT activate it until you complete it entirely and are ready to accept guests or no more than one month before that time. Ideally, you make your listing live one to three weeks before you are ready to accept your first guest. This is because, on average, most reservations are coming right around 30 days before the check-in date.

As you start out, follow my NLCS (refer to *Chapter 7.22 What Is The New Listing Calendar Strategy?*). FPGs will snap up your aesthetically pleasing and optimized listing like you wouldn't believe.

Emergency Contact

This is like insurance. Hopefully, you will never use it, but it's a must. An emergency contact is one person the guest can get in touch with for any urgent issue that needs to be dealt with ASAP.

This person needs to be available 24/7. It can be you, your cleaner, your trusted friend, your neighbor, property manager, a maintenance person, local college student, anyone who meets the above criteria: available and reachable 24/7. You'll need to work out a payment deal in advance with this person. In exchange for their availability, you will pay a premium.

If you have everything figured out, which you will within the first couple months, this person may never be called.

You want to let the guest know who this person is. You also want to be clear that this person is *only* for emergencies and that all else should be communicated through the OTA or whatever your system becomes.

Does it seem like a lot of work? It is, but the point is that you are doing everything from the start instead of figuring it out along the way. You don't have to do any of the above right away. You can start with low-quality photos. You can first hire a bad cleaning team, then realize you need to pay top dollar to rid yourself of the myriad of cleaning issues and poor reviews. I've done it. I've been a host of many properties, I'm a property manager, I've worked for a property management company with over 70 Airbnbs. I've experienced it all.

Ready. Set. Host.

The above was primarily focused on getting your space, both online and offline, ready for your first guest. Now that your space is in order, you have a whole new set of decisions to focus on: automation, guest experience, revenue maximization. We'll cover these now. We're only half way through so buckle up.

I know you want to be in the top 10% of hosts and experience all the associated benefits. What are those, you ask?

For one, it means that when the slow season hits (*Chapter 7.17 How Do I Get More Reservations During Slow Season?*), you will be the least affected.

Slow season, for the majority of hosts, means plummeting of occupancy *with* a lowered nightly rate.

The latter scenario scares the living crap out of me, especially because I'm responsible for others' income as a property manager, and I earn a commission based on their income.

Let's prepare ourselves now to lessen any potential negative impacts of the unknown future.

Take solace in the fact that I highly value both my time and energy. I am not telling you anything that you don't need to know. This is why my writing style is as always, no-fluff.

Let's get to it.

Understand That Guests Do Not Read Lengthy Listing Details

It is well known in the STR community that guests don't read. While that's true, I think hosts are often communicating the wrong information at the wrong time.

Respect your guest's attention at all times (see Chapter *1.8 The Vacation Rental Commandments*) by being succinct and communicating only what the guest needs to know at the time they need to know it (see Chapter *1.5 The Reservation Flow*).

Create a Floor Plan

If you rent out anything besides a room, I strongly suggest creating a floor plan. This perfectly sets your guests' expectations. **Mismanaged expectations result in negative reviews**.

You can create one for free with various online tools. I require these on all of my listings, whether owned or managed. I talk more about this in *Chapter 3.5 Photos*.

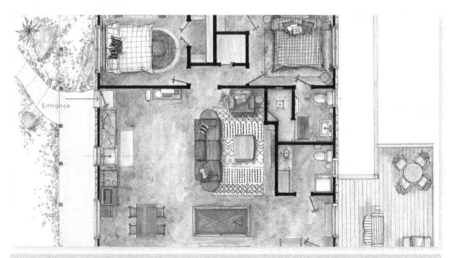

Example of a floor plan sold on my website. Remember, the bonus items include all photos in color.

Automate Your Messages

The reservation process, as you'll soon find out, is consistent in that you'll end up making the same responses over and over again. This does not add to the guest experience. In fact, it decreases it because they have to ask you these basic questions and wait for your response.

The good news is that you can fully automate this part of your hosting. I talk more about this in *Chapter 4.3 How To Message Your Guest*.

Identify Noise Complaints Before They Happen

For some listings, there is an ever-present risk of guests throwing parties, or simply being loud after a night of drinking. You're already friends with your neighbor, and they know what you're doing and why, right? Most people are ok with STRs, though I've come into contact with a few difficult neighbors who just seemed unwilling to cooperate.

Even though parties *do* happen in STR rentals just like the occasional parties thrown by a long-term renter, you still want to minimize this risk.

Even good guests are allowed to get rowdy sometimes. But, we have a secondary line of defense for these instances. They're called noise monitors. They record either noise in the form of decibel levels or the number of devices connected to the Wi-Fi network. Either way, they are designed to pre-emptively alert you to an impending or in-progress party.

In the bonus items, you will find my recommended tool under 'Noise Monitors'.

Create a Digital Guidebook

One of the best things you can do to increase guest satisfaction and automate your time is to create a digital guidebook. You will present it to the guest as a sort of house manual that contains relevant information needed for check-in and to enjoy your rental.

This is so important because of the reservation flow. If the guest books a month in advance, you do not want to send them check-in, Wi-Fi, and parking information upon reservation confirmation. At this point of the reservation the information is irrelevant.

This is doubly true if you have a really important house rule they must follow. If you tell them a month before check-in, they will forget. Instead, this should be communicated near the actual check-in date or upon arrival.

This is covered in depth in *Chapter 4.4 Digital Guidebook*.

Manage Your Nightly Rate and Calendar

Pricing is a hot topic and something you must become proficient at. It's what most hosts want to talk about when they purchase a one-on-one consultation with me.

That's why I've dedicated an entire section to the topic in this book, post regular free YouTube videos, and cover it in detail in my course.

I have developed a strategy that I've used successfully for years and it only takes up to two minutes per week, per listing. I'll share it with you in *Part 5: Pricing*.

Should You Allow Events In Your Rental?

It is a personal choice and also depends on if your space would be sought after for events. Events are not only parties, but commercial and short film shoots, weddings, etc. Before you go with the almost automatic 'no' response, consider the following.

In addition to widening the pool of FPGs, especially during slow season, there are other benefits. *Most* events are professional operations. This means they are going to be careful with your stuff. They've done this before and have processes around making the experience as smooth as possible for you (such as replacing any moved furniture, not scratching the floors).

They will pay a higher rate as it's a commercial use, and they will not sleep in your space. Many events are held mid-day. Sometimes it can be an evening event, but they never sleep in your space except in the case of some company off-sites which are not really events anyway. They are meetings.

Keep in mind that you will have additional folks in your home above your max occupancy, typically.

As a new host you will encounter more questions along your journey, and you'll find many of those more specific question along with the associated answers in *Part 7: Bonus Content:*

Questions and Answers. I have answered them there as they're also relevant to existing hosts.

Ready. Set. Host?

This STR stuff is a bit more complicated than you thought, right? It's like poker. You can learn to play in five minutes, but you can spend a lifetime improving to master the game.

With this chapter, I only wanted to introduce you to the many aspects of hosting. I hope it didn't feel like information overload.

If it all doesn't immediately make sense, don't worry. Each chapter will fill in more gaps. You'll be an expert at the end of this book.

We're taking it slow. The next part will introduce a little more about your instructor-author, me, and some other foundational concepts you should know before you dive into the main content.

Part 1

INTRODUCTION

1.1 WHO IS THIS BOOK FOR?

This book in meant to be an all-in-one guide for new, interested, and experienced short-term rental hosts and real estate investors alike, with one exception.

You don't need to have 100 properties to have short-term rental success.

In fact, if your plan is to acquire a highly leveraged real-estate portfolio with other people's money via syndicates worth tens of millions of dollars, the information presented in this book may fall short for you.

As you'll soon learn, I'm about doing more with less. I'm about maximizing the ROI from each rental investment rather than meeting minimal requirements. I'm not always buying. I sit back and wait until the economy creates a buyer's environment further ensuring a successful investment choice.

If you identify with the above, this book was written for you.

If you are totally new to the short-term rental life, how many industries can you name where you're virtually guaranteed to make money? Oh brother, hotels had it so good for so long!

This book is for people who understand that a book is the closest we've gotten to that scene from *The Matrix* when Trinity's brain is uploaded with information on how to fly. Do you remember that scene? If not, picture someone with facial expressions part orgasmic part painful for a few seconds and afterwards she knows how to fly a plane.

Referenced scene from *The Matrix*

SCAN ME

By the end of this book, you will have gained my decade worth of experience in the short-term rental space helping hosts around the world from third-world countries to 16-bedroom penthouses in premium cities. And, if you choose, I hope you'll further join me via the course.

1.2 STRUCTURE OF THE BOOK

This book does not need to be read from start to finish.

Think of the preface and the introduction as the first thirty minutes of a movie. While it might not be the most exciting part of the movie, it sets the foundation of the story. It communicates what you need for maximum enjoyment and understanding during the rest of the film.

With that said, if you prefer to jump right in, skip to *Part 2: Vacation Rental Market Analysis.*

It is preferable that you read one complete part at a time to get a full picture of the topic at hand.

This book is laid out according to how an investor or rental owner approaches the STR industry *and* in terms of troubleshooting problems when they arise.

First, and most importantly, you need to understand how to find and analyze a market and more than that, a micro-neighborhood and individual property. If you do this step incorrectly, you're working harder, not smarter. We'll explore this topic in *Part 2: Vacation Rental Market Analysis.*

Once you have a rental, you'll need to perfect your online presence. It's also step one of three when troubleshooting problems with your rental. Is your online listing optimized? This includes my strategy for removing negative reviews. It's the easiest part of the business to correct, and we'll explore this topic in *Part 3: Build and Optimize Your Listing.*

The second stop on the troubleshooting highway is your hospitality, which ultimately shows up in your review rating. Is the guest experience optimized? We'll cover this topic in *Part 4: Elevate Your Hospitality.*

Pricing is a hot topic, and the third and final tool in our troubleshooting arsenal. I break down the art and science of pricing into two levels each of which gets its own chapter. We'll cover this topic in *Part 5: Pricing*.

After some time, many STR hosts will venture into the direct booking world which entails creating your own online presence to get reservations outside of the OTA platforms. This trend is happening sooner and sooner for new hosts. We'll cover this topic in *Part 6: Direct Bookings*.

In *Part 7: Bonus Content: Questions and Answers* I will answer a variety of common questions unique to the STR world.

Finally, and maybe the most popular section, will be *Part 8: How To Rank #1 On Airbnb*. After all, that's basically what we all want. It will solve all our problems. While many of the ranking factors are a result of being a good host anyway, there are some hacks that will be discussed. After years of personal experience and help from data scientists, I know how to rank high in Airbnb search.

1.3 MY PHILOSOPHY

It's important you know my philosophy, which acts as a guiding principle for my strategies in operating rental properties, to see if yours aligns with mine. If they do not, then it's like relying on some random person to tell you where to vacation. What if they're not like you? What if they like mountains, and you like beaches? What if they like to visit religious buildings and museums, and you couldn't care less? On the other hand, if you asked someone who was similar to you, then your chances of success relying on their info are greater.

As it relates to this book, there are going to be two overarching philosophies.

First, no fluff. I'm allergic to it. I'm not here to entertain you. I'm here to educate you.

Get out the highlighter or get familiar with the highlight feature on your e-reader. My aim is to deliver an astounding level of value in 400 pages.

Second, I believe my time is my most valuable asset. I know my hourly rate, and I try not to do anything in business that doesn't increase that rate.

I'm constantly measuring my time value, or that hourly rate. For a given activity, how much extra time do I need to spend on it versus how much extra benefit or return on investment am I receiving?

Your time, like mine, is better spent learning a new skill, building your personal relationships, or enjoying a hobby if the return on the business is low.

This is who I am as a person. It's how I think about life, how I teach, and how I learn. And it's no different to how I run my STR.

It's the Pareto Principle, which states that 20% of the input is responsible for 80% of the output, at work, and I hope my readers understand and agree with this.

1.4 THE RIGHT MINDSET

I used to advertise a 694% return on your nightly rate within one week after optimization. In other words, if you charged $100 per night, you could expect six or seven nights of reservations within just one week of my magic.

to me ▾

the agent i spoke to checked with someone on why there was a disparity between the listings...she basically said it was complicated and she didn't know exactly why, but that the listing you optimized appeared to be easier to read, was more approachable, and ranked higher as a result...

for my other listing, i just replicated basically what you did...

Prior customer summarizing Airbnb's response as to why the listing I optimized ranked higher comapred to when he applied the same concepts on his own to a second listing.

Long ago, I stopped advertising that and not because it's not true. In fact, the vast majority of hosts (75%) who work with me earn an increase of reservations compared to the week prior.

I stopped because I noticed it attracted too many hosts with the wrong mindset.

The ones that wanted the quick fix. The magic bullet.

Or, it made otherwise well-intentioned hosts focus on something that really didn't matter... just like views or search rank (see *Chapter 1.7 Views vs. Conversion vs. Rank*).

I realized that I was focusing hosts' attention on something short-term when vacation rentals require a long-term strategy.

The wrong mindset is short-term focused.

It's the difference between the employee and the executive.

The employee is doing daily tasks and putting out fires. The executive is planning for the future and working to limit excessive or future fires.

Even the current good employees, the ones who get promoted, the future executives, they are already thinking with a long-term approach.

Even though you may be an employee in your day job, I want you to understand that you are the executive of your rental. I will help you to start thinking like one, too.

This concept is so important and applies to so many facets of STRs that you must repeat out loud right now:

I am a host with a long-term mindset.

I focus on long-term strategies.

I am a problem solver. Every negative experience has a potential solution.

I filter out the noise and the short-term advice.

The right mindset is the only mindset.

The right mindset will solve all my problems and make me the best host I can be.

Profitable Properties is the best book I've ever read (aha!).

You can stop talking out loud like a lunatic now.

Year after year, season after season, continuously optimizing and problem solving are the key to success.

Years ago, while staying at an Airbnb in Hong Kong, I recorded a sloppy video for my YouTube channel talking about this.

Before arriving to the city, I noticed one of the listings that I was interested in was low-quality and generic. Given how expensive Hong Kong was, I reached out, explained what I do, and offered to help the host in exchange for a discount.

The host responded that he didn't need any help, that he was experiencing a lot of interest. I ended up booking this listing anyways.

When I arrived, I noticed the listing was even worse than his online presence. It was lacking many basic amenities including Wi-Fi. While the reviews weren't terrible, they also weren't stellar.

In the video I said, "his listing is slowly going to go downhill. He is slowly going to do worse and worse."

Well, I just checked his listing, and it's still live with a fully open calendar at $68 per night and only 17 reviews. When I booked it year ago I paid $67 per night.

This experience made "it" click for me.

I had always received messages from hosts saying the same thing: "I don't know what happened. I started off strong, but now (three, six, nine months later) I am not getting reservations."

Oftentimes, they give up.

This Hong Kong host fit the profile. He started off strong and was satisfied. Uninterested in any feedback. Things were doing well at the moment. Why improve?

This Hong Kong host had the wrong mindset, focusing on the short-term. He would reach out to me months later.

Here's another all-too-common mindset problem example: cancelling a reservation because you think you can get more money. Maybe you can make a little extra money on one reservation, but that's a short-term mindset.

Cancellations are one of the worst things you can do. Even though they're technically allowed sometimes, I notice a decline in interest after these "allowed" cancellations.

When you set up your rental, you have a bunch of decisions to make ("*one-of-a-hundred*"). Wi-Fi being an important one. Did you opt for the cheaper and slower service or the high-speed, reliable option?

Short-term mindset: saving money today on cheaper Wi-Fi demonstrates poor understanding of the effect this decision has on the future.

Long-term mindset: pay the premium for great Wi-Fi, and let it be a competitive advantage. High cost now, but with an understanding that returns come in the long-term via better reviews, higher occupancy, and increased nightly rates. You also avoid complaints.

Cleaners are another *great* example. A lot of STR experts preach getting the cheapest cleaners and then those experts offer strategies to pay them even less. This boggles my mind! Any good host knows you need to be paranoid about cleaning because all it takes for some guests is a single pubic hair in the shower drain or on the toilet seat for a less than five-star review. I call it "The 1 Pubic Hair Rule." You are cleaning to the cleaning standard of the pickiest/most cleanly guest. There's one well known Airbnb expert who preaches the cheap-cleaner strategy all the time on his social media. You know what he doesn't talk about so much? His listings with sub 4.5 ratings.

Getting the cheapest cleaners is a horrible idea. Trust me, I know. I've negotiated deals with individual cleaners, with cleaning companies, with laundromats, and it always worked out poorly.

This goes right back to the last chapter. Am I going to pay more for a market-rate cleaner who will save me time and avoid complaints, or am I going with the cheap cleaner whose poor performance will take more of my time and possibly money in the long run? You already know my answer.

There are *so* many fringe benefits you get with paying your cleaners well. We talk all about this in *Chapter 4.5 Cleaning Process*.

To wrap up this conversation, I want to provide one more real-life example of how a seemingly unimportant decision today has unknown, real costs in the future.

While I was staying in an Airbnb in Panama City, Panama, I quickly learned that the host hadn't properly secured the vent for the stove. It basically didn't work, and the host had opted not to fix it. Fine. But what are the long-term effects of this judgement? Twice a day when I cooked, I had to open the balcony doors to cool down the house and get rid of extra smoke all while blasting the A/C to avoid having a heat stroke in the 100-degree weather (38°C for my international readers).

The simple kitchen vent fix cost the equivalent of the extra, prolonged A/C usage and decreased the guest experience. Details matter.

1.5 THE RESERVATION FLOW

The reservation flow is an important foundational concept and will be relevant throughout the book. It allows us to communicate with the guest efficiently.

Each reservation, from the guest perspective, follows a very similar path: the FPG searches, reserves, checks in, stays, and checks out.

Understanding the big picture reservation flow allows us to get the details of the communication right. In other words, when to communicate what so that it's most relevant. If you know the reservation flow, then you would know that adding in check-out rules or parking instructions at the time of booking is inappropriate. It may sound obvious but misunderstanding the reservation flow and, thus, communication errors are common and affect the entire operation.

First, the FPG will search for a suitable listing. There is information they are looking for at this point in their booking journey. Specifically, what are you offering in exchange for the price? There is also information they do not need at this time which we will save for later.

For example, selling the neighborhood in the listing is unwise in most instances. At this point the guest has already chosen where they want to go. The FPG does not use an OTA as a travel guide.

Next, the FPG will either book a listing right away, will come back to search various times and ultimately book, or will not book.

We have strategies to *optimize* each of these outcomes. Yes, even when the FPG doesn't book, we can engage them to add us to their wishlist or follow us on social media.

Assuming the FPG reserves your space and becomes a future guest (hip-hip-HORAY), we now have another set of relevant information to communicate depending on the booking lead time—the time in advance of the check-in date that the guest books (this measure becomes very important with messaging and pricing, covered later in the book in detail or refer back to *iii. Terminology*).

Next, the guest arrives on check-in day and, again, there is relevant information to be communicated. However, we start our check-in communication early because the guest typically gets nervous if they haven't received this info within *three* days before arrival. To avoid unnecessary communication, we'll send out a message with check-in info just before the guest is likely to reach out to us.

When the guest is in our space, it's common for them to encounter problems within the first 24 hours. So, we'll ensure they know we're available, if needed.

Finally, we have check-out day! Stressful for both you and the guest. And, super important because it's the last memory the guest will have before the OTA asks them to write a review while they're at the airport waiting for their flight. There are ways to earn some extra goodwill at this point which help the review and increase the number of reviewing guests.

I'll share one with you now. I provide free airport lounge passes knowing that 90% of guests won't use them because they're running late, but I still get the benefit of having made the offer.

Recently I heard a host say that it's common in her market to require guests to take out the trash, load dirty dishes and start the dishwasher, and clean out the fridge. Wow! If I were in that market, I would make it my competitive advantage in not having the guest work for me upon checkout.

Now we know how to respect our guests' attention (Vacation Rental Commandment #2) and deliver them a truly phenomenal experience via excellent hospitality, something lacking from short-term rentals today, from start to finish. All of this sets you up for success not only in good times, but also in bad times.

1.6 MY OVERALL STRATEGY FOCUS

Conversion and automation are my gold standard concepts. A lot of my strategies have to do with increasing both your conversion *and* your automation. (Conversion is how many guests who view your listing actually then book it.)

There is one exception, and it is the Level 3 host. They are now so good at the game that they are optimizing at the more nuanced levels to eke out an extra 1-2%. But that 1-2% represents great value. When applicable, I'll mention those concepts only relevant to the Level 3 host.

I'm also highly focused on conversion. That's the ultimate goal for many of my strategies. You're a business owner now. You measure expenses against revenue to get your net profit. And, ultimately, it comes down to how often a guest reserved your listing. Every little thing comes back to conversion.

From how I fill in my host profile to how I message my guest to foundation concepts like photos, title, and text—all are optimized for conversion. Not views. Not search rank.

1.7 VIEWS VS. CONVERSION VS. RANK

There's a lot of hoopla out there around views and rank, two things whose importance pales in comparison to conversion.

We will go over this in detail in *Chapter 3.1 Why Airbnb Search Is Not Static Like Google*, but I want to share a story with you from a recent consultation call.

The Airbnb host challenged me on my stance that search rank doesn't matter. He was experiencing poor occupancy, and he argued that search rank does matter because it would tell him *why* he is experiencing poor occupancy. Was it due to a low search rank or something else?

Let's go with this reasoning. Let's say we *could* confirm that his poor occupancy was due to a low search rank. What would we do to increase that search rank to boost his occupancy?

Answer: Exactly the same things that we would have done anyway.

There's no button you can push to increase your search rank. (Well, there is kind of one we'll go over in *Part 8: How To Rank #1 On Airbnb*.) You can't pay for placement. If you could, then knowing your search rank might be helpful. A poor search rank is a symptom. We have to address the underlying cause(s).

What do we do to increase our search rank? Remember, our three-step troubleshooting process? First, we will optimize our online listing to make it as attractive to our FPGs as the competition.

Second, we will optimize our hospitality to increase our review rating.

Third, we will fine-tune our pricing to ensure we're booking just as many low demand days as high demand days.

Okay. But let's go back to the beginning. We've identified that we have a high search rank, but still suffer poor occupancy. Besides the fact that this is an unrealistic reality, to fix our new situation we would...what...do exactly the same things that we should do anyway.

Our online listing needs to be fine-tuned because we have a low conversion rate. We're unlikely to rank high with a low rating so that's probably not it, but still probably could be improved. And, finally, our price may just be too high.

And this is ignoring the fact that you can't even know your search rank.

Booking.com says,

> "we can tailor each guest's search results for them, rather than presenting the same properties to everyone." [1]

VRBO says,

> "ranking is combined with an individual traveler's preferences — including stay dates, search filters, and other personalization factors — to determine where your property shows up in their search results." [2]

Finally, Airbnb says,

> "[our search rank] model is responsible for ordering the listings available according to the guest's likelihood of booking." [3]

---

[1] https://partner.booking.com/en-gb/help/growing-your-business/analytics-reports/all-about-ranking-search-results-and-visibility

[2] https://host.expediagroup.com/vrbo/en-us/resources/improve-performance/market-rank-and-search-position

[3] https://arxiv.org/pdf/1810.09591.pdf

That reference is an interesting internal technical paper from the data science team titled *Applying Deep Learning To Airbnb Search* that gives a very detailed working model of how search works and how to rank highly if you're interested in learn more.

1.8 THE VACATION RENTAL COMMANDMENTS

Before we jump into arguably the most important section of the book (*Part 2: Vacation Rental Market Analysis*), I want to share my five vacation rental commandments.

They should be front and center in everything you do as it relates to hosting. They'll bring you to the almighty Level 3 status, if you choose.

They're a summary of my time working directly with STRs in more than 95 countries, staying as an Airbnb guest more than 2,000 nights, and hosting more than 10,000 reservations since 2013.

They are in order of importance.

1. Entrepreneurial Mindset

If you're an STR host, you are an entrepreneur. If that's too scary, think of yourself as a small business owner.

After all, you are running a business. You're providing capital in the form of buying furniture and paying for services.

You're the marketing department by listing your space online to convince an FPG to buy your product.

You're accounting in that you'll be collecting payments, paying taxes, and tracking expenses.

Research and development come in the form of acquiring knowledge (i.e. reading my book and, later, venturing to my website, Instagram, or YouTube and those of other experts), testing, and improving.

You even have an online reputation to maintain. That's public relations.

An entrepreneur's greatest asset is their mind. Mostly, what an entrepreneur does is think through a myriad of opportunities and problems for the optimal solution. It's the right mindset that leads to success.

2. Respect The Guests' Attention

Most hosts disobey this commandment, often and repeatedly. If you keep this in mind in everything you do, you will be one of the most competitive listings in your market.

To know if you're respecting your guests' attention, here are two questions to ask yourself:

- Have you used the fewest possible words both in your online listing and via messaging?
- Have you simplified all processes for the guest (check-in, using amenities, etc.)?

3. Learn How To Be a Marketer

If you're like most hosts, you are an employee for a portion of your life at your day job which may be totally unrelated to your hosting duties. But when you're a host, you transform into a hospitality entrepreneur who needs to be a master marketer.

After all, you're trying to convince an FPG to reserve your listing over hundreds of others. That requires skill.

When it comes to marketing, it's a two-step process:

1. Ensure the FPG is a great fit for what you offer, then,
2. Get them excited about booking your space.

4. Communication Keys

Communicate only that information relevant to your guest at the time they need it in line with the reservation flow.

Clear communication with your guest will help you avoid many potential problems.

This is one of the reasons why I suggest you try to become a regular guest in the STRs of others and experience a range of hospitality. You will discover good and bad things about how other hosts operate. It's our version of a trade show.

5. Hospitality Matters

This encompasses everything from responding to guest complaints quickly and professionally, to going above and beyond while your guest is at your property, to thinking of nice gestures for your guest throughout the booking process.

Are you doing anything special that might set you apart from your competition?

Just last week there was a festival here in Colombia called 'Noche de las Velitas' (Night of the Candles) where people light candles in front of their home, on the street, or on the balcony. I had my team explain the holiday to the guests checking in that afternoon and gave them some candles to participate.

If the guest left something behind, are you the type to charge them to return it? Or, worse, just ignore it so you don't have to send it back?

If so, then you're breaking this commandment. Even though it's the guest's fault for leaving something behind, it's your mindset that we need to adjust as it comes out in all of your hosting abilities.

As you might have noticed, some of the above commandments overlap.

Part 2

VACATION RENTAL MARKET ANALYSIS

2.1 INTRODUCTION

"You need to be doing $50,000, in my head that's your goal."

"Actually, my calculation is that I can do $80,000 per year."

"Hm....how so...how'd you get to that number?"

After explaining my rationale: "I don't doubt that's possible. It's just that we haven't seen an $80,000 home yet."

This was a conversation before I bought *The Belmonte Penthouse* which had generated $42,000 annually for each of the three years prior to my purchase.

In my first year, I didn't make $80,000. I made $156,000.

In this section I'm going to take you along my journey in how I found and chose the market, the neighborhood, and the micro-neighborhood for my STR investment. We will go over my method in running the numbers prior to signing the contract whether that's to buy or rent. You will be able to apply my process to your next investment no matter where you are on the planet. It includes both soft and hard data.

I know some people simply don't have time to get to know a specific market by spending time there or simply lack the interest in doing so. They'd prefer to buy properties from afar. In *Chapter 2.6 Alternative Method To Finding Profitable Rentals,* I will outline a strategy in using hard data to identify a profitable investment in that scenario.

I started my short-term rental investment search in 2020 in Medellin, Colombia where I'm writing this chapter.

As you know, I call it *The Belmonte Penthouse,* and, if you follow me on Instagram or YouTube, you probably already know the history of this purchase which was more than twice my original budget.

This was a BIG decision for me.

Part of my confidence was having traveled through dozens and dozens of cities across the globe and having lived in

Medellin for a total of two years over various trips. Part of my research included an electric scooter. I rode all around that city trying to discover the *micro-neighborhoods* which we will learn about later.

Even though it is a third-world country, even though it had to be an all-cash deal and my Colombian lawyer thought I was crazy to pay such an absurd price, I completed the deal because my confidence level was very high. By the end of this section your confidence level will be high prior to your first or next real-estate investment.

And it has turned out (so far!) to be a phenomenal real estate investment, even better than most real estate professionals make. My cash-on-cash (CoC) return, a common measure in the real estate industry, was 27% in year one while being loose with expenses. Year two is almost complete and on pace for over 30%.

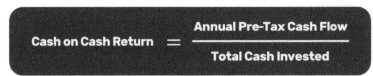

Remember, I didn't leverage this purchase with a loan, so my denominator (lower number) is the full purchase price of the apartment. Because of this, my cap rate, another popular real estate return measure, would equal the same return percentage.

For reference, a good CoC return for an STR is 10%, and a home run is above 20%. Had I financed the deal with a mortgage, my CoC would have been around 90%. Needless to say, my deep market and micro-market analysis and the strategies I used to make the investment have paid off very well. At least so far. Much in life is a marathon, and this is no different. Luckily, I think in decades.

Are you ready to move on?

> The most important thing you can do to set yourself up for success in the STR space, all but guarantee it, is choosing the right home in the right micro-neighborhood in the right market. We're first going to find your ideal market.

2.2 STEP 1: IDENTIFY A MARKET

Humans are lazy, and we're going to make that our advantage. Most investors will go to the main markets simply because those markets are more well-known.

My market preference: places with unique guest demand, well-known for something but not by the general public.

By the end of this chapter, you'll understand why the above is my personal preference.

First order of business is identifying a suitable and profitable market. I break down markets into two categories: discovered and undiscovered.

None of the following four steps is more important than the other.

Discovered vs. Undiscovered Markets

You can think of them like a professional versus a semi-professional athlete. As a professional athlete, there's more upside (revenue potential) in the discovered markets (the professional leagues), but there's also a lot more competition. The bar is higher.

As an amateur in the big leagues, you're going to have a tough time. But in an undiscovered market (i.e. the minor leagues), you have greater opportunity to rise to the top. Most people won't have heard of you or your market. While your earning potential won't be as high as the professional, your likelihood of success is greater due to less competition.

It's not a perfect metaphor, but it's good enough for now.

I prefer undiscovered markets, but that's not at the exclusion of discovered ones, which have their benefits. We know there are a lot of guest arrivals in discovered markets. That's a huge plus. One side of the equation (demand) figured out. And, sometimes, demand is harder to track down. We'll talk about supply shortly.

An undiscovered market is less well known. An ideal undiscovered market has strong guest demand but is off the radar of the general public (causing less supply). This creates stellar investment opportunities.

I prefer undiscovered markets because there are fewer STRs.

Here are some examples of undiscovered markets and where the demand comes from.

If you're a freediver, you're likely to discover Roatan, Honduras as a top worldwide destination during your research.

If you're going bald, you're likely to discover Istanbul, Turkey as a top reliable and budget alternative for hair transplant surgery.

If you want to learn Spanish abroad, you're likely to find Antigua, Guatemala while searching for best places to learn the language.

Or Cali, Colombia if you are a salsa dancer. Or Red Sea, Egypt if you're a wind surfer.

For other adventure sports like kite-surfing or sky-diving, there are certain hot spots in this world. Same with mediation or yoga where you'll find parts of India.

State or national parks can be undiscovered markets.

There are tons of other examples. In fact, I'd argue there are more examples of undiscovered markets than discovered ones because there are 36,000 cities on our planet.

I will not tell you where to invest because it's a very personal decision. I get many hosts asking me this very question. While there may not be such a thing as a stupid question, there are lazy questions. When I get this question, I often encourage the person not to invest as I don't think it's the right time for them. Their potential downside is too high.

I had one host re-ask this question over and over in the course of a 45-minute call. He wanted me to give him a list of the best markets. "Where would you invest?" he asked me. But the thing is, where I would invest might not be best and could be a bad idea for him.

Going back to predictable, off-the-radar demand, did you notice something about the above examples?

These are all activities with year-round demand. The Red Sea is known for wind surfing because there's wind all year round!

A bonus in both a discovered and undiscovered market is the potential to do short-, medium-, and long-term rentals. These markets have guest demand from a variety of population segments (vacationers, digital nomads, work travel, conference, vacation home renovators, etc.). Markets with a diverse set of guest demands are ideal. Nashville, Tennessee is a great example as it brings in sports fans, partiers (bachelor and bachelorette), conference-goers, and those attending university events. Look for this as it limits your downside.

Let's look at discovered markets. Austin, Texas is a discovered market. They have some giant conferences like South by Southwest. And this brings me to my next point: discovered versus undiscovered data.

When I refer to discovered data, I'm referring to more common data points. Overall guest arrivals or number of conferences are two examples. Better data would be to measure the conference capacity of a city (this is an undiscovered data point, which means fewer people are looking at it as a metric). A single large event can be moved, thus devastating your revenues and property value.

You know what can't be moved so easily? Hospitals and stadiums and colleges.

Austin, Texas is the definition of a discovered market. They also have a clear low and high season. The summers are very hot. The peak seasons run only from September to November and March to May.

On the world stage, Bali is a discovered market. It also has harsh seasonality due to unbearable rain, flooding the roads and making living conditions poor. Luckily. it's so close to Australia!

Discovered markets are easy to spot: Paris, New York, London, popular beach or island destinations, Toronto....

Supply vs. Demand

In my experience, people usually look at these equally important measures in isolation. creating potential for a bad investment.

Let's take a simplistic example of two markets, one discovered and one undiscovered.

The discovered market has 100 vacation rentals (supply) and 1000 guest arrivals (demand) per year. This means that, on average, each rental will receive 10 reservations each year.

The undiscovered market has 25 vacation rentals and 400 guest arrivals per year. This means that, on average, each rental will receive 16 reservations each year.

In the undiscovered market, demand (guest arrivals) dropped by 60%, but supply dropped by 75% (rentals). Because the supply dropped by more than demand, even though the guest arrivals were so much lower, it seems to be a more profitable market because more guests are trying to reserve fewer rentals (i.e. it's an underserved vacation rental market).

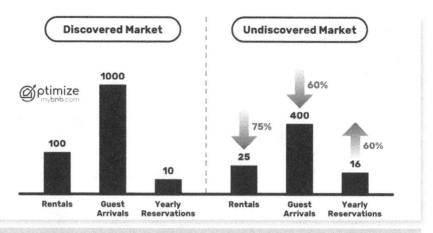

You can see that although the guest arrivals decreased by 60% in the undiscovered market, rentals dropped by even more (75%) thus causing an overall increase in average yearly reservations per rental.

This is a very simplistic example and not based on reality whatsoever because there are a dozen other relevant factors to consider, but it highlights the relationship between supply and demand. You need to keep both in mind. We'll go over the other factors, like, oh, revenue potential (!), in *Chapter 2.5 Step 4: Running The Numbers.*

The supply and demand relationship is also valid for home size. Just as there is a supply and demand relationship for a market, there is also one for each size home (studio, 1-bedroom, 2-bedroom, etc.). Even though 88% of reservations are for less than four guests, causing flawed thinking that a 1- or 2-bedroom home would be best, this stat is wildly misleading as we will further discuss in *Chapter 2.4 Step 3: Identify a Property.*

But right now, let's stick to the market level supply and demand relationship.

A discovered market will have both more rentals (supply) and more guest arrivals (demand). If you're in the top percentile of hosts, you can expect to secure more of these reservations. But there are only so many top hosts and the competition is greater, so you really have to be on your A game.

Why go to a competitive, discovered market when there are plenty of undiscovered markets?

One valid reason is that you want to vacation there. A wonderful feature of vacation rentals is being able to block off dates on the calendar for when you want to use your investment.

Personal interests aside, our job is to understand the relationship between supply and demand in our pursuit of profitability. Undiscovered markets will, in general, have less supply (fewer rentals). We can get a good estimate of this by going to Airbnb directly. While understanding there are more OTAs out there and there could be rental companies with large inventories and completely off the OTAs, it's a fine place to start, as Airbnb is the market leader.

A good indication of the relationship between supply and demand is when 30% of listings have more than 10 reviews. This is assuming they are year-round rentals. If this stat is satisfied but the reviews go back years, it means that these homes are only rented out on a part-time basis. This nullifies our initial research.

If you're seeing many rentals with hundreds of reviews, you're probably looking at a discovered market.

Before we move on, I want to call your attention to one more thing to consider while researching market demand, and that is future market demand. All markets go in cycles. Some cycles are long. Some short. Most cycles repeat.

I'll take Medellin as an international example of a hot market with a bright future.

I'm referring to future demand. Medellin was the most dangerous place on the planet and world-renowned for this fact. This was true for two decades. Since about the early 2000s the city has been on an upward trend. Even today, Medellin in many people's minds is synonymous with Pablo Escobar even though the man has been dead for nearly 30 years.

This misapprehension creates a really unique and enticing opportunity. While of course the visitor should take the minimal precautions, Medellin is overwhelmingly safe, not to mention incredibly cheap. It also brings in repeat vacationers, digital nomads, and real-estate and agricultural investors. In recent years, I've seen more and more young Europeans coming for a couple weeks in their gap year.

Now, the notion of future supply is going to be your guesstimate. You will have to understand the market and the potential for future growth and potential downsides. This isn't about me selling the Medellin market to you, but by my estimation, this market is hot, it's growing fast, the future is bright, and the locals don't seem to be interested in Airbnb as much as foreign investors.

Of course, being in a South American market has its risks, and those need to be accounted for. One of these risks is currency devaluation. Since I bought the rental apartment, the currency has devalued from between 10-25%. If you're investing in the USA or a developed nation like Australia, the UK, or most of Europe, this is not as much a concern as the USD, AUD, GBP, and EUR, respectively, are viewed as stable currencies.

Online Lists

"I found this list on large, mid, and up-and-coming markets and I was wondering if you could take a look and tell me if any stand out to you? There's a ton!"

After browsing the list from a popular vacation rental data company for a few moments, I said, "I see an 'Investor Score'. What is that?"

"I have no clue."

This answer scared me.

While online lists are a fine place to start your research, they should not be relied upon. For reference, for brainstorming, sure. But if you rely on someone else to tell you where to invest, you're in for a world of hurt.

In a few chapters I'll show you why these lists are nearly useless.

Investing is hard. There are a lot of experts out there snapping up the best deals. And there are lots of expert scammers out there presenting themselves as experts and ready to sell you something that doesn't further your financial freedom.

I'll never forget the time I spoke to a host who already made a poor investment based on one of these for-lack-of-a-better-word scammers.

In this case, the caller had purchased an apartment in one these pre-identified hot markets only to realize the local short-term rental laws only allowed reservations for 32-nights or longer. Yikes! Some of you reading this, your heart just sunk. All but guaranteed failure. Why?

Anyone searching for 28 nights (which gives the monthly discount on Airbnb) or even 30 nights will not see this host's listing. On OTA platforms, search inquiries really start to fall after 28 nights. As you get to 32 nights, it's like you're on the 10th page of a Google search results list. Double yikes! That's nearly no one.

I'm sure he'll get a reservation, at rock bottom rates, but then what happens when he has a gap of 10 or 20 or 30 nights. Yikes! Yikes! Yikes! I'm sick to my stomach just writing this.

This host could expect a maximum of around 50% occupancy based on these restrictions. Additionally, he'll have less money to make improvements so he's in for a very painful future.

Why did this happen?

Because this host was looking for and found a direct answer of where to invest. Whether it's an online list or a guru, be very cautious. I hope I've communicated thoroughly in this chapter the importance of identifying your own undiscovered market.

> The most important thing you can do to set yourself up for success, all but guarantee it, in the STR space is choosing the right home in the right micro-neighborhood in the right market. I hope you now have the confidence and strategy to brainstorm and find those undiscovered markets.

2.3 STEP 2: IDENTIFYING A MICRO-NEIGHBORHOOD

While you can identify a market from your living room couch, Step 2 and Step 3 become more difficult if you don't visit in person due to the soft data that becomes more important.

Soft data are things like how much traffic the street has, how safe the route walking to the nearest popular street is, or how likely it is that a building were erected that would ruin your view.

As you know, it's my preference to visit in person to identify the best micro-neighborhoods. It doesn't mean you have to live there for a year before making a decision. But, going in person for more than a couple nights is important.

A micro-neighborhood is a specific area of the larger neighborhood, sometimes a street or around a feature like a park, which will increase your profits due to the ideal location.

I also understand it can be difficult and time consuming to visit in person. For these situations, I have two alternatives.

First, in *Chapter 2.6 Alternative Method To Find An STR Investment*, I introduce a strategy to identify these micro-neighborhoods by using data alone. This strategy will still require your time, and it is a very reliable process, but you will not need to visit the market to identify the most profitable micro-neighborhoods.

Second, if you want a fully passive STR investment, you could engage a professional company offering these services, many of which exist today. They do everything: identify the market, buy, hold, and manage the rental, and sell it years later. Your investment portfolio gets exposure to the industry, but you don't own the underlying asset directly. You share in the profits, but with limited risk. Of course, this means your ROI will be lower. If you go this route you would evaluate the *company* and make an investment based on that.

In the Deal Sheet under 'Passive STR Investments' you will find the two companies that I invest with. One is restricted to accredited investors in the USA with a $25,000 minimum investment. The other is open to all investors with a minimum investment of $100. If you want more information, scan the QR code.

Bonus Item
– Deal Sheet

SCAN ME

Back to the topic at hand.

So, you've identified your vacation rental market, or a few of them. Now, you have to study the different neighborhoods in order to identify your preferred micro-neighborhood.

I recently met a gentleman doing Airbnb rental arbitrage here in Medellin. He has a large rental, just like mine. He has a hot tub, just like mine. His home is in Poblado, the main touristy area, just like mine. But his home is not in the same micro-neighborhood.

He's making $6,000 per month with an estimated high-end target of $10,000. I am making $14,000 with the potential for $18,000 a month.

Again, we're both in the same city, with the same size home, the same neighborhood, similar amenities, even with similar expenses, but drastically different revenues. Why?

I don't talk much about neighborhoods for a reason. **Micro-neighborhoods are much more important.** For example, one neighborhood might have a highway cutting through it, making STR ownership unprofitable on one side but profitable on the other.

His home is in the hills. While it has a nice view, much better than mine, it's far away from where his guests want to go. It would require up to a half-hour taxi ride for anything from a lunch to going out at night and everything in between.

Additionally, when tourists come to Medellin for the first time, they hear about Lleras Park (the 'll' is pronounced like the 'll' in tortillas; YEH-ras Park). And only Lleras Park. Medellin is unique in that there is one central, main point of tourism. And that's especially true for first-time arrivals.

Another problem of a home that far out is the maps on OTAs. His location is outside of where a typical FPG would be looking on the map which means his listing doesn't show up for many of these FPGs.

Same market. Same neighborhood. Very different micro-neighborhoods. My title even says how far away Lleras Park is from my rental (eight minutes on foot) because I know how important this one fact is to FPGs.

Let's assume a guest booked both of our places, and we're in a market that see's repeat guests year after year. The guest is more likely to return to mine for their next trip because, while it's walkable to all the nightlife, it also is not noisy. You can sleep at night! The best of both worlds. This is soft data. As you continue your investment journey, keep this hidden factor in mind: what percentage of guests return and how frequently?

Let's take an even finer example to demonstrate the effect of micro-neighborhoods on your success.

When searching for an apartment in the Poblado neighborhood of Medellin, I made note of two streets next to each other. Specifically, 'Calle 6' and 'Calle 5G'. Calle in Spanish means street. I know, they get creative with their street names. They are side-by-side. Calle 5G was an acceptable street. Calle 6, even though I visited a beautiful penthouse with a rooftop jacuzzi and gorgeous view, was unacceptable.

The decision came down to the incline of each street. Soft data. Calle 6 was twice as steep, yet too near Lleras Park to call a taxi. Additionally, it was a dead-end street, and taxis often got lost. Soft data. My guests would be forced to walk and return up a hill any time they wanted a coffee, food, cigarettes, or to go out at night. Even if you were in pretty good shape, you'd be short of breath each time you returned home. It's not a pleasant experience. They'd be unlikely to return, and it might even affect the review.

I knew all of this not only because of my exploring of the micro-neighborhoods, but also because I stayed nearby as a guest and had first-hand experience walking these streets.

Ideally, you will be a tourist in your potential market so that you can have first-hand experience of what the guest is looking for, even if they don't know, and also what they will experience in daily life. This is soft data, and I hope you're starting to see its importance.

There's another popular neighborhood in Medellin called Laureles. But my local knowledge told me that guests who choose this neighborhood are already familiar with Medellin, have smaller budgets, typically stay longer which further cuts into profits, and are more likely to make a direct booking off the OTAs. None of this is necessarily bad, but for my goals, it was not ideal.

I wanted first-time arrivals, shorter stays, and wealthier guests. The data confirmed my local knowledge that the neighborhood of Poblado, and specifically the micro-neighborhood of Lleras Park, was where I wanted to make an investment.

Other Considerations

There's another location also only an eight-minute walk from Lleras Park except that it's separated by two main thoroughfares. That's two long stoplights, crossing some less-than-safe streets every time you want to go to the main area. One of the ways a micro-neighborhood is defined is by the streets: highways and main thoroughfares.

Parks can also be a micro-neighborhood defining feature. In Madrid, Spain there is a park called El Retiro. West side is good. East side is bad. East Side has fewer Metro lines and for being so close, creates an extra 30 minutes of transit any time you want to go to the main tourist area.

Be wary of flight paths or trains causing daily noise and inconveniences to the guest.

Are you near the main entrance of the super-mega concerts of Coachella or Stagecoach in Indio, California or 25 minutes away? This becomes even more important for locations with repeat guests who start to understand the micro-neighborhoods themselves because they know which are hilly, unsafe, or simply less convenient for their trip.

Are you privy to the workings of city politics and local planning commissions? Is there a future metro line or other city development planned for the future changing the dynamics of neighborhoods? We touch on this in the prior chapter about future demand.

When I arrived in Medellin in 2018, I stayed in the micro-neighborhood called Manila. It was fine, but nothing special. Today, it's buzzing with new developments and is ideally located to various hot spots including Lleras Park. I saw this future demand in 2020 when searching for a rental and was going to buy an apartment there until the Colombian owner disappeared (story for another time) causing me to restart my search and leading me, ultimately, to *The Belmonte Penthouse.*

Are you near a theme park, famed golf course, river rafting, well-known hiking spots, cruise ship stops?

Knowing your FPG also comes into play here, which I'll cover in *Part 3: Build and Optimize Your Listing.*

If your FPG is coming for the party and restaurants then your micro-neighborhood should not only be in this area, but in the best micro-spot of this area. Close enough, but not too close. Soft data.

Or are they coming to New York and likely to use the subway? Being near a stop might prove very wise. Or are they coming for medical treatment over a couple weeks? Then being able to access the hospital without getting on the freeway full of traffic might be important.

> The most important thing you can do to set yourself up for success, all but guarantee it, in the STR space is choosing the right home in the right micro-neighborhood in the right market. I hope you now have the confidence and strategy to brainstorm and find the best micro-neighborhoods.

2.4 STEP 3:
IDENTIFY A PROPERTY

In the last two chapters, if we zoom out, we're trying to find the biggest differential between supply and demand at both the market and micro-neighborhood levels. We're not looking individually at supply or demand, but the relationship between the two.

When it comes down to identifying a specific property, there are a few things to consider. Not only do you want to consider the actual property, how it looks, how old the building is, etc., but you also want to consider the differential between supply and demand in terms of home size.

During my profitable property search and based on my research in Step 2, I was able to be micro-focused, and my agent knew that. He stopped trying to sell me on certain properties, because he knew I was looking at everything so specifically and in such detail that he knew he would be wasting his time. He sent me the photo, stats, and address, and most of the time it was a no. But he knew I was serious about buying.

Advice: if you engage a real estate agent, but you're not serious about buying, they will stop sending you leads and will be hesitant to put in much work in the future when you are.

Many agents even gave up on me as a serious buyer. Throughout my entire process I was in contact with nine and seven of them stopped sending me properties quite

quickly. Or, maybe it was me. One agent, when presented with my detailed list of requirements, said in 30 years he'd never seen anything like it. If you're curious to see what that list looked like, you'll find it in the bonus items. I'm unsure if that was a compliment, but I think not because he didn't send me any leads. He said he didn't have any that fit all my requirements. That's ok. I'm here to ensure a profitable investment.

Bonus Item: Google Sheet - List of requirements for Medellin search

SCAN ME

Investing is very serious business for me, especially when I'm doing so in a foreign country and on an all-cash deal. I did it because I knew, after going through this process, what a successful investment looked like and where it would be located. My confidence level was high. Whether you're investing in your home country or abroad, the process is the same.

In fact, all future investments will be documented in my course.

I knew to a very high degree of certainty that if I found what I was looking for, it would be a success.

I knew exactly what I wanted, where I wanted it, and at what price.

What I didn't know, and part of what I'll cover in this chapter, is what size home is most profitable. For that, I need some data.

It's really all about finding the demand. But demand is not as easily knowable as supply.

Supply data you can easily obtain. How many homes are available in the market? Any data tool will give you that information.

As a side note, supply data gets trickier the more detailed you get. There might be 1,000 rentals in your market, but how many are truly competition? How many are on your level? How many are renting out year-round? Is the owner a hospitality professional like you? That becomes more difficult, with more assumptions, but doable. The profits are hiding in the details. You will be a master of the details.

We want to know how many available rentals are there for studios all the way up to 5-bedrooms in most markets. You also want to consider bathrooms.

A 3-bedroom, 1-bathroom (3/1) versus a 3-bedroom, 3.5-bathroom (3/3.5) tells you a good bit of information. A 3/1 is probably an old building, it's probably not a luxury design whereas a 3/3.5 is a newer building or updated unit and probably has a more modern or luxury feel.

This matters when we "run the numbers" in the next chapter as luxury homes cost more and better be earning more revenue as a result for them to be a profitable investment.

But right now, we want to run the numbers in a more general sense to figure out what will make a profitable investment.

The process looks like this: First, we get the total supply of each size home, hopefully in our ideal neighborhood. Then, we get the occupancy per size. Ideally, you can get the occupancy on a monthly basis. This is important due to seasonality.

Finally, get the Average Daily Rate (ADR) by size of home. We'll use a short-term rental data tool to get the data, and with it we can arrive at the estimated yearly revenue.

Below I'll present a simplified example where you can start to see how there's an $18,000 increase in yearly revenue from 3-bedroom to 4-bedroom which is a clue to demand. You can also see the occupancy fall for 2-, 4-, and 5-bedroom homes.

Size of Home	Supply	Occupancy	ADR	Yearly Revenue
1-bedroom	745	78%	$148	$42,206
2-bedroom	638	71%	$174	$45,137
3-bedroom	523	84%	$182	$55,872
4-bedroom	235	70%	$288	$73,655
5-bedroom	135	50%	$426	$77,670

Table 2.4.1 Yearly Revenue Per Size Home Based On Data

I want to be clear that the above example is too simplistic as it's an average. As you know, there are winners and losers in every market. You'd want to filter out the obvious dud results, those listings that have terrible ratings, the outliers, etc. The above can be thought of as the 50th percentile. Some listings in each category could be making twice the average, or more.

With this information, before seeing how much a home costs and wasting your time running those numbers, you will have a good idea of what a profitable investment property should cost.

A payback period is how long it takes you to recoup the full cost of the investment. In our example, the investment was the purchase price of the home. If the 2-bedroom home making $45,000 per year costs $400,000, your payback period is 8.9 years.

In the vacation rental industry, a good payback period is five years. More than seven should not be considered as a good investment in my opinion. We want an excellent investment, and anything around four years is excellent.

If we want a payback period of five years, this is our budget per home.

Size of Home	Yearly Rev * Payback Period	Maximum Cost of Home
1-bedroom	$42,206 * 5	$211,030
2-bedroom	$45,137 * 5	$225,685
3-bedroom	$55,872 * 5	$279,360
4-bedroom	$73,655 * 5	$368,275
5-bedroom	$77,670 * 5	$388,350

Table 2.4.2 Calculating Maximum Cost of Home For 5-Year Payback Period

Apologies to my readers in the USA to whom these numbers look ridiculous, but for 80% of the planet these numbers are reasonable. Homes in many desirable areas across America easily cost in the millions. If it's easier, you can think of these as the down payment. Regardless of the numbers, the strategy remains. While it's true that a payback period differs for different markets, it's also true that the quicker the payback, the better the investment. So, why would you want to invest in a market where the average payback period is six, seven, or eight years? The longer time horizon increases your risk.

It's important to know what our home should maximally cost at each size to make a good investment because typically a larger home, in the same area, will incrementally increase in cost like this:

Size of Home	Average Cost of Home
1-bedroom	$205,000
2-bedroom	$235,000
3-bedroom	$254,000
4-bedroom	$289,000
5-bedroom	$318,000

Table 2.4.3 Average Home Value In Market Per Size Home

This narrows our focus to 3-, 4-, and 5-bedroom homes because it allows for us to buy a slightly nicer than average home fetching us a slightly nicer than average return. We're off to a good start!

Let's see what that looks like:

Size of Home	Yearly Revenue	Average Cost of Home	Maximum Cost of Home	Spread
1-bedroom	$42,206	$205,000	$211,030	$6,030
2-bedroom	$45,137	$235,000	$225,685	($9,315)
3-bedroom	$55,872	$254,000	$279,360	$25,360
4-bedroom	$73,655	$289,000	$368,275	$79,275
5-bedroom	$77,670	$318,000	$388,350	$70,350

Table 2.4.4 Calculating Most Profitable Home Size

With the table above, you can see the average cost of the home is less than your maximum cost limit for a payback period of five years if the spread (right-most column) is positive. We know that a 2-bedroom home is likely to be a bad investment in this market.

A 4-bedroom home gives you a surplus of almost $80,000 to work with when looking for your investment. It means you can get a nicer 4-bedroom home likely to result in higher profits. The middle column is the average cost of a home in our example micro-neighborhood which means you would likely get average returns (average home gets you average returns) if you bought a home for that amount.

Although this analysis is an important one, it is just one of many ways you can analyze your profitable property. And, you should be using as many different methods as possible to get the clearest picture. I think this is absolutely essential, and in the online course I will be using a variety of analyses for my next short-term rental investment.

Other Considerations

Besides the cost and location, the home layout is also to be considered:

- Is it an open-plan layout?
- Are the ceilings high?
- What about the size of the bathrooms and shower?
- One or two levels?
- Do the doors roll or swing open?
- What are the unique features, cover photo opportunities?
- Is there a pool or gym? Other communal facilities?
- What's on the ground floor of the apartment building? Nothing or a desirable café?
- Does the sun hit in the morning or in the afternoon? If it hits in the afternoon/evening time, does the home get overly hot?

- Is there potential for construction across the road which would ruin the view and set you up for noise complaints and less revenue over the next 2-3 years?
- Is there a convenience store down the street?
- Is the immediate neighborhood flat? Would your FPGs care?
- Do the bedrooms share a wall, decreasing privacy?
- If it's in a building, what's the vibe? What floor? Where is your parking spot located?

Regarding the last point, as a guest, it's always disappointing yet common to be on a low level without a view. And this is often hidden in the photos.

The above is more soft data to be considered.

During my search, my local knowledge told me that there was a plethora of studio, 1-, and 2- bedroom apartments, and there were various projects going up and planned that would add an additional quantity of smaller sized STRs. This further convinced me to raise my budget and go for a larger home.

Additionally, there is a more defined nightly rate cap on smaller units. Even if it's a nice one-bedroom, at a certain point dictated by the cost of two-bedrooms, that FPG will decide on a larger space—because they *always* want the largest space they can get for their money. This is the cap. But as you get up to 3-, 4-, and 5-bedroom homes, there is less of a cap because there are fewer homes available. This cap is further diminished when the home is unique.

Look for structural features. Multi-level homes are unique, and highlight features like a giant balcony or unique flooring or windows all make a home unique. Even how the light enters the home is a factor to be considered. I was in a very nice looking home in Ubud, Bali, but it was on the side of mountain where it was always dark and gloomy based on how the sun rose and set. I swear I felt depressed and unproductive in that space based on how the light hit it each day.

Spaces are also important. Remember, spaces are unique features of one area or room. They make things more complex and sometimes feel larger. If you have a backyard, that can be one or many spaces. The pool is one space. The BBQ area is another space. If you put up a gazebo, that counts as a space. In the living room, if you have a space for the TV and couch and another space with an armchair and small table to read, these are two spaces.

When I visited *The Belmonte Penthouse*, I noticed a river in front of the building. This does two awesome and unexpected things. First, it creates a soothing sound. Second, it neutralizes some of the noise from nearby traffic and Lleras Park, the rowdy party zone.

There was also a similarly designed hotel, in that guests booking my place typically also like the design of the hotel, two buildings away. This has also proven to be very useful because, if there are more than four guests who want a central meeting place but their own private room to sleep, the overflow can go to this hotel. I've recommended that hotel many times to complete a reservation.

Some of the other unique features in my rental are a "Sky Shower" (it's a semi-outdoor show with a glass roof), a bar area, a garden patio, separate living room in the master bedroom, and a massive, thick wooden dining table.

During your search, you shouldn't be too hasty. You should see many options because not only do you not always know what you are looking for, but sometimes you don't know what you are going to find. At the outset of my search, for example, looking for a river or to be near a fancy hotel was not something I was thinking about, but it has added value to my STR business.

> The most important thing you can do to set yourself up for success, all but guarantee it, in the STR space is choosing the right home in the right micro-neighborhood in the right market. I hope you now have the confidence and strategy to brainstorm and find the best properties in your chosen micro-neighborhood.

2.5 STEP 4: RUNNING THE NUMBERS

The Belmonte Penthouse

12-month revenue prior to purchase = $45,000
Expectation based on running the numbers = $126,000
12-month revenue after purchase = $156,000

Always remember: **when you are running the numbers on individual properties, you are the output.**

What I mean is that the final numbers come from you. Not from the data. The data helps. It helps a lot. But it's an input. Your analysis and agreement of the numbers, is the output. This will become clear by the end of this chapter. If I were to rely solely on the data as provided by external parties, I may have missed out on an opportunity generating 27% annual return.

In my case, this was a prior Airbnb, so I had existing revenue data to work from. This is getting more and more common.

However, if I hadn't had that hard data, then I could have used an online data analytics tool to make the same estimates that I got from numbers provided by the owner. These tools tend to be pretty accurate if you know what you're doing. We'll talk more about this in the next chapter.

You can also go directly to Airbnb or another OTA and search for your competition, look at their nightly rates, and look at their future calendar occupancy.

You want as many data points as you can get. I created a very simple yet accurate revenue calculator on my website. It estimated my revenue at between $127,750 and $164,250. Not bad for only four questions. Scan the QR code to try it (and be sure to watch the video explanation!)

OptimizeMyBnb.com
STR Revenue
Calculator

SCAN ME

AIRBNB REVENUE CALCULATOR

🏷 Nightly Rate: `500`

👥 Number of guests: `4`

🏢 City Population: `3000000`

🏠 Your place is: `Entire Home or Apartment ⌄`

▦ Calculate

Your Yearly Estimated Airbnb Revenue Is: 127,750 - 164,250

This should be combined with your own estimates including ways in which you believe you can increase the revenue.

My deal was a really unique situation where it was a true win-win. The prior owner was using a property manager and making $45,000 per year renting about eight days per month at $500 per night.

In talking with the prior owner, he was thrilled and was selling to me for a markup of nearly twice what he had bought the place for three years prior.

The apartment wasn't listed publicly, but the owner was happy to sell it. After running the numbers, I was more than happy to buy it.

And I was happy to buy it because, after running the numbers, even my conservative estimates showed me making a tremendous profit well above what the prior owner was doing.

There are a lot of assumptions that go into making these revenue and expense predictions—and this is where my skills and experience come in to benefit you. Let's see what I'm talking about by getting into the details of my story.

What predictions and assumptions did I make to get from revenue of $45,000 per year to $126,000, and how did I underestimate that by a full $30,000?

The Belmonte Penthouse Analysis

Let's first examine what the prior owner was doing.

He was renting out this 4-bedroom, 4-bath apartment for approximately eight nights per month at $500 per night. This was essentially the weekends.

His property manager did not use any dynamic pricing tool.

There were no weekly or monthly discounts encouraging tack-on days or longer-term rentals during slower periods.

They were offering free airport pickup with a reservation of three nights or longer.

They had set maximum guests at four.

They were offering daily cleaning.

Next, let's start with my revenue side calculations.

My original calculations were as follows:

I would increase occupancy to eight guests and charge a premium after the fifth guest. This would widen my pool of reservations as anyone searching for five to eight guests would now see my listing and at a slight increase in price.

I estimated an increase in occupancy by half from 8 to 12 nights per month with dynamic pricing.

I estimated a 25% weekend premium given the strong weekend booking pattern ($625 per night Fridays and Saturdays).

I also would discount midweek and assumed this would add up to an additional eight nights at $400 (or $3,200 total).

Because the prior owner offered no long-stay discounts, he got no long-stay bookings. The local competition was offering somewhere between no discount and 35%.

I understood the home was going to be used more as a party/social house, and my initial idea was to book more week-long or longer reservations that would decrease the parties and damage. I would offer a 50% weekly discount for revenue of $1,750 per week-long reservation.

I didn't anticipate any month-long reservations.

This brought me a monthly estimated revenue of roughly:

($625 x 8 weekend nights) + ($400 x 8 weekday nights) + (a weeklong booking at a 50% discount) = $9,950

I factored in an additional $500 for the extra guest fee assuming I would get about one per month.

You'll notice occupancy is missing from the above analysis, and that is because in Medellin the entire year is one long busy season. The climate ranges from 65-85° F (18-28° C) year-round, and their summertime which runs from November to February just means there is less rain. Even when it does rain, it's usually for an hour or two per day.

If you are dealing in a market with seasons, then you will have to estimate a change in rates and occupancy. For example, in busy season you may be able to get $500 per night at

90% occupancy for five months, but low season prices are only $250 at 60% occupancy for seven months.

> In the bonus items, I have included a simple Excel spreadsheet with formulas that can help you with this math.

Bonus item:
Google Sheet
- Monthly Revenue
Estimates

SCAN ME

General Expense Estimates

Expense estimates are much easier to make than revenue. And all over the world, expenses are standard. There are two types of expenses: fixed and variable.

Fixed expenses are cash outflows no matter what (even if you have zero reservations), like mortgage payments, property taxes, and insurance.

Variable expenses are associated with usage. These are things like toilet paper (consumables) or electricity costs (utilities), all of which will rise with more reservations. Repairs and maintenance costs will also increase.

Paying someone to check your guests in, any transportation costs, providing extras like flowers or welcome gifts, property manager costs—all of these things you would know and should add to the expense calculation.

The Belmonte Penthouse Incorrect Assumptions

I had many revelations related to revenues and expenses, but some of the larger ones were all related to how I priced my listing.

While the weekend days were Friday and Saturday and the demand was roughly an increase of 25%, the rates would sometimes go to $1,000 nightly (a 100% increase above average nightly rate). This was uncommon, but rates in the $700 to $800 range happened with more regularity. Additionally, Thursday and Sunday also commanded premiums of 10%.

A lot of this was adjusted automatically by the dynamic pricing tool once I dialed in my base price. We'll learn about that and pricing customizations in *Part 5: Pricing*.

Monday to Wednesday typically go for $320 at the cheapest, not $400.

My biggest realization was that I needed to eliminate my last-minute discount which is a staple pricing customization for the majority of STRs. (This adjusts the nightly rate so that, after a certain point, the closer you get to the actual booking date, the lower the rate is.) I published a video about this unique situation on my YouTube. To sum it up, while my average booking lead time is 25 days, the majority of my bookings come in the next 15 days *or* more than 45 days in advance.

I had been offering a gradual discount of 40% starting at 25 days out. However, after I realized that nearly half of my bookings are reserved within just two weeks of check-in date, this last-minute discount no longer made sense and I promptly removed it.

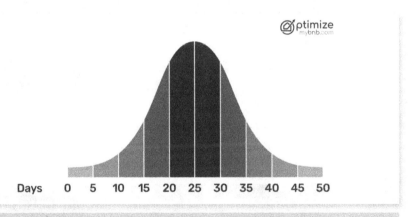

A normal bell curve for a rental with a 25-day booking lead time.

For most listings with a 25-day booking lead time, your bookings will look like the above chart. Most will come between 15 and 35 days. This is a normal bell curve.

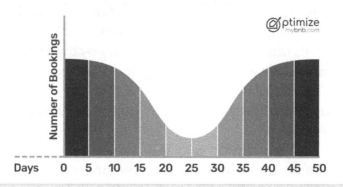

The inverse bell curve of *The Belmonte Penthouse* where the BLT is still 25-days but most bookings are made within 15-days and further than 35 days into the future.

Above is my bell curve and, as you can see, it's inverse! I figured this out after some time observing my booking patterns, then I analyzed all the data to confirm my suspicions. I think this is more common than you might think and encourage you to analyze your booking lead time. Here is that YouTube video.

Video: Booking Lead Time Analysis For *The Belmonte Penthouse*

SCAN ME

While I did get one month-long and one week-long reservation, I quickly removed these longer-term discounts due to my occupancy estimate being way off. My occupancy has been 100% some months, and overall it sits at 94% yearly. This means that I don't need to offer any discounts unless it is my personal preference for longer reservations.

> The most important thing you can do to set yourself up for success, all but guarantee it, in the STR space is choosing the right home in the right micro-neighborhood in the right market. Once you've carried out that research, you should have a deep understanding of the market and be able to run the numbers with a high degree of confidence.

2.6 ALTERNATE METHOD TO FIND AN STR INVESTMENT

There's another reliable and effective way to find a profitable vacation rental anywhere in the world with data alone. That means you don't have to visit in person. It works, but you have to be comfortable analyzing raw data.

This process has four steps:

First, you will extract market data from an online STR data and analytics tool.

Second, you will organize that data by average revenue to identify the most profitable neighborhoods and home sizes in the market. Here, you will need to identify and remove bad data for a more accurate analysis.

Third, you will start to analyze the vacation rentals in the identified neighborhood to determine what drives the revenue of the successful rentals and what the unsuccessful ones are doing wrong.

Fourth and final, you need to find properties that match your profit profile.

In the accompanying course, I will be documenting my next short-term rental investment—which will be in the USA—using this strategy, and I hope you'll join me!

Let's get started.

Step 1

After you have selected a market, you need to find a data tool that will allow you to download and analyze the data. You'll find my recommended data tool in the Deal Sheet.

Typically, these tools show you a pleasant-looking graphical dashboard. They are not so useful for our purposes because the data is too broad. Even if they show top and bottom performing rentals by percentile, we want to get as granular as we can.

Once we have the data, before we can analyze it, we need to remove the bad data. Bad data is an important topic that can create material errors in our analysis and we will return to it a few times in this chapter.

In this case, bad data would be any piece of data for individual properties with less than 300 days tracked. This simply leaves too much to the imagination to be useful and can potentially affect our results.

Maybe the rental started in busy season, so if we were to extrapolate 9-month data to 12-months, occupancy and revenue would likely be overstated as those three missing months were the slow season and thus less profitable. Alternatively, maybe they got started during slow season leading to a likely material *understatement* of extrapolated annual data.

Regardless, be sure that, whatever data tool you use, it identifies the minimum days tracked. Ideally, they can tell you what actual dates are missing from the prior year if less than a full year was tracked.

Assuming we are looking to invest and rent out an entire home, any private or shared room data is also to be considered bad data and should be removed.

We need to know how a 4-bedroom on one side of the city compares to a 4-bedroom on the other. In fact, we need to see how everything from a studio to an 8-bedroom mansion, if there is one, performs in every identifiable neighborhood of the city.

This way we will be able to identify, at the same time, both the most profitably-sized homes (how many bedrooms and bathrooms) and the most profitable neighborhoods of the market.

Step 2

Now that we have only valid data, we'll want to organize this data by neighborhood and by bedroom/bathroom size. Your data tool will identify neighborhoods in any variety of ways, sometimes zip code or sometimes actual neighborhood names like Soho or Lleras Park. Either works fine at this point.

After organizing, we will easily be able to identify the most profitable neighborhoods plus the most profitably-sized homes. It's often the case that you'll see a jump in revenue by just adding a single bedroom and/or bathroom.

To simplify the example, I'll ignore bathrooms. It'll look like this:

	1-bedroom	2-bedroom	3-bedroom	4-bedroom
Zone 1	$68,000	$71,000	$75,000	$79,000
Zone 2	$59,000	$64,000	$66,000	$67,000
Zone 3	$77,000	$79,000	$96,000	$99,000
Zone 4	$97,000	$103,000	$111,000	$118,000

Table 2.6.1 Organized Yearly Revenue Data By Neighborhood From Data Tool

You can probably see that Zone 3 seems to be where we want to start and, specifically, there, 3-bedrooms jump $17,000, or 22%, in revenue by just adding one bedroom. Our hope is that the cost of a home from 2-bedroom to 3-bedroom in this zone doesn't also jump by 22%.

But to go to a 4th bedroom might not make sense as a 4-bedroom home will cost more than 3-bedroom home, but the increase in revenue is only an additional $3,000, or 3%.

It's a clue as to demand, but we'll need to verify it all in step 3.

We're using Burger King logic here. McDonalds spends millions deciding what street corner will be most profitable. Then, Burger King opens up across the street.

That is to say, we're going to discover what is already working and replicate. We are confident in our abilities at hosting, at running a vacation rental, so our edge will come in how we do that compared to our local competition. We're starting ourselves off with an advantage. We'll know we're in the right neighborhood.

A noteworthy difference between this method and those covered in the prior chapters is that we're ignoring future demand and market changes. Up-and-coming markets will be invisible to us using this method without local market knowledge.

By this point, we have extracted the data, understood the data, removed the bad data, and sorted the data so that we can further identify where the most profitable neighborhoods (we're calling them zones) are in the market.

The next step is to dig in to both Zone 3 and Zone 4 above to figure out what is driving revenue. The above numbers are averages, so there will be some listings above and below the average.

Step 3

Step three is probably the most fun for me. We're going to start analyzing each of the listings in the most profitable zones.

We'll need to remove more bad data. Any listings where the link doesn't work or has fewer than 20 reviews is too incomplete to be relied upon for such an important decision.

Any listings with revenue significantly higher than the rest are suspicious, and we'll investigate. It could be a combination listing, meaning that one home is split up into multiple listings. The larger listing has a higher price, but it's not getting booked out often because any time one of the smaller listings gets a reservation, the larger listing gets an automatic calendar block for those dates as their calendars are synced to avoid a double booking.

But the data tool probably can't tell the difference because it looks like a legit booking pattern. So, the data tool is recording revenue for the larger listing even though it's actually a blocked date. This is bad data and prime example of how you are the output and data is the input.

Now that we have good data, let's start with Zone 4. While rentals in this zone make more money, we can clearly see after clicking on a few listings that the homes in this zone are going to cost $2M+. We'd be paying double the price for the home, for less than double the income. Bad deal.

Moving on to Zone 3. Open up every listing link no matter the platform. Take note of the listings above and below the averages. What you're doing now is identifying what drives revenue. You're going to notice the higher-grossing listings have nice photos plus they may all have some common amenity. Do they all have large backyards or a hot tub or two living rooms? How do the kitchens look? Are there more luxurious finishes like stainless steel appliances and granite countertops?

If you don't notice much difference between the listings, the difference may come down to revenue management. Remember *The Belmonte Penthouse* property manager had it listed at $500 per night for the entire year. They were missing out both on weekday revenue at a lower price and weekend revenue at a higher price. If that property manager was doing his or her job, they would have doubled the income with a revenue management strategy. We'll go over this in *Chapter 5.4 Weekly Occupancy Management*.

Now you need to do two things:

1. Make a list of what drives revenue
2. Plot the locations on a map

By making a list of what drives revenue, we will know what amenities are a must for our future rental property purchase. By plotting the locations of the highest-grossing listings, we will know what micro-neighborhood will further give us a competitive advantage. If all are located on one side of a highway or near a park, knowing this is valuable. You don't even need to know what it is that the best rentals are clustered around (a stadium, a concert venue, downtown, etc.), but if all the homes are in the southeastern part of the zone, you'll want to note this. Remember the Burger King Logic.

What you are doing with this process is putting yourself in the guest's shoes during their search. The guest, our paying customer, is examining all the available options and deciding based on them. Let's say you noticed that all the best homes have a small putting green next to a large outdoor pool. Whether or not the guest was specifically looking for a putting green at the outset of their search, they're telling you that by the time they are ready to make a reservation, those homes with the putting green represent the best value.

Thus, the homes with a putting green next to a larger pool, whether that's because it photographs well or many of the FPGs like golf or whatever reason, are getting the majority of reservations.

Does that make sense? Of the available options, whether or not the booking guest realizes it, the putting green *is* the thing that separates the *best* from the merely *good* homes. Even if the booking guest doesn't necessarily want a putting green, through their search they've realized these homes represent the best value. Why book a home without a putting green when you can get one for the same price?

This is your starting point or the minimum requirements. Maybe you even try to beat out the competition and change the market dynamic by adding some other amenity you know will be in demand?

Now that we're confident where to buy, how big of a home to buy, and what features that home needs, it's time to find properties that match.

Step 4

If you're in a part of the world with organized real estate listings, this search will be quick and easy. You can go on a website like Zillow in the US and find what is available in your area, even specifying home size and other filters.

If you don't have this type of platform in your country, or it's not common to list on public directories when you want to sell (thus making it a little more involved to buy), consider it your competitive advantage.

Even though it can be harder to locate deals in this environment, the seller will have fewer offers to review.

Regardless of whether you are using an online platform, a real-estate agent, your local contacts, or a local person to knock on doors, the process is the same.

In our example, that average 3-bedroom in Zone 3 is making $96,000. But that's the average. The homes in the higher end are making around $110,000, and that will be our goal, if not $120,000. We are confident in our abilities in hosting. We know we are a great host and will be one of the best in this market. Every market has winners and losers. We are a winner.

As we discussed in the last chapter, we want to purchase a home valued at no more than five times yearly revenue or $480,000.

Now it's just a matter of finding desirable homes that match this price. Check online how many were sold within our specifications under that price in the last year, or ask the real estate agent.

A quick piece of advice regarding real-estate agents. I find that buyers place too much value on their opinions. I suggest you use a real-estate agent's opinion on the market or any individual property as a single data point, and only if they also invest in the local market.

It's beautiful how easy this is, right? After your analysis of the data, you know what the ideal home looks like, where it is, how big it is, what amenities it has. Then you only need to find one for sale.

Sometimes, it's not possible. Fine. You saved yourself a poor investment. But from my experience, the majority of times, you're going to find many profitable deals.

Before we move on I want to briefly talk about another popular STR strategy, and that is rental arbitrage. The gentlemen from my example in *Chapter 2.3 Step 2: Identifying a Micro-Neighborhood* was doing rental arbitrage. Rental arbitrage is for people who want to get into STRs but don't have the capital for a down payment or property management experience. Instead, they look to rent a property at lower long-term rates and list it on an OTA at higher short-term rates, thus pocketing the difference.

I'm not a rental arbitrage expert and don't feel qualified to speak at length about this subject. That's the bad news.

The good news is that Brian Page, the person who wrote my foreword is the owner and creator of the most popular rental arbitrage course and has just written his own introductory book. Scan the QR code to learn more.

Learn More About The *BNB Formula*.

SCAN ME

Conclusion

This method has its place in the short-term rental market analysis portion of your hosting success. It helps with the demand data which is harder to get. Supply side data is much easier except for identifying the good listings. It's one thing to know there are 1,000 active listings in a market. But it's another to know there are 15 that are truly competitive to what you will want to do in the neighborhood that you want to do it in.

You have two options for this strategy. You can implement it yourself with what you just learned. If you are visual, I have published videos on my YouTube. Search "vacation rental market analysis" on my channel to find it.

Or, you can purchase it done-for-you.

Featured Product Discount - Vacation Rental Market Analysis

The Vacation Rental Market Analysis analyzes the data from your chosen market and produces an Excel document of all the data. At the end you get a consultation call with a member of my team to explain all the details and to answer your questions.

Find your 5% discount code in the 'Featured Product Discounts' PDF of the bonus items.

Featured Product Discount - Vacation Rental Market Analysis

SCAN ME

> The most important thing you can do to set yourself up for success, all but guarantee it, in the STR space is choosing the right home in the right neighborhood in the right market. Once you've gone through that data, you should have a deep understanding of the market and know what exactly you need to achieve market dominance.

2.7 A NOTE ABOUT HARD DATA AND DATA TOOLS

Numbers lie. Most data is inaccurate. It sounds grave, and it is. I'm saying that as an accountant. At Airbnb, I worked as a Certified Public Accountant in the Finance department. I know numbers.

Whenever you see an official-looking, impressively-designed chart or a stat or some other data, from here on out you should do one of two things:

1. Verify what's behind that number/data before relying on it.
2. Assume it's false and do not rely on it at all.

Straight false. As bad as an outright lie. And it might be.

I'm serious about this. Not knowing this will cost you money and potentially a catastrophic amount.

Let me give you one simple example. Let's say you're using my strategy in the prior chapter to identify listings with high revenue. You found some! They seem like a great deal if you look at that yearly total revenue number. But what if you didn't know that this STR data tool calculated yearly revenue for any listing that is active for more than 180 days. In other words, any listing that was active for between 181 and 365 days would show a yearly revenue number. But, let's say your high season is six months, or about 181 days, and that's only when you list your space.

Let's say during high season you make $100,000 and during low season you would make $50,000. But in this example, you're not listing during low season, only high season. So, this data tool only has 180+ days, or half, the required data. They want to present their customer with more data and what looks to be complete data.

What does this data company do? They assign a yearly income for this property at $200,000. That's 33% more than the $150,000 this property would normally earn.

This was actually a true example from a popular online STR data company. This specific data inaccuracy has been fixed. But there are others.

If you do not understand what is behind a number, then you shouldn't rely on it.

That's the bad news.

The good news is that we can use it as our competitive advantage because most people don't know this about data, or wouldn't amend their behavior if they did.

If you take the time to investigate what's behind the number, then you will earn a competitive advantage so great that your chances of success skyrocket and are all but guaranteed.

When To Use Data?

I get a version of the following question often enough that it warrants its own section: "What do you think of this data tool?" or "Is that data tool worth it?"

My follow up is the same: "What do you want to get from the data tool?" "What are you looking for?" "Why do you want STR data?"

The answer is usually that they don't know. They just kinda feel it's the right, professional thing to do. They've heard the name on forums, etc.

Here's the answer: If you don't know why or what data you want, then you shouldn't subscribe to the tool.

There are only two reasons why you should be looking at STR data:

1. You have a specific question that you believe can be answered with it.
2. You have a desire to understand data and how it can help you.

Maybe you heard me speak on a podcast prompting flexible cancellation policy as a rank booster and my reasoning sounded convincing. Then you wondered how many of your local competitors were on the different cancellation policies. This might be a reason to use one of these tools.

Or maybe you're investigating adding a hot tub to your home and wanted to research the revenue and occupancy data of competitors with hot tubs to get a better idea of whether or not the investment will pay off.

A Final Caution

Data is valuable, but it's one input. Remember, you are the output. I hope that you've learned a variety of strategies in this section that will further your confidence in your investment.

You should use hard data. But not at the exclusion of other kinds of observations. If I only used hard data, I might have missed out on *The Belmonte Penthouse*. The data told me I could make around $50,000 annually. I knew this because the owner showed me his dashboard. If we use our five-year payback period, I would have had $200,000 to spend on this apartment. But it cost much more than that. Thus, I would have had to decline the opportunity.

But I saw that the owner had made some gross errors in the management of this property. Soft data. Some simple ones that I believed would have a giant revenue impact. For example, the photo of the hot tub was the very last photo. Hot tubs are highly sought after in this market, yet the majority of FPGs didn't even know this place had one! By moving the photo up and highlighting this amenity in the title I knew would have a revenue impact. By my estimation, featuring the hot tub would have increased occupancy by 5-10%. Talk about ROI!

I also understood that the prior owner had a strong preference to avoid problems and parties, even to the detriment of revenue. That's why he set a limit of four guests in a 4-bedroom, 2,500 square-foot (230 square meter) space. Changing that to eight guests not only gave me my $1,000+ nights, double what the prior owner was making, but also these reservations have been couples or families, my best guests! Talk about a win-win!

Data is one input.

> The most important thing you can do to set yourself up for success, all but guarantee it, in the STR space is choosing the right home in the right micro-neighborhood in the right market. Once you've gone through the data and in combination with your market knowledge and observations, you should have the confidence to achieve market dominance.

2.8 HIGH ROI INVESTMENTS FOR YOUR SPACE

A host once asked me: "There are so many things that I can spend money on. Where can I spend money and get the highest return on investment? Where does it make sense to spend the limited dollars I have?"

This is a rockstar question.

Of course, choosing the right market, micro-neighborhood, home, and knowing how to analyze data are of paramount importance. Now that you already have your home, however, let's focus on the things that can bring the most added value.

First, let's define ROI or Return on Investment. It's a measurement of how much profit you will make from an expense.

Really, all expenses related to a revenue-producing asset (like your STR) can be considered an investment (and not an expense). But for the purpose of this chapter, I am speaking of only the things that will improve the guest experience and/ or increase the nightly rate you can charge.

The highest ROI upgrades you can make will result in the largest increases to both your nightly and occupancy rates.

As a simplistic example, if you spend $500 on an upgrade and earn $900 from that upgrade in a year, your return on investment is $400, or 80% for the year. Outstanding.

We are also concerned with our break-even point which is when the return equals the cost. In our example, if we made the investment in January, and it returned $500 by September, our break-even period is nine months.

A More Detailed Example

Let's say you decided to spend $500 on turning a bed in one of your bedrooms into a bunk bed.

This means a few things to you:

- It increases your nightly rate by allowing an additional guest
- It increases your variable costs due to an additional guest (water usage, increased cleaning time, extra towels to replace, etc.)

- It ideally increases your occupancy because you found an unfulfilled market demand

Ideally, you made some assumptions and calculations related to this investment to decide whether or not it would net a positive ROI.

Let's assume that, after numerous requests for a cot or air mattress, you realized that many families who book your listing want an extra bed. Your assumptions lead you to believe that with an extra bed you could:

- charge an extra $25 per night
- increase your occupancy by 9%

Let's assume your average occupancy is 70%, or 255 booked nights per year.

At 76% occupancy (70% * 1.09), you will book an additional 23 nights each year. If we multiply those extra nights by $25 per night, you will earn $575 related to the addition of the bunk bed in the first year.

As to whether or not this is a good investment...you guessed it, some assumptions are to be made like the additional costs which we left out from this example.

An extra guest means an extra set of sheets to launder, extra cleaning time, extra utilities and consumables, extra liability.

In the end, let's say the host decided the extra revenue in terms of nightly rate and occupancy was greater than the additional costs thus making it a worthwhile investment.

You might be asking how the host got to these initial numbers, that 9% increase in occupancy and $25 extra per night?

First, the host did market research using Airbnb or an STR data tool. Then, the host saw the prices that the competition was charging with six beds (let's assume our host had five beds before the addition of the bunk bed) and the occupancy they were getting. Finally, he compared that to his existing STR operation and made some educated assumptions to arrive at specific numbers needed to make the decision.

The following are eight upgrades you can make to your STR which could increase your overall ROI.

Exterior Design or Landscaping

Do something with your outdoor space whether that's a rooftop patio pictured above, a private balcony, or a backyard. You don't have to go crazy. Add some seating, a hammock, a BBQ, whatever makes sense for you, your space, and your FPG, but do something.

If you have any unused outdoor space, this upgrade is probably going to be the biggest bang for your buck. Below we'll talk about adding extra rooms, but you'd first want to work with what you already have.

If you have outdoor space that is not useable, the first step is to make it useable. That could be mowing the lawn, pulling weeds, or adding some furniture like a picnic table and umbrella. This adds to the appeal and functionality of your listing and improves online presentation.

If you have outdoor space that is already being used, you could upgrade it with some professional landscaping or think of specific amenities to add like a firepit, hammock, or high-end barbecue.

Interior Design

A nicely designed listing wins at every price point.

If your budget doesn't allow for a full home interior design, start with only one of the high-traffic rooms like the kitchen, living room, bathroom, or bedroom.

Doing just one room will give you an excellent cover photo, a very important part of your success.

I consider lighting part of interior design, and it can have a big effect on the look and feel of your space. For a bigger project, think about accent lighting or, as an easier alternative, track lights for the ceiling. Make lights dimmable when possible.

The interior of a past, potential short-term rental investment.

Interior design is an overlooked hosting strategy probably because it can be expensive. It's so overlooked and so important at the same time that I'll talk a little more about it with examples in *Chapter 7.19 How Much Does Interior Design Matter?*

Additional Beds

This one is obvious, but it may not make sense for every host for a couple of reasons.

Adding an extra bed adds an extra guest. The more guests, the increased potential for noise. If it's possible that by adding an extra bed, you will piss off your neighbors, it's not a good idea.

You can always pre-emptively counteract parties and loud noise with a noise monitor. (If you didn't read the preface, you can find my recommendation under 'Noise Monitor' in the Deal Sheet.)

However, if you are in an area that seems to have demand for an extra bed, this could be a very worthwhile upgrade.

Up-to-date Appliances and Fixtures

I used to manage an Airbnb in a highly sought-after location with so much potential, but the host would not make any of my suggested upgrades.

For example, the shower was old and moldy even after a deep clean. I'd get a complaint one of every three guests about the look of the shower or that the handle made it hard to get hot water. As the host would not upgrade, I had to constantly pretend that it was the first time I was hearing of this issue and that I'd get it looked at after the guest checked out.

The home also had a nice backyard with a view, but it had a ratty, old hammock, uncomfortable outdoor furniture, and mud instead of grass.

Aesthetics: Paint and Flooring

It's amazing what a fresh coat of paint can do to your property value. Now you know why homes for sale always get fresh paint and small touchups to the walls. It delivers a return on investment. New paint instantly makes your vacation rental feel newer.

New flooring accomplishes the same thing. It's best to do this in combination with interior or exterior design upgrades.

Additional Amenities

Remember our landscaped backyard? What about adding a hot tub? Or a BBQ? Trampoline? Hammock? Bicycle? Electric scooter? Bedside reading lamp? The options are endless.

One Palm Springs host wanted my opinion on adding an observatory to their property. Yes, like the thing you gaze up into space with. Now we're thinking! With a very short discussion, I knew this was a very good idea. Today it has nearly 200 reviews at 4.99 rating.

Observatory | Hot Tub | Game Room | Fire Pit| View

Soon (*Chapter 3.6 The Title*) you will recognize the title of that listing as an OptimizeMyBnb.com hallmark. Beautiful isn't it?

Or maybe you notice the average length of stay in your area is 15 days, but your average is only five days. Maybe adding a washer/dryer will have you welcoming more long-term guests? Read more about medium-term guests in *Chapter 7.15 How Can I Get More Medium-term Bookings?*

It doesn't even have to be anything physical. How about an HBO or Netflix subscription, a free weekly cleaning, or a Custom Guest Itinerary?

Consumables or Features Upgrades

You see how these look unique or high-end? The host also went above and beyond getting four types of soap.

This host provided high-end hand and body soap, shampoo, and conditioner. And, guess what? He charged 25% more than his competition. Details.

Everyone wants to charge the most and be the best, but few think about the details.

Are you trying to cater to a high-end guest, but providing discount shampoo and conditioner?

Do you have a nice kitchen, but are missing some nice avocado oil and pink Himalayan salt? How about a cheese grater or strainer?

Are your towels the fluffiest and softest you could find, or are you opting for the cheaper alternative? If near water, do you provide separate beach towels?

Do you have one of those tiny rusted out showerheads or a large one dispensing copious amounts of easily-adjustable warm water?

This is a 12" showerhead from a prior Airbnb I stayed in as a guest and it was fabulous. Adding a bathroom heater, typically in the ceiling, especially in colder areas could prove to have a high ROI and encourage repeat guests.

Additional 'Spaces' and Space That Is Usable

Do you lock up a room? How much extra could you make by opening it up?

Do you have an expansive backyard or deck area that you could make usable?

I recently rented a large home with some friends, and there was a neat loft that went totally unused. The host could have added some bean bags and a daybed to add another space.

How about an unused corner where you could add a bookshelf and arm chair?

The host from the intro who inspired this chapter had an extra side room that he didn't know what to do with. It was a room, but not a 'space'.

After doing some market research, we decided that turning it into a game room might make the most sense as he welcomes families and groups of friends or couples. He'll added a card table, an arcade game, some board games, and he's even got a new cover photo!

New Rooms

You can always add on to your home. This is the highest cost, but also has the highest potential for return and increased resale value.

Based on my research with the Vacation Rental Market Analysis, the simple act of adding a bathroom, dining room, bedroom, or office could net some serious extra dough each year.

I'm currently considering purchasing a 2,300 square-foot (213 square meter), 1-bedroom apartment in Medellin, Colombia. I would turn it into a 2-bedroom and estimate I could earn an extra $24,000 per year plus $56,000 upon sale. This would be an involved multi-month project featuring many headaches, but the returns are all but guaranteed. Two bedrooms are worth more than one.

I hope I've gotten your creative juices flowing. What do you think will be your next or has been your last high ROI upgrade? Let me know on Instagram or on my website.

Anything that will increase your pool of FPGs has the potential to be a great investment decision. On top of that, don't forget about simply making your space child-, pet-, or business-travel friendly. We'll cover these topics in *Part 7: Bonus Content: Questions and Answers.*

Let's move on to how best to present yourself online.

Part 3

BUILD AND OPTIMIZE YOUR LISTING

3.1 WHY AIRBNB SEARCH IS NOT STATIC LIKE GOOGLE

"I don't show up on the first page of search!"

Echoed often. Heard daily. But alas, almost always a waste of time and energy.

An Airbnb, VRBO, and Booking.com search is not static like Google or YouTube, both of whom are moving away from this model, as well. Two people who search 'Kazakhstan travel guide' on the same day on Google are going to get the same, or very similar, results. But, any two users who search for an Airbnb in 'Saigon, Vietnam' can and do see different search results.

Don't believe me? Search 'Optimize My Airbnb' in Google. No matter where in the world you are, here's what you will see in the top results:

- My main website
- Amazon page for my first book
- The book website
- My YouTube

This is true because, on a traditional search engine like Google, the website owner will target specific keywords to rank high for (i.e. 'travel guide Kazakhstan'). On OTAs, you are trying to target the FPG, not the keyword.

Google creates its search results by using a robot to 'crawl' all internet web pages to render *some* of those web pages which it *doesn't* control as search results.

On the other hand, the OTAs control almost all of the content on their website and can see directly into the end users' account (viewed listings, reviews received and given, prices paid, searches, preferences for design features, etc.).

Another big difference between the OTAs like Airbnb and Google is that Google does not face a limit of results. Any piece of information can be viewed an unlimited number of times while a listing can only be seen for a particular set of dates until it's booked.

In fact, a better search engine comparison might be eBay as they have limited inventory, but even their inventory is not unique (an iPhone is an iPhone) unlike an STR.

While it's true that some listings tend to consistently show up towards the top of an OTA search and others consistently show up towards the bottom, knowing the exact search position for a listing is impossible except on a search-by-search basis and depending on dates and filters selected.

A much better indicator of listing health is your calendar's occupancy rate. We'll talk more about this in *Chapter 5.5 Common Calendar Occupancies*.

What Is Static Search?

Think of websites. Most websites are static, meaning all users see the same information.

For the techies out there, technically a website is dynamic if the user can interact with it and get a different result, but for our purposes, the information is the same no matter what the user decides to do on the website.

A static *search* means that all users see the same results as in the above example search of 'Optimize My Airbnb'.

For a search of 'women's heels', everyone is going to see the same results on Google. These are static search results.

This works well when the user (not the platform) knows best what they are searching for. The 'women's heels' searcher may want black heels with white laces and red soles in size seven, but searching this specifically would actually exclude many relevant results. Instead, the user searches something generic and quickly identifies their preferred choice among the results. **The user knows exactly what they want**.

However, static search results start to become less useful when the user is not exactly sure what they want. We run into the paradox of choice which says that when the user has too many options, they don't know which to choose—and click away having made no choice. Not good for OTA bottom lines.

Enter dynamic search.

What Is Dynamic Search?

Let's say you want to go to Bondi Beach, Australia. However, unlike our search for 'women's heels', the user has never been to Australia let alone Bondi Beach. They do not know where they want to stay, what the average prices are, etc.

In this case, the search engine (OTAs) knows better than the user what they want. And this improves with the more information the search engine has about the user.

This is dynamic search.

Since 2018, Airbnb has used a dynamic search based largely on artificial intelligence. The other OTAs soon followed suit. Any two users will see different results. The results can be slightly different or vastly different. A single mid-week business traveler in Chicago is going to see different results than a family of six booking for a weekend vacation in Chicago.

The best, most relevant listings will always appear towards the top of search results. However, as most markets have hundreds of top listings (sometimes thousands), it's the OTA's job to deliver the user the most relevant listings so they can make a quick decision and are more likely to click that 'Make a Reservation' button.

Why Do OTAs Use Dynamic Search?

It's about delivering the user the best experience and increasing the bottom line (increasing their conversion rate, or how often people move from search to make that reservation!).

Unlike Google, the OTAs can track the user's behavior with 100% accuracy from the initial search to post-reservation review.

The OTA knows if you usually travel by yourself. They know what your typical price range is. They even know if you seem to prefer balconies or backyards.

It goes further with Airbnb. Based on photo recognition technology, Airbnb even knows if you prefer a bohemian or minimalist design. Even before your first search on the platform, Airbnb already has enough data on you to personalize the results!

Based on your prior behavior on the platform, the OTA can start to deliver highly curated and relevant results for each user.

They do this for two reasons.

First, it earns the company more money. If the OTA user sees their dream home bookable for their upcoming vacation, do you think they'll opt for that or the generic hotel?

Dynamic search earns the OTA more money by increasing the probability that the FPG will make a reservation because the OTA is only showing the listings that the FPG most probably will like.

Second, it increases the user experience. Remember the last time you went to purchase toothpaste? Or the last time you made your guest buy laundry detergent because you don't provide it? Oh wait, that never happened because you *do* provide detergent. Don't get me started as a guest. Not only is it inconvenient, but there's an entire aisle full of laundry detergent options.

Anyhoo...

There are a million choices, and it's hard to understand which is the best toothpaste or laundry detergent for your needs. You can think of this as static search (all shoppers are shown the same options). On top of that, if you've ever been to a foreign country, buying these common amenities is even more difficult when presented in a foreign language. In fact, I once purchased what looked to be normal butter, but it was actually butter infused with chocolate. You end up purchasing randomly either by price or name brand.

The OTAs don't want you to reserve a home randomly.

So, what if your personal expert was there to hand you the best option? This is dynamic. Each user gets a different offer based on who they are.

Dynamic search increases the user experience by speeding up the decision-making process and helping identify a good fit better than the guest can do for themselves.

As a guest, when I search for an Airbnb, I'm often presented over 300 possibilities even after I've selected dates, price, and a very specific neighborhood on the map.

If Airbnb can delivery me a listing that they know with a high degree of accuracy will get a 5-star review from me upon check-out, I'll be more likely to make a reservation in the future, and I'll be more likely to tell my friends about Airbnb when the topic undoubtedly comes up.

How To Track Your Airbnb Search Rank

In a truly dynamic search environment, it's not reasonably possible to track your search rank because of the number of possible search results. Add in filters, and it becomes a waste of time.

I have a YouTuber friend with nearly a million followers. I was asking him some advice for my own channel, and he told me that, due to recent algorithmic changes, he's given up on spending much time trying to rank for keywords on that platform. That's because YouTube knows there are too many options, and they're probably better at showing the user what they might want to see especially with enough search behavior history. I believe all search is moving in this direction.

Moving back to OTAs, if we look simply at the date search filter, you would have to see a result for each day, plus each 2-day period, plus each 3-day period, etc. based on your maximum night limit. Even if you knew this for a particular date, your search rank will change based on any upcoming reservation, modifications, and cancellations to existing reservations in your market. It will also change based on number of guests (Airbnb prefers a cheaper average cost per bed). And that's ignoring any future listings that will go live. Keep in mind, all new listings get a limited search rank boost on Airbnb. If that weren't enough, your rank would also change based on the zoom level of the map.

In a static search environment like Google, your website's search rank is known in the short term. But on Airbnb and the other OTAs, a new and optimized listing can go live in 30 minutes and rank on the first page.

While there are tools that track your OTA search rank, I urge you to use them as just another data point, if at all. Do not make them a central point of your optimization process because it's not where your precious time is most valuably spent. Even though 'know your search rank' is such a sellable idea just like 'make tons of passive income without owning any real estate' is, search rankings break down as useful strategies in the real world.

Regardless of your search rank, you should still be trying to be the best host you can be, trying to offer every guest the best experience you can, and trying to continually improve for those 5-star reviews. By doing this, your rank takes care of itself. Personally, I do not pay attention to my search rank in favor of my occupancy rate. I go over this in *Part 5: Pricing*.

3.2 KNOW YOUR FPG

Although this chapter will be short, it could be the most important one for you, especially if you've never given this concept any thought.

Imagine a chocolate company not knowing why their customer buys their chocolate. Or a concert venue being unaware of what kinds of music are popular with surrounding populations.

My point is that all businesses have customers, and successful businesses know their customer. In the world of vacation rentals, I refer to the customer as a Future Potential Guest, or FPG.

I want to break guests down into two categories:

1. All FPGs coming to your area
2. Those FPGs who are ideal for your space

Las Vegas draws a few different types of FPGs. Most people probably think of the partiers coming for gambling, for fine dining, and for the nightclubs. Your penthouse in Wynn Resort might be a great option for the high-roller FPG or your 4-bedroom apartment just off the main strip might be a great option for budget bachelor parties or college students.

But did you know Las Vegas is a family vacation destination, too? There are not only a ton of neat, family-friendly things to do within the city, but less than an hour away there are many nature-based and family-friendly outdoor tourist activities. These families will visit Red Rock Canyon National Park and the ever-popular Hoover Dam, the largest reservoir in the United States.

Then we have Nellis Air Force Base, a 15-minute drive from the northern part of the Strip. Military bases bring all sorts of short-term visitors, including families, special instructors, and significant others.

Las Vegas is also a popular choice for conferences, employee trainings, and traveling entertainment groups that will require short-term accommodations.

These are only some of the FPG segments coming to Las Vegas. Before you close this book and start looking for a real estate agent in Las Vegas, however, you should know that Clark County heavily prohibits short-term rentals. This is to be expected with such powerful and wealthy hotel groups in the area.

Here is how you get to know what types of FPGs are coming to a particular market and why they're coming. It's actually not very difficult to find this information, especially for the discovered markets. Google searches bring up a plethora of results: "What to do in Las Vegas?" You could also poke around popular travel forums. If the FPG demand is so niche that it's hard to find, then it's probably not going to be profitable unless you see future growth or the opportunity presented is unique.

Whether you already have a listing or are in the market to buy one, you'll need to know your *ideal* FPG. Cater to as many as possible, but be realistic.

Is your single-family home with a backyard in between the Las Vegas airport and the Hoover Dam? Maybe a family with a pet would prefer your home. Or, maybe a family with three young, loud children prefers to rent a home with some space between the neighborhoods over an apartment sharing a wall with them. Maybe you highlight your fenced backyard, or the fence around the pool for child safety. Maybe you highlight that you have board games, a washer/dryer, high chair, and/or a Pack'n'Play.

Maybe you knew your FPG so well that you knew their main concern was impeccable sanitization, and, by highlighting this in the title and photos, you secure yourself extra bookings in that tough STR market. Knowing your FPG equals ROI.

Maybe installing a tiki bar in the backyard or surround sound system throughout the house will be bad investments not desired by your FPG in the single-family home with a fence backyard, but maybe it turns into a good investment for the Wynn Penthouse. Knowing your FPG helps make these decisions easier.

Or maybe you're in a digital-nomad friendly city, and your ideal FPG is a remote worker. You'll want to highlight the desk, office chair, fast Wi-Fi, and that quiet space for concentration, "The Concentration Den". I can see the title and branding now!

In *The Belmonte Penthouse*, I had originally highlighted the well-designed kitchen opening up to the jacuzzi room in the top five photos and summary text. My ideal FPG was families and longer reservations. But after some time, my true FPG just wouldn't go away. They would also pay top dollar. My true FPG are groups of men in their 30s or 40s coming for a few days to party and dine out. After understanding this, I moved the kitchen towards the end of the photos, de-emphasized the fully-stocked kitchen in the text, and offered daily breakfast and cleaning instead.

A Note About Airbnb

When you reject a booking on Airbnb, it's very bad for you. Airbnb defaults to thinking you're sexist or racist or otherwise deficient. They may even pause your listing for review if they think you do it too often.

To be clear, Airbnb compares your individual acceptance rate to your market. If you reject three bookings this month and so does your competition, then it's in line with the average, and there is no consequence (probably), or the consequence is equal between all listings. In reality, even a single rejection has high potential to negatively affect your search rank (see *Part 8: How To Rank #1 On Airbnb*).

I believe Airbnb's stance inhibits your ability to cater to your preferred and ideal FPG.

Airbnb further inhibits the host to cater to their ideal FPG with the poor selection of filters the platform offers to the searching guests. These ineffective filters are largely ignored by the hosts, anyway. There are many rentals with certain amenities in the home, but the home would not appear in search for that amenity because the host hasn't selected it.

Airbnb doesn't encourage hosts to fill out their amenities properly, and they add so many marginally relevant amenities like a hockey rink or baking sheet, most of which the guest cannot filter for on P2 anyways (refer back to *iii. Terminology* or wait for the next chapter where I explain this concept in detail). It's hard to keep up with.

This really inhibits your ability to attract and host your ideal FPG. And this is evident on Airbnb and in vacation rentals in general by having all listings trying to cater to all types of guests (overly generic). That's partly why other niche OTAs have popped up. There are niche OTA websites for families, travelers with pets, nurses, marijuana lovers, etc.

Even though Airbnb makes it difficult to target your ideal FPG, you should still know your ideal FPG and cater to them as best you can. This will be a running theme throughout this section as these well-targeted listings still seem to perform the best. And if you decide to pursue a direct booking strategy as covered in *Part 6: Direct Bookings*, this will become even more important.

3.3 KNOW YOUR SPACE

The prior chapter and this one come down to maximizing your positive reviews and minimizing the negative ones. Remember, *negative reviews are the result of mismanaged expectations.* We want a certain type of FPG, the one that is the best fit for our offer. The last chapter discussed the importance of knowing your FPG, why they're coming to your market, and how you can maximize your amenities to cater to your ideal FPG.

In this chapter, we want to be clear about what we're actually offering, both in terms of our rental and our neighborhood, to avoid bad reviews resulting from a guest booking a rental that's not correct for them. If your listing is in the heart of the party district, do you really want to attract a family by adding board games and other family amenities?

Recently, I received a Super Host Optimization (SHO) order on my website. As I always do, I quickly reviewed the listing. I saw poor reviews. By my estimation, the host needed to improve their hospitality. A SHO doesn't help much with that so I refunded the money and requested this host book a consultation call with me so we could identify the root problem and fix it. Below is a short excerpt of our conversation.

My question: "Is the building clean?" His answer: "No."
My question: "Is it quiet?" His answer: "No."

When I say "Know Your Space", I am talking about your offer which is the physical space, the layout, the benefits and the drawbacks. I am also talking about where it's located in the building, in the community, in the neighborhood.

PRO TIP:

Telling the guest your building is the newest in the area is important because there's a big difference in a building that is three versus 30 years old. This is especially important in vacation rental markets with a lot of buildings in the same area with apartments that look the same. It's hard for the guest to decide.

Is the bedroom window next to the common area where the smokers gather and chit chat all night long? Might be fine for a partier who smokes, but not for a remote worker there for a month who's into marathons.

By default, you as the host know all this. The guest does not. You are selling a clean and quiet offering, but that's not actually what was being offered by the host on the consultation call.

Sometimes, you have to tell the guest what you're *not* offering. Today, if you don't provide Wi-Fi, because this is standard and expected, you must say that you do not provide Wi-Fi. Simply not clicking Wi-Fi as an amenity is not enough. Doing that will result in negative reviews.

I originally thought the fellow on the call was just a bad host, but what I learned was simply that he needed to better communicate his offer. You don't want a guest thinking they're booking a room at the Ritz but getting a budget space.

At the same time, don't assume the guest has done deep market research and knows all the micro-neighborhoods or even the cost of an average listing versus a budget listing. They don't. You do. You must tell them.

The reason for this host's poor reviews was not poor hosting, but mismanaged expectations. He had an underwhelming home in an underwhelming neighborhood. He didn't communicate this, and his reviews suffered.

Be honest about your offering. You want to attract those who are a good fit and discourage those who are not. Something that one FPG views as a negative might be a positive for another. Maybe someone is looking for a budget listing, and the neighborhood doesn't matter because all they will be doing is attending seminars all day and staying in at night. Or maybe a fit young woman prefers a rental with no elevator while that would be a nightmare for an elderly gent.

A friend of mine recently left a negative review for their recent Airbnb trip. When I asked why, she said that the host had too many rules. Upon further investigation, the rule that really bothered my friend was that the host required total silence at all times. It did sound a little restrictive because even talking on the phone was not allowed. Why did my friend leave a negative review? Say it together now: mismanaged expectations! For some FPGs, total silence is a bonus. For others, it results in a negative review.

Here's what I wrote for the host from the beginning of this chapter to use in his listing: *Book my Airbnb if you are a budget traveler and want a central location. Please note the building is old and somewhat rundown but my Airbnb is clean and ready for you!*

Just be honest!

**If you promise a 5-star listing
and deliver a 4-star listing,
you'll get a 3-star review.**

3 Pros and 2 Cons

There's another strategy you can implement to communicate the negatives in a soft way, and that is with the '3 Pros and 2 Cons' strategy.

When a host sets out to create a listing, they often do a great job of identifying the positives. After all, they're trying to sell their space. They're in the sales mindset which oftentimes purposefully overlooks any downsides.

This is a powerful short-term strategy that may come back to haunt them in the long-term via negative reviews as it did to our host above. Even one negative review could haunt you for months. That's because the negative reviews are more important to an FPG than the positive ones.

The listing could look great in the photos and text, but if the guest arrives to a home right next to a busy freeway and separated only by a four-foot-tall fence (true story), they're going to feel slighted. It's likely the guest mentions the noise and lack of privacy in their review and leaves you with fewer than five stars.

If we manage expectations and let the FPG know about what they're getting into up front, our problems go away.

How do we implement this strategy?

Simply list three things guests love about your listing and two things guests don't love about it.

You'd rather pass on a guest who's not a good fit than book them and get a negative review, never mind the marginal extra revenue. Ideally, this strategy allows the guest to decide for themselves that they're not a good fit, even before reaching out to you.

How could our example host above, with the clean rental in a stodgy building, implement this strategy?

Three things guests love about our space: central location, budget price, pristine interior. Two cons: the building is a bit run-down and in an up-and-coming but not yet gentrified neighborhood.

A Word of Caution

Don't force yourself to think of negatives. They should only be noteworthy things likely to lead to a negative review. If you have a run-of-the-mill, standard home with not many exciting features but not any real downsides, skip this. Don't fret.

Additionally, avoid listing negatives that only affect a small group of guests. Living above a bar that stays open until 2am on Friday and Saturday is a negative for the majority of guests. As noisy nights are a predictable and regular event, mention it in the listing.

However, living in an area where electricity goes out once or twice a month for a few hours at a time is probably not something you should mention. It is not predictable and rare. And it would probably seem worse than it is to the FPG.

If you rent out your downstairs and have kids upstairs that make noise occasionally, you'll want to consider whether or not to put this in your listing.

Remember our example host above who said his space wasn't quiet? He was referring to his neighbors who have children. My next question was whether any past guest had complained about it. As soon as the host answered 'no', I knew we should leave it out.

Putting something as innocent and straightforward as 'I live upstairs with two young children who occasionally make some noise' could be understood as 'there's going to be a bunch of noise from kids upstairs, pounding footsteps all day, no sleep at night.' In this case, if the noise is occasional, I would leave it out and test to see if this is affecting your reviews.

Alternatively, I once had a physically-disabled person book my first listing in San Francisco which was reached by climbing 42 steps. This was not ideal for him, resulting in a lackluster review. I added a photo of the stairs which I felt would only deter those who didn't want stairs, which being in San Francisco, was a small segment of my pool of FPGs.

You have to consider the cost/benefit of disclosure. Will disclosing the piece of information cost you more than the benefit it brings you? Some considerations, like health and safety, should be disclosed at all times no matter how many guests it effects.

3.4 HOW DOES THE FPG ACTUALLY SEARCH?

The following chapter is directly relevant for guest search behavior on Airbnb, but the concepts can still be applied, in large part, to all OTAs.

Let's first get out of the way how the FPG does *not* search.

FPGs do not use Airbnb to decide *where* to travel. It's a platform used to decide where to *stay*.

This is important, so please keep it in mind.

"We think that the listing's plus is the location. The property is in Fajardo, Puerto Rico."

This host thinks their selling point is the same as every other vacation rental, a common misstep.

On Airbnb, the FPG has already made their mind up about where they want to go the moment they enter a destination in the search box. They may have even made their mind up on the neighborhood they want to be in.

With few exceptions, your location is not your selling point as that doesn't provide any competitive advantage. (The exception is when, for example, your listing is within walking distance of the hospital the nurse is doing her course at or the college the guest's child is graduating from.)

This goes straight back to *Chapter 1.5 The Reservation Flow*. I really meant it when I said to keep this in mind for everything. A lot of this chapter is about the same topic. As an FPG comes on to Airbnb.com, they also follow a typical flow to the reservation. We're going to discuss that here and how you can *optimize* each portion of the process to increase your conversion rate.

P1 – No Optimization

Remember that P1, P2, P3 refer to the three search pages on Airbnb before the guest can make a reservation. First up, P1, is rather unextraordinary. We cannot optimize anything on this page. The guest must type in, at the very least, a location to start a search. And, we hope but have no control over them searching for our location.

While they don't have to input dates or number of guests, serious FPGs will do this. P1 is where the FPG can enter the number of adults, infants, and even pets.

P2 – To Get The Click

Potential Optimizations: Map location, cover photo and top five photos, price, ratings, number of beds, title

Here the guest will typically apply some filters. The most common filter is whether they want an entire place, private room, or shared room like a hostel. These are basic differences, and many FPGs use this filter.

There are cases where a city might not legally label your offering as an entire home, but it has a bathroom, kitchen, and all amenities a home would have. Check your local regulations if choosing entire home in this situation to make sure it is legal. If you can, it's preferable to select entire home as they fetch more revenue. FPGs with higher budgets are searching for entire homes.

The next potential and common filter is price. Airbnb shows the average price for the selected filters and map location. Most FPGs are likely to use this filter, especially if you have many listings in your area (more than a few pages of search results in your neighborhood). Rather than every price category, the FPG is typically searching towards the low end, in the middle, or towards the high end with a variance of plus or minus 25%. That means if the average price is $100 per night, a common search is up to $50 to $75, between $75 and $125, and $125 to $150+. Your price is set based on market demand, that is occupancy, and that will have an entire section dedicated to it (*Part 5: Pricing*).

Most searches start with these two filters. If there are a lot of listings, the FPG may come back to select more filters. They will also select an additional filter if they're a frequent Airbnb guest and know they definitely want something like a dedicated workspace, washer and dryer, or full kitchen.

On P2, the FPG is looking for the features and amenities they know they want in their future Airbnb. And filtering out those which don't have them. On mobile, they will click open individually each listing they have interest in moving to P3 then back to P2 for the selection of additional listings. On desktop, they may open various tabs while staying on P2.

Our first real optimization is on location. You should be most accurate with your listing location, but you can also put your listing wherever you want. Literally on Airbnb when setting your location as a host, you can type an address and move the pin wherever you want on the map.

Because on Airbnb you're allowed to show a general location which is essentially a circle on the map hovering over a few block radii, it can make sense to move it a few blocks closer to a touristy hot spot. Map location is a ranking factor. After all, if the FPG zooms on that touristy hot spot and you're not on the map, you have exactly a zero percent chance of getting booked. Don't move your pin halfway across town, but a few blocks is okay.

The next optimization is easy, it's the number of bedrooms and beds. Ensure your number of bedrooms is accurately listed on Airbnb. Airbnb only counts certain sleeping arrangements as beds, but you want to show more beds. If they count a sofa as a bed but not a floor mattress, I'd default to selecting the sofa. In the guest's eyes, they're equivalent, and you'll appear in more searches with more beds. (And here is where I have to say that Airbnb has been known to change its rules as soon as people like me publish such hacks!)

As the FPG is going through all the listings on P2, they're also taking note of the rating. While an average FPG won't know the difference between a 4.9 and 4.8 listing, they will start to notice the fewer and fewer listings at 4.6 and below. At this level, they'll understand that right around 4.6 and below are the bad Airbnb listings.

That's not to say it doesn't matter if you have a 4.8 versus a 4.9. It does. If you are being compared on P3 to a 4.9 and you're a 4.8, this could very well be the ultimate deciding factor. I know it's hard, but strive for a 5.0. Hard, but not difficult. You'll have to swallow your pride occasionally and learn how to remove negative reviews which I'll teach you below.

As the FPG flips through the smaller photos on P2, and they will flip fast, they are confirming their wants. You might have a half a second per photo to communicate what you need to the FPG. This is why we will make our photos crystal clear and a main focus.

Remember what P2 is for? The FPG has a list of wants. You need to know what they are and communicate them in the first five photos. If the FPG wants a kids' room, and they don't see it in the first few photos, they may move on from your listing.

If it's not evidently clear from the photos on P2 that you have what the guest is looking for, they will move on in all cases except when they really like your listing. Maybe it's the design, or they are fishing for a deal and will send an inquiry.

The majority of FPGs will get to no more than the third page before they get burnt out with so many options. But, remember, don't obsess about your search rank. It's not knowable or very difficult to know. Focus on optimization and your occupancy instead.

PRO TIP:

If you have many similar-looking listings, say in the same building, make your photos as different as you possibly can between each listing. If you have the same photos and the guest has already looked at one of your listings and decided it was not a good fit, then are likely to skip over all remaining listings with that same cover photo or set of photos. Alternately, let's say the FPG did click on one of the listings. They're likely to not click on any of the others because they think all the listings that look similar are just a copy of the already opened listing. **Differentiating your listings gets more clicks to P3.**

There's one more strategy that I'd like to share with you to implement on P2. It's a pricing strategy and entails raising your calendar prices at the same time offering a discount. Let's call it a "creative" discount. It also allows you to keep your listing with a one-night minimum and thus appear in more searches. However, if someone books one night only they will pay a premium of your choosing. The strategy needs to be explained visually and so if you'd like to learn it, please scan the QR code.

Video - "Creative" Discount

SCAN ME

P3 – To Get The Reservation

Optimizations: Photo layout and captions, reviews, text, title

Remember P2 is where the FPG is looking for what they want, and P3 is where they confirm that you have the things that they want.

For example, the FPG may want a 2-bedroom with an office space, large living room, a balcony, and a king bed. She'll be looking for it on P2 and on P3, where she'll find more details, she'll be confirming everything to make a final decision.

The whole point of **P3 is to eliminate any confusion and communicate fully what the FPG is getting in exchange for their money.** You also have an opportunity with the text and photo captions to communicate any additional amenities, even ones they didn't know they wanted or weren't shown or which weren't clearly available from the photos. That could be a 77" smart TV with HBO, all sports packages, Netflix, and other subscriptions. Or it could be a special memory foam mattress. Or 500Mbps dedicated Wi-Fi.

But let's start where the FPG will start, with the photos. If, for example, the FPG wants a full kitchen with a full fridge and you don't clearly show that, you're out. We'll cover photos more in the next chapter.

When I was searching for an Airbnb in Belo Horizonte, Brazil, one of the final options had 'penthouse' in the title. It looked nice, but then I saw stairs on the outside leading to something. Then I saw a photo of a 2-story building with no caption. *Was this a penthouse? A 2nd story penthouse? Was it an apartment building? Would there be security?* I clicked out of that listing.

In Airbnb, don't assign photos to rooms. This is where you tell Airbnb which photo is for which room. Visually it's suboptimal, and you lose control of your photo layout. Photo layout is super important and under-appreciated. Once you do assign photos to rooms, you cannot undo it without deleting and reuploading all your photos.

Your first opportunity to present the FPG with additional amenities you offer is with the photos and their captions. The photo captions are easily missed because the FPG is, well, looking at the photos and not reading text.

What are your special amenities that can be shown off in the photos? Rain showerhead, free beach chairs and towels, fancy coffee maker, board games, projector TV, hammock....

Your second opportunity is maybe the most important part of the entire listing: the text. That's because if the guest is reading your text, that means they are close to making that reservation. They just are trying to confirm something, or get a little bit more information.

For me, text is where conversion kicks in. Don't say a bunch of nothing like most hosts! This is your chance to present the guest with things you know they want, but that they might not even know they want. Know your FPG!

What are you offering that wasn't already immensely clear from the photos:

- Heated floors
- 1,000-thread count sheets
- King bed
- 500Mbps Wi-Fi
- Digital lock
- Early check-in
- Walkability of your neighborhood

We'll discuss more about text in three of the upcoming chapters, but suffice it to say the guest reading text is at the end of their booking journey. They are comparing you with other listings that they also like, that are probably similarly priced, in similar locations, and with similar ratings. This is your chance—and why knowing your FPG is so important so you can sell them now when it matters!

The next part of P3 the host can optimize is the reviews. The FPG might go down to reviews even before reading the text, and what they'll do there is look for negative keywords:

- Bad
- Smelly
- Slow
- Not
- Loud
- Dirty

They're scanning for negative, typically longer reviews. The FPG will not read the entire review. You can optimize the reviews by responding to them. There's a very specific way to respond to reviews for maximum impact which we'll cover later in this section.

House Rules are next. Some guests may not even look at them. They include the cancellation policy. But the same holds: eliminate, don't create, confusion.

If you're the best listing in town, you can get away with extra strict rules. But overly stringent House Rules *can* turn away guests. Keep rules short and few in number. Don't repeat yourself. Don't list irrelevant things like check-out instructions here. Take a look at your competition to see what they're doing. Do list the necessary things the guest needs to know to ensure they're booking the right rental, to avoid any unnecessary issues, and to fully enjoy their stay.

The End – The Message

You did it. The FPG is seriously considering your listing. They will now do one of three things:

1. Book right away (we'll optimize this outcome via our automated messages)
2. Click away (no optimization to be done)
3. Send a message

If the FPG is sending a message here, they are seeking additional clarification or asking for a discount.

If that clarification has already been answered in your listing, you can simply answer it again or use a strategy to verify the guest has read it. The strategy is simple, and it consists of adding a word at the end of the text and asking the guest to send that word with their initial inquiry. I use 'banana pancakes' if I implement this strategy.

After doing this, when you have undoubtedly received a message without the keyword, inform the guest that you find reservations go smoothest when you know the guest has read the entire listing. Most of the time, the guest will catch on and reply with the secret code word.

If not, either you saved yourself a future headache or time as the guest wasn't ready to book.

But if you decide to reply which is my recommendation (unless you have a lot of peculiarities with your home or rules) then the same rules apply. Your goal is to eliminate any confusion.

If the FPG asks about your guest policy, about luggage storage, about parking, the worst thing you can do is be unclear and/or delay.

Let's take asking for a discount as a common example. You will either give a discount or not. Do that. And do that right away. Or lose the guest.

I'll illustrate with a personal example. Booking a trip, I chose two listings and sent a message to each asking for a discount.

Both hosts got back to me right away. One said no to the discount. The other asked me to wait, as they were occupied and needed to discuss it with their partner.

This put me in a predicament. I had two listings in the same location, price range, and similar review score, so equally desirable. I knew the definitive price of one listing. The other listing, I was waiting to hear back and didn't know how long it would take. The host could respond in an hour or the next day or forget altogether. In the meantime, the other listing or both could get booked up. That would be terrible because I'd have to search all over. I knew I didn't want to do that, even if I had to pay a little more. The second host did get back to me with a discount, but it was too late. I had already booked the other listing which I was happy with, pretty confident about, and for which I knew the final price.

Provide clarity for the guest and as quickly as possible.

3.5 PHOTOS

I'm here to tell you that all roads *don't* lead to Rome. Optimizing everything about your photos is low-hanging fruit. When finished reading this chapter, you'll be in the top 5% of all listings in terms of anything and everything related to photos.

Buckle up because this is going to be a long journey. We will be covering the following:

- Optimal number of photos per listing size
- Types of photos
- The all-important cover photo plus the next four (just as important)
- Photo layout options
- How to optimize photo captions

Towards the end we'll discuss how to prepare for a photo shoot, why you don't have to hire a professional photographer, and how to take your own photos if you so choose (and the benefits in choosing this). Let's dive in!

How Many Photos?

Fewer than you think. For some of you, far less than you think. In no instance are 50 photos needed. Or 40. The typical, smaller rental should have between 12 and 15 photos. Larger rentals might have upwards of 30. If you take nothing else from this chapter, know that it's better to limit the number of photos in your listing. It's okay to leave some things up to the imagination. In general, we'll have one photo per space, and a space does not equal a room.

Let's run through an example of a typical 2-bedroom home with one cool/bonus feature:

1. Bedroom #1
2. Bedroom #2
3. Bathroom #1
4. Bathroom #2
5. Kitchen
6. Kitchen Bonus
7. Dining Room
8. Living Room
9. Office or desk space
10. Balcony or patio
11. Garage with beach gear and some workout equipment
12. Exterior Twilight
13. Review Photo
14. Floor Plan
15. Neighborhood

POP QUIZ:

If you have a super-cool 4-bedroom rental with a hot tub, a fifth bathroom, a few balconies, a bar area, and in-building community amenities like a pool, gym, and lounge, how many photos would be optimal?

We'd be at something like 25, especially if the bedrooms and bathrooms look very similar as they do in many vacation rentals. If you have four bedrooms and they all look very similar, you actually don't need to show the 4th bedroom. It makes no difference to the FPG, who won't even notice. Same thing with bathrooms and balcony space.

In general, the number of photos your listing should have should be no fewer than 10 and no more than about 35 as the home size increases from studio to five-bedroom.

Types of Photos

There are 10 types of photos. Depending on your rental, you can expect to have between two and seven types in your listing.

The first type of photo I call 'Basic'. These are photos of the bedroom, bathroom, kitchen, dining room, living room, office/desk space, and outdoor space like a patio, porch, or balcony.

The second type of photo I call 'Bonus'. These are photos of your special features like pool (or pool table), hot tub, rooftop, firepit, community amenities, art gallery (see below), etc. These are also photos of special amenities like a super-cool coffee maker, a giant projector with a theatre-style screen, or a wet bar. It could also be of the kitchen with all the drawers and cabinets opened up showing off the goods in your "fully-equipped kitchen".

The third type of photo I call 'Exterior', and the name speaks for itself. Generally, you do not want to add a photo of the exterior of the building or home as it's unnecessary and potentially causes a security risk. The only exception is if your exterior is unique. The litmus test is whether or not a photo of the exterior of your home shows the guest more than simply the exterior. Does it communicate that this home is fancy or luxurious? Is there an outdoor, second-level walkway? Maybe it's three levels all with balconies? Is there a luxurious garden in the foreground?

A good exterior photo. This photo communicates more information about the surroundings and the wood on the porch suggests a fireplace and included firewood.

The fourth photo I call 'Views'. These are photos of any special views that you may have. Typically, I'm not a fan of 'Views' photos as your view is probably not spectacular and probably similar to much of your competition. The guest is probably not booking for the view. On top of that, when hosts add a 'Views' photo, they tend to add more than one. A few of each angle, a few of the sunset, a few of the sunrise, one of each season in the year. Or, worse, a photo of a dolphin in the ocean or some wildlife. Overkill.

I think some of you reading this right now are laughing. You have 50 photos, 10 of which are of the sunset and views. Admit it! Ha! If you do add a 'Views' photo, limit it to one, maximum two. There are two possible exceptions. The first comes into play generally in nature destinations where the view is more in-demand, and you don't have a neighbor to your immediate left and right. Remember, it's what makes you unique. If, indeed, you *do* have the best view in town *and* a guest will book because of it and that feature can be easily communicated with a single photo, then maybe you should think about adding it. Or combine two 'Views' photos into one. Two cropped horizontal photos, one of sunset and one of sunrise. The second exception is if you have a good view of a famous landmark or something unique. Here are some examples:

The fifth type of photo I call 'Bird's Eye', a photo taken from above with a drone. You're still trying to communicate something to the FPG. What is it? Maybe it shows that you have no neighbors? Maybe your distance from the beach? Maybe the size of the lot? If you do this photo, it might be a good idea to make your surroundings black and white to have the FPG focus on your listing. Towards the end of this chapter, I offer a Featured Product Discount for my Edited Photos product which does this for you.

The sixth type of photo I call 'Neighborhood Photo.' This is a photo that shows your expertise as a host and demonstrates an extra benefit offered to the reserving guest. It's local, insider knowledge. What it is not is a general photo of your neighborhood, a photo of a popular street, café, bar, or tourist destination. These photos are useless, and I hereby ban them. If the FPG can find it with a quick Google search, it's not a 'Neighborhood Photo' as defined here. If you think your proximity really is your selling point (it's probably not), then put it in the title. Typically, a neighborhood photo needs a caption. I added this caption to the following photo which was a property I managed for many years: Book for my local tip how to enjoy Muir Woods without having to book or pay for parking!

The seventh type of photo I call 'Twilight.' This is a photo of the exterior or backyard at dusk. Turn on all the lights inside and outside. Ideally the sky is a purple or pink shade, if not you can edit it in later. This is only valid for homes and not apartments and can be combined with an exterior photo.

Be sure to claim the bonus items for these images in color. How beautiful is this photo!

The eighth type of photo I call 'Review'. It's a designed photo that serves to bring one of your extra stellar reviews higher up on P3. We'll caption this photo as something like 'Be sure to check out the rest of my five-star reviews below.' I have a video on my YouTube of how to do a simple version of this easily with a screenshot on your desktop computer (search 'review photo' on my channel). In the accompanying course, I show an advanced technique that makes such photos a bit more visually appealing.

The above review is for *The Belmonte Penthouse*. A designed review photo is included with Super Host Optimizations and Optimized Host.

The ninth type of photo I call 'Layout'. A layout photo shows more than one space. Remember, a space is a distinct part of a room. We want to avoid layout photos because they're harder for the FPG to process quickly. We replace this photo in favor of the much better 'Floor Plan' which I discuss next.

This is not an ideal photo because there's too much going on and too much detail, especially for mobile. Layout photos show a lot of space, but the FPG isn't giving each photo the needed attention to process all the detail. We've got the kitchen, living room, and balcony in the background with a door open to the right, but the focus is mostly on the dining table.

The tenth type of photo I call 'Floor Plan', and it's an astoundingly beautiful (if I don't say so myself) custom-hand-drawn, to-scale, and color-coordinated digital floor plan that matches the exact layout and colors of your STR. Use it for Airbnb, Booking, VRBO, and your direct booking website.

Featured Product Discount - Custom Floor Plan

It can be drawn in 3D or 2D. For basic listings, it makes a great cover photo. For all listings, it helps set the guest expectations while setting you apart from your competition. The FPG likely has never seen this photo before, they're going to give your listing more attention thus they're more likely to book your listing (things that get our attention are most persuasive).

Featured
Product Discount
- Floor Plan

SCAN ME

Find your 15% discount code in the 'Featured Product Discounts' PDF of the bonus items.

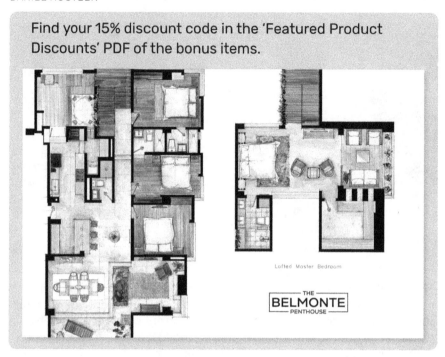

Lofted Master Bedroom

THE
BELMONTE
PENTHOUSE

There's another type of photo that I'm not including because they should never be included in your online listing. These are close up or detail photos. Photographers are creative people, and so they like to take creative photos. I'm referring to the details of your fireplace trim, the orchid on the balcony, or the centerpiece of the dining room table. While these may be good for social media, you'd never add these to your online listing.

Before we move on to the next section, I have a special note for studio and 1-bedroom rentals. The number of photos stays the same. You'll probably have around a dozen. The types of photos stay consistent, though you might make them a bit more nuanced.

Maybe in this case you take a photo of the TV from the couch and a photo of the couch and armchair from the TV. Maybe you take a photo of the kitchen and one of the stovetop with all the pots and pans plus the condiments to one side and the blender or coffee maker to the other. Maybe you take a photo of the digital lock indicating easy self-check-in. Or maybe you take a photo of the board games, pet toys and water bowl, or full-sized mirror with aesthetically pleasing green plant on the side.

When you have a smaller rental, you have more liberty to add a few extra common amenities to the photo section.

The First Five Photos – Important!

The first five photos consist of the cover photo plus the next four photos. On a typical desktop screen, the FPG is shown a preview of the first five photos on P3 without any additional clicks. On a mobile screen, there is no preview but in both cases on P2, the FPG will flip through about five photos before moving on.

The cover photo should be your best photo. The feature or amenity that separates you from your competition. The thing your ideal FPG is looking for. The most visually pleasing photo. Something that's going to stop the scroll and get the click.

Perform a search in your market and have a look at what your competition is doing. Are they all showing the same amenity like an outdoor pool or the same colors like a light-colored living room or bathroom? Unless yours is clearly the best, it's probably not a wise decision to do the same. At least, throw in some orange or red or blue or green.

Whenever I go to Bali, I'm always surprised to see the majority of photos showing the nice backyard with the turquoise pool. They look great! But they all blur together when all of your competition has a very similar backyard. The only one or two that stand out are the very best options. I've optimized numerous listings in this saturated market, and they're killing it by helping the guest differentiate between loads of similarly looking listings.

Remember the layout photo from above (not to be confused with the floor plan)? *Never* use a layout photo as your cover photo. There's too much detail in those photos, especially for a cover photo, especially if the FPG is using a mobile device, especially if the FPG happens to be older. I'm in my 30s and my eyes have already started short-circuiting. Help that older person by anticipating and providing a useful, clear image.

The cover photo needs to be of one main feature, your best thing, which is easy to do with a larger and fancier home. Its purpose is to get the click. But what if you have a basic, no-frills home? In that case, I want you to do something crazy like paint one of the walls a different color or buy or create your own floor plan. This can be your eye-catching cover photo.

Your next four photos should be of four different rooms or spaces, and they should be the next best rooms, spaces, features, or amenities.

An alternative layout strategy is to take the guest on a journey as if they were checking into the home, starting at or near the front entrance, then moving through the living room, the kitchen, the dining room, the first bedroom, then bathroom, all the way out to the backyard. It *can* work for fancy homes where all the photos are gorgeous, but generally you should be leading with your top five photos.

Photo Captions

Photo captions are not important until they are. And they are precisely when the FPG is actually reading them. You'll learn more about why text is so important and underleveraged in the upcoming chapters. For now, I'm going to teach you some easy ways to *optimize* your photo captions.

There are three rules. First, you want to label spaces. I like to use brackets to identify my rooms: [ ]

[Social Bathroom]
[Master Bedroom, Upstairs]

Simple as that. Add the room and what level they are on in your home, if applicable. Sometimes it's obvious that we're looking at a kitchen, but we label them all for consistency.

The FPG is not familiar with your home so things that appear obvious to you may not be for them, at least not immediately. And remember how little time the FPG moves through each photo.

Second, use captions to call out non-obvious things or anything you want to draw additional attention to. Does the closed door in the back corner of the bedroom lead to a private balcony, a walk-in closet, or an ensuite bathroom?

Maybe we have a proper and comfy office chair at the desk and want to give ourselves one more opportunity to ensure the FPG notices it.

Maybe we don't have a TV, but a projector hanging down from the ceiling shown at the top of the photo. This would be a good idea to call out that there's an 85" projector in the living room. Don't want the FPG missing that!

Maybe the shower doubles as a sauna.

Maybe your small backyard in the big city apartment is extra cool because it's so uncommon. The guest might not know this, so tell them. Time to sell, baby!

[Bathroom #1] Strong water pressure!

Third, place the guest in the space.

[Bedroom #3] Just behind you is a wall-mounted HDTV

[Dining Room] That door to the left leads to your private balcony with sunrise views.

[Living Room] Imagine yourself relaxing with good conversation, a glass of wine, and friends....

Another option is to add a review snippet as the caption (no more than 10 words, but ideally around five), or your YouTube channel name for a video walkthrough or your Instagram page for more photos. You can also add any of these to your text descriptions which we'll cover soon. But, don't overdo it!

[Dining Room] "So happy our family of 8 could spread out on the giant dining table."

Here are a few "do nots". Don't write generic stuff. Every photo does not need a caption, so no need to force it. And don't be wordy. No more than 15 words.

The Photo Shoot

The all-important photo shoot. For a successful photo shoot you'll need to hire a stager and a photographer. I've learned that these are two very different skills, though I believe they're complementary.

The stager will help you organize and prop your home so that it shows well in photos. This person will do things like hide cables, add or adjust lighting, organize or remove clutter, rearrange or remove furniture or amenities, and add visually appealing things like plants on the coffee table or a bowl of fruit to your kitchen.

You might be thinking that you can do the staging yourself. And I'd agree. You can absolutely do it yourself. If not, invite that friend over who's good at organizing and design.

I want to highlight the difference between staging and interior design. Interior design comes before staging. Interior design is more comprehensive. It looks at the entire space from the beginning to make it look bigger or be more functional or achieve a desired effect, feeling, or ambiance. Staging is taking what you already have and adding (or, sometimes subtracting!) minor details to make it look good for photos or in-person presentation.

The photographer will come and take photos of the space with their high-end DSLR camera. Typically, you will find a photographer as a referral or on an online platform. Ensure that you see their prior work. You should be seeking photographers who specialize in vacation rentals. If not vacation rentals, then residential photography. There are a wide range of photographers who specialize in nature photos, portraits, weddings, etc. You'll want the same photographers real estate agents use.

But beware of one photographer who is known and used in one market. I've seen some markets where 50% of the photos are from the same photographer. The photos look great, individually! But just like our Bali backyards, they no longer stand out because all of the competition has the same style.

Photographers will not do any, or very limited, staging. Some might send you a short list of things to do before their arrival. Most photographers do have the lighting figured out as this is essential for a good photo and means less editing later. They should lightly edit the photos afterwards.

Most will require payment prior to sending the final photos. You should try to withhold some of the final payment until after you see and approve the final edited photos. You might not like the way they were edited or how they otherwise turned out which creates additional fees for the photographer, if you've already paid them.

To avoid this situation, you should be reviewing at least some of the photos during the actual photo shoot. You don't want to see the photos for the first time after you send full payment only to see the ceiling is half of the photo.

Do You Need Professional Photos?

Once upon a time, I always recommended professional photos for all online listings. Nowadays, I only recommend hosts with ultra-luxury homes opt for professional photos. That's right, about 99% of this book's readers do not need to hire a professional photographer.

There's nothing wrong with hiring a professional photographer. I repeat, I have no objection to you paying money for a professional photographer. I've done it many times. But I've learned that the individual host can usually do equally well with a little instruction.

After all, we know how important quality photos are to the success of a listing, so why do we so easily outsource this task?

You're probably thinking one of two things right about now.

You might be thinking that you're not good at taking photos. But that's only because it's not natural for you, and you never gave it much thought. Did you expect to be a good cook or endurance athlete without much practice? Where else in life can we do something without practicing and become good at whatever that is? So why do we think like that for photos?

I didn't think I was a good photographer, either. When friends asked me to take a photo of them, I did, but often to see their unsatisfactory facial expressions upon viewing said photo. The good news is that taking photos of inanimate objects is a lot easier than of humans. Your sofa is less picky!

In the next section, you'll learn how to take great photos. It's really pretty easy and fun.

The other thing you might be thinking of is all the crappy listing photos that you know someone took with their camera phone. If you were thinking that and laughing at me for giving such terrible advice, hold on. Let's be clear. I'm not comparing crappy camera phone photos to professional photos.

I'm comparing professional-looking photos taken by you on your camera phone at your convenience to professional photos taken by a photographer at their convenience and your cost.

Where did all this come from? Why did I go from recommending professional photos to doing it yourself?

It all starts with my rental. I wanted the absolute best photos I could find. To get them, I decided to hire seven photographers. I thought that I'd take some from one and some from another plus I'd have a bunch of content for my Instagram page which we'll discuss in *Part 6: Direct Bookings*.

What I came to learn through this experience was that staging was just as important as photos, yet totally ignored by professional photographers. I welcomed them into my home, it was ready to go, and I told them to have at it. I explained that they should move around and shoot anything they wanted for the perfect photo.

Time and time again, I was disappointed. It's not that they were horrible photos. At least not most of them.

But they were underwhelming. And the angles were sub-optimal. This could have been subjective. Judge for yourself with the QR code below. But I felt it wasn't a subjective opinion when the final photographer came by. He happened to be from Airbnb. At the start he told me that it would take about an hour. I followed him around and took a look at all the photos he was taking. I suggested new angles to him. I suggested some staging changes like moving plants around, etc. I even added a cleverly-placed rose to some of the photos. At the third hour, I made note of the time. I was not expecting his response. The Airbnb photographer said that he didn't mind at all because he was learning so much from me. I was shocked!

I felt confident in the instruction I was giving to him, but to have a professional photographer tell me that was flattering and concerning.

Going into this experiment, I thought that I was paying not only for a professional camera, but more importantly for the creative eye of the photographer. That largely didn't turn out to be true.

I realized that I might not be using my time and money wisely here. At the same time, I realized that if I could teach a professional photographer about the right angels for my listing, why couldn't I teach others?

**If you'd like to have a look at
The Belmonte Penthouse photos,
scan the QR code.**

The Belmonte Penthouse
Airbnb Listing

SCAN ME

To summarize, you can definitely hire a professional photographer, and your photos will probably turn out just fine. There's nothing wrong with this route. However, I want you to know that with a little training you can take awesome photos yourself.

Awesome photos consist of four things: staging, lighting, angles, and editing.

How To Use Your Phone To Take Better Photos

I hope I have inspired a little confidence and intrigue about taking your own photos. I want to start off with the benefits of taking your own photos:

1. Save money
2. Do it on your schedule
3. Retake photos as rooms/layouts/amenities change
4. Take photos when the light is optimal for each room

Our overall goal with photos, whether a professional takes them or you do, is to make them as easily processable by the FPG as possible. Many of the strategies I'll show you below make photos more enjoyable to look at and easier to decipher even though the FPG doesn't consciously realize it. It's the same reason why when you go to Las Vegas for the first time only to wonder why you spent eight hours in the casino and don't feel tired. (The casino pumps in fresh, pure oxygen, has removed all clocks and windows, sets the light to resemble dawn, picks *optimized* music to keep your brain active, and uses a host of other factors the casino goer doesn't consciously realize.)

One note before we move on. I think the first three benefits above are rather obvious. What I mean by the fourth is that each room/amenity might photograph best at a different time of day. One example would be of a jacuzzi with nice lighting. You'd probably want to take that in the evening while you'd want to shoot the outdoor patio in the middle of the day.

Here are the settings or additional items you'll need.

1. A modern camera phone from the past two years
2. Microfiber cloth to clean the camera lens

3. (optional) Tripod
4. Turn on HDR mode; all camera phones have it
5. Turn on camera gridlines

You can purchase a tripod for 20 bucks, and it will help stabilize the photos, but is not necessary. I only used it for one of my photos. HDR stands for High Dynamic Range, and it helps produce a better photo. Whenever you see a photo where the window is blown out and white, that could be partially or fully fixed with HDR. Gridlines are those two vertical and horizontal lines on your camera screen when taking photos. It will help with straight lines, a concept we will discuss in a bit.

When you're actually taking the photos on your phone, you'll just use the automatic settings which are great for almost every photo.

Let's start with some general best practices for taking great photos.

Open all shades and turn on all lights.

Organize and declutter. Declutter and organize. And, do it some more. Anything that doesn't need to be in the photos should not be in the photos. We'll cover what that means by room in a bit, but for now I want you to remove or hide any cables. Even when you think you've decluttered enough; the photo may *still* look cluttered. You looking at a room and a photo of the same room are two very different things. The only thing that matters is if the *photo* looks decluttered and organized.

Similarly, regarding angles, take a bunch of them and decide on the best later. There's a noticeable difference between what looks good in person vs. what looks good on camera.

Take more photos than you think. But not too many. You don't want to go through 500 photos.

Take photos at waist level and straight on. Cameras tilted down or up produce unpleasant photos. They give us those tilted lines in the photo (see below for an example of what I mean), and it's one of the things the FPG doesn't consciously notice but that makes the photo hard to look at. *This is the most common error when owners take their own photos.*

Can you see the photo converging at the bottom? I've added white lines to help you and it's due to the camera phone being tilted slightly upwards. This can be mostly corrected with photo editing.

Have fun! I really enjoyed my time taking photos, figuring out which rooms looked better at which times of the day, moving things around. Play music, invite a friend over, make it a date. Enjoy the journey!

Remember to take photos of individual spaces, not necessarily rooms. And to limit or avoid layout photos. If you take a layout photo and you have an open home, only one should make its way into the final listing, if you must, and even that one towards the end. Promise me?

When rooms don't have good light or lack windows, use the flash or the night mode setting (sometimes automatic) on your camera. Or use the flash/night mode anyways and compare the two photos. I find that often a night mode photo, even in a well-lit room, turns out more vibrant.

Open doors generally create an inviting atmosphere. When taking photos, however, if the door doesn't need to be in the photo then either close it or move the camera angle to show whatever is on the other side of that space.

The open door to the right serves no purpose for the photo.

Make things look presentable. Put your marketing hat on. If you're presenting your FPG with a nice foldout sofa bed, but the photo of it is angled down with a couple pillows randomly on there and no sheets, that's not presentable.

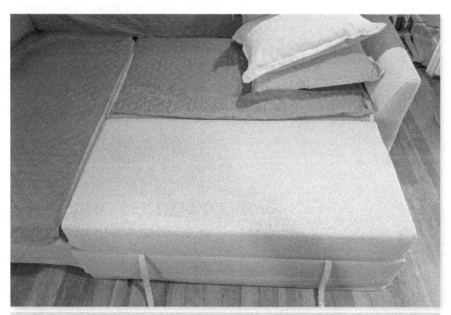

A sad, poorly taken photo with a poorly staged sofabed.

Following these general rules will make your photos among the top 5% of photos.

Next, let's consider some specifics room by room.

Bedroom. Folding the sheets into the bedframe, if possible, looks best in my opinion. Duvet, bedspread, or other covering that drapes and hides the bedrails is also optimal. More pillows look better. Turn on the bedside lamp. Always shoot bedrooms from one corner to the other.

Bathroom. Remove the trashcan, plunger, and toilet cleaner. Add a hand towel. Open the shower curtains. Always show the shower and sink. Ideally the toilet is also shown, but it's not necessary. Most toilets are similar. As long as you can see a portion of the toilet, that's sufficient. Close the toilet lid. If the bathroom is tight, you can take two vertical photos and stitch them together or take one panoramic photo (all newer phones have this option).

Kitchen. The kitchen is not the dining room, even though they're physically nearby each other. These are two individual spaces. Add a dish towel, and fold it neatly. Remove trashcan. Beware of reflections on appliances. Think about adding a bowl of fruit or some other ornament to the counter top.

Living Room. Avoid showing the backs of sofas. If something is blocking your view at waist level, either step to the side, choose a different angle, or move it out of the way. Yes, you are allowed to move the entire sofa if it doesn't serve the photo.

Outdoors. Always take the photo with the sun behind you. The 'golden hour' (one hour before sunset or after sunrise) is ideal. Layout photos are fine here showing an expansive backyard.

Whew! You did it. You now know whether or not you want to hire a professional photographer. If you do it yourself, you have the skills to do it well. But to push you over the edge, if you so choose, I'm going to offer you the next Featured

Product Discount on my Edited Photos plus a neat course I personally took to help teach myself all this excellence.

Featured Product Discount - Edited Photos

After you take your photos, send them to me, I'll select which are the best, and my designer will apply individual edits to each photo. Whether you want to make the sky blue, add the Netflix logo onto the TV or a fire to the fireplace, remove glare from windows, it can be done. Scan the QR code to see more examples.

Find your 10% discount code in the 'Featured Product Discounts' PDF of the bonus items.

Featured Product Discount – Edited Photos

SCAN ME

The course I recommend specifically teaches you how to take photos with your smartphone and can be found under 'Mobile Photography' on the Deal Sheet. The creator has agreed to a $50 reader discount plus choosing and editing of your first five photos.

3.6 THE TITLE

Eighty-five percent of vacation rental hosts are not getting this important *optimization* right. Remember, it's just one-of-a-hundred optimizations you can make to be a success. But it's low-hanging fruit and rather important, so let's get it right.

What Is The Title For?

Please remember this:

The title is for your guest. It's not for you.

What that means is to avoid adding anything to the title that helps you, and not the guest. Looking at you, property managers! These could be identifying the property with a number or code. Instead assign an internal name allowed within most OTAs and all PMS.

Don't do this: Energy 1603 1b/1ba NEW Pool Views

This is a live title on Airbnb right now, and you'll soon understand why it's so poorly optimized.

Emojis and Special Characters

If the OTA allows these, then I suggest you use them in order to differentiate yourself from your competition and draw more attention to your listing. But do so sparingly. One or two emojis.

(By the way, this won't work with Airbnb, which has been on a crusade to eradicate all emojis from titles, and they appear to have succeeded.)

Length of Title

Use every character permitted in your title. The title can be thought of as the very first piece of text the FPG will read from your listing, so it is even more important than the summary text. If the OTA tells you your title is too long, then shorten it just enough.

There used to be a valuable title hack where you could use a third-party tool to add extra characters. It's why my title is so long. Unfortunately, shortly after I announced the hack publicly, it was eliminated which was a huge bummer. I think Airbnb is listening....

How To Craft An Optimized Title

It's one of the easiest things you'll do as an Airbnb host. And it's one of those things within your control. Not everything will be in your control, but the title is, so let's do it right. You've already gotten to know your ideal FPG. Whatever they want and you have, the most important things, should go in your title.

Here's an example of an optimized title:

Walk Score 99 | Early Check | 1G | PetsOK | WD | King

I fit six amenities in there. Be sure that you are listing the most useful things to your FPG, not what you consider cool. Let's say you live in a big city, in a popular neighborhood, and cater to families. The rooftop is definitely cool and sexy, but your onsite parking garage might actually be the thing that is more sought after because fewer competing properties offer it.

Your garage, though not glamorous, is the thing that most sets you apart from the competition. So you'd put this first, then maybe the rooftop hot tub depending on what else…. what?...the FPG values (not what you offer).

People read from left to right, and up to down. So, the left-most item should be the most sought-after amenity.

You'll want to pack as much important information into those 50 or so precious characters as you can. When possible, use abbreviations like turning 'minutes' into 'min' (15min to airport) and always use 'to' instead of 'from' (i.e. 15min fromto airport) to save two characters. Above I saved the "/" character from W/D. Do you know what W/D is? It doesn't matter. The title is to be used to arouse interest. I also didn't use 'in' for 'check-in' nor 'Wi-Fi' after 1G. It should encourage the guest to read the text. In this case:

- Walk Score 99 (walk to grocery, cafes, gym, dining, nightlife)
- Onsite washer + dryer
- Early check-in for direct bookings
- 1 gig Wi-Fi speed
- King memory foam mattress in master

If you're near a popular location like a stadium, beach, or music venue then it *might* make sense to add your distance to (not from!) that location, especially if it makes a difference whether you're 5min or 15min to it. Some people have a strong preference to be very near the beach, and the difference between a 5- and 15-minute walk could be significant. Even though the map shows your location, it's obvious to many hosts that guests don't pay it much attention as we get questions about how far we are from X popular location near our home all the time.

In *The Belmonte Penthouse*, Lleras Park is such a popular and well-known destination that I put my distance in the title.

Finally, don't worry if you do not have a luxurious STR with a sauna, onsite bowling alley, private chef, tennis courts, golf carts. Any of the following can work for basic rentals:

- Keyless Entry
- Smart TV
- 100Mbps Wi-Fi
- Early Check-in/Late Check-out or luggage storage
- Fully stocked and equipped kitchen
- Netflix
- Desk or office chair
- Ground level
- Corner unit
- Hammock
- Fireplace
- Keurig coffee machine
- Garden
- Office

Things To Avoid

Let's run a little experiment. I typed in United States on Airbnb and narrowed down the map to the middle of the country landing on Fort Collins, Colorado. Here is a selection of the titles:

Mid-Century modern 3 bed/3 bath near City Park 9

OLD TOWN 2 bed Unit; Walk-bike; Private; Gorgeous

Private Studio in Old Town

Uniquely Modern Old Town Gem with Private Hot Tub!

Spacious modern town home close to CSU/old town

The Nest near Old Town & Breweries

Cozy Cabin near Old-Town

Ugh!

Remember when we talked about how your location isn't your selling point? Does the above not make this point abundantly clear?

Let's take a closer look.

The FPG may not know anything about your specific neighborhood, so telling them is not going to encourage them to book (so save those title words for something that is).

Or, the neighborhood is so popular that the FPG already knows about it and whether or not your home is there. If they want to stay in Old Town, they've probably already narrowed the map.

If the guest has narrowed the map to Old Town, none of these listings are unique. On top of that, descriptive words like 'modern', 'private', 'spacious', and 'cozy' do nothing for an FPG.

Even words like 'mid-century', 'studio', 'town home', and 'cabin', which are slightly better, should still be removed because the guest will know from the photos.

For my ever-popular 'luxury' or 'renovated' listings out there, the photos will allow the FPG to make that decision for themselves. Instead, tell the FPG *why* your place is luxury (heated towel racks in bathroom, private concierge, airport transit, etc.) or *what* was renovated.

I classify all of these words in quotes above as generic adjectives and hereby ban them permanently from your title.

I'd also avoid CAPITALIZATIONS because they take up more room than lowercase words. This means less of your title is shown on screen, especially if that screen happens to be a mobile phone or tablet. They also can give off the scammy vibe. We've all received the following email or text: WINNER WINNER CHICKEN DINNER! CLAIM YOUR 1ST PLACE PRIZE OF $1,000,000 RESPOND NOW!!!

Airbnb Title Generator

Still stuck?

I've developed a free tool to help you. I call it the "Airbnb Title Generator", and you can access it via the QR code. Simply answer as many questions as you can and, optionally, click to open 'Show more questions'. Then, click 'generate'. The more questions you answer, the more title suggestions you'll get.

At the bottom you'll have an option to include emojis in the title. By default, 'no' is selected.

Then just copy and paste your unique and optimized title into your listing.

3.7 SUMMARY TEXT

At this point creating your text sections will also be easy as you've already done the hard work in getting to know your FPG and your listing.

The summary text, no matter the OTA, is going to be the text at the very top of the listing page. This is the most important text box. If the FPG reads anything, this is it.

In this chapter and the next I'll share best practices on how to optimize all text sections plus a few tricks.

Here are your general best practices for text and how they relate to the Vacation Rental Commandments:

- Never add fluff or useless information (Respect The Guests' Attention)
- Don't treat the FPG as a child and repeat yourself (Respect The Guests' Attention)
- Keep the text as clear as possible (Be A Marketer)
- Only present information the guest needs prior to making a reservation (Communication Keys)

Let's explore how to put those abstract best practices into play.

The goal is to set your listing apart from those of your competition and get the FPG excited about booking that listing. Your job is to present them with all the reasons, in easily digestible bits, why they should book. Bullet points will be a main feature of your summary text. This is the most efficient and straightforward way to communicate what value you have to offer at the price.

We've already gone over many potential bullet points above, but here are some more:

- Dimmable lights
- Sonos sound system (or Bluetooth speaker)
- Theatre style projector screen
- Daily cleaning (or breakfast)
- Fenced backyard w/ firepit
- Heated pool
- Private balcony (or patio)
- Bathroom/Towel heaters

If my home is bike- or transit-friendly and my FPG is likely to value this, I'll mention the Bike Score or Transit Score. You can find yours by going to www.WalkScore.com and inputting your address. Think about including bikes with your rental or securing a deal with a nearby bike shop. Or provide transit cards preloaded with a few trips. Entrepreneurial mindset. If you are thinking of these as costs and not investments, please go back to read *Chapter 1.4 The Right Mindset*. The right question is whether or not such perks will produce an ROI.

Numbers draw attention. Keep that in mind and mix them throughout the bullet points:

- Bike Score 95 (nearby bike rentals, flat, dedicated bike lanes)
- 88" HDTV
- 325Mbps Wi-Fi
- 1,750ft² / 170m² cabin
- 12" rain showerhead

- 3-level penthouse
- 180° views from private rooftop
- Onsite, garage parking for 2 vehicles
- 8min walk to Lleras Park
- 29th floor

If you don't know your Wi-Fi speed, go to www.Fast.com the next time you're in the rental to find out. Some hosts put screenshots in the photos, but I advise against it. If an FPG is that concerned about the Wi-Fi speed, they will check the text.

Towards the bottom of your summary text, you can put your distance to (remember *to* and not *from*) no more than three popular locations, and only if you think your FPG wants to know. I also like to separate this section with a space and a different type of bullet point:

» 20min drive to ✈ SFO
» 6min walk to downtown

How To Highlight Reviews In Summary Text

If you'd like to highlight reviews in your summary text, and I suggest that you do, identify them with a different bullet point. You are allowed to use emojis in the summary text, but do so sparingly. I identify review quotes with a star like this:

★"...one of the best stays in Medellin."
★"Danny was hands down the best host I ever had."

Notice the snippets I chose are short and talk about one aspect only. Ideally less than 10 words. Highlight something fantastic. "This home was really perfect" is okay if you don't have anything better, but to me it sounds a little bland.

CTA = Call To Action

What if we could get some FPGs viewing our listing, but not yet ready to make a reservation, to still help us out. Let's ask viewers to save our listing to their wishlist, which is a positive indication for the Airbnb search algorithm. FMI refer to *Part 8: How To Rank #1 On Airbnb* to learn why.

Add my listing to your wishlist by clicking the ♥ in the upper-right corner.

Or, let's say we want to be more direct:

I want you! Tell me what I can do to be your host.

You can also add "Send me a message now."

Suggestions are persuasive. Stick your hand out to someone, even a stranger, and they'll shake it.

Ask someone to cut in line because you're in a hurry, and most will allow it.

I Call It "The Blurb"

Sometimes you can summarize your whole experience, or the main parts of it, with a short blurb at the top of the summary text. This is one or two short sentences.

"Villa Serenity comes with a chef, butler, housekeeper, gardener, and chauffeur. No need to worry about anything besides relaxing."

You can also use "The Blurb" anytime you can better communicate various bullet points into one.

"3500ft² / 325m² villa on a 1-acre gated lot!"

That's four things we're communicating in nine words (size of home, type of property, size of lot, privacy). Everything *optimized*. Our competition stands no chance.

Here's another:

"1960s ranch style home on 2 acres with 2,400ft² / 225m² indoor space."

Here's a really good blurb:

"Super private, pet-friendly 13 acre solar powered*, modern farmhouse 2 hours from NYC in Catskills." Ufff, sexy!

171

If you were familiar with the area, as most booking guests will be in this case, you'd know what Catskills is and the desirability of the location.

For a list of everything in this chapter and the next plus real-life examples of summary text, blurbs, CTAs, review quotes, and a list of preferred bullet points, scan the QR code below to access the bonus items. Every list/ section can be copied and pasted.

Bonus Item – Selection of copy/paste items for listing text

SCAN ME

3.8 OTHER TEXT AND HOUSE RULES

Nearly three-quarters of all listings do not use all available text boxes. I don't want you going in and adding a bunch of fluff and otherwise useless text, but there are ways to *optimize* every single text box. Even if that means adding your YouTube channel name or other social media account like Instagram or Facebook for more photos. "Check out *The Belmonte Penthouse* on YouTube for a video walkthrough!"

The text boxes below are labeled as they are in Airbnb and in that order. We already know the most important text is the title, closely followed up by the summary text. As you read further on in this chapter, even if the text boxes are renamed or you're using a different OTA, remember this: fewer FPGs read text which is lower on the page and/or requires additional clicks. Just because fewer are reading down, doesn't make them any less important. Those that are reading are still giving you a chance to convert them into a paying guest.

The Space

"The Space" text box is to be used as spillover from the summary section, if any. The summary text should be punchy. You should not be listing everything up there, only enough to get the FPG interested, the top six to eight best features. We don't want to overwhelm the FPG with 15 bullet points. "The Space" is where the rest of your cool amenities and features go.

Anything that needs further explaining can also go here. For example, maybe you have a heated pool, but need to explain that it comes at an additional cost. Put an asterisk (*) to the right (heated pool*) and explain it here or in the house rules which we'll cover as the last section of this chapter.

If you're pet-friendly, but only for small dogs or with an extra cost or if you need to let the FPG know that your dog also lives on site, this should all be done just below the summary section.

But what if you have a basic listing and can't think of any other text? We still want to fill in all text boxes and *optimize* any way we can. In this case, you can add your Airbnb link for credit:

→ Share your home on Airbnb to pay for your next trip. Use my link to receive a bonus: https://www.airbnb.com/r/drusteen

If you don't want to put that, I have a few more general options for you:

→ We use only green / organic / non-scented cleaning materials

Another option is to add a few common questions and answers. Don't overdo it. Two or three maximum.

Q: Is early check-in allowed?
A: Yes, if the listing has been empty. Otherwise, you can store your luggage on-site starting at 12pm.

Q: Is smoking allowed?
A: We allow vaping, e-cigarettes, and smoking on the balcony or in the front of the house as long as the windows are closed.

Q: Are there any restrictions on the community amenities?
A: Only those registered on the booking are allowed.

Guest Access

This one is pretty easy:

→ Entire space is included in this rental. Please, make yourself at home.

If there is something extra you want to call attention to or something is off limits, say so:

→ Entire space plus all building amenities are included in this rental. Please, make yourself at home.

Or

→ Entire space minus the garage/locked closet in bathroom are included in this rental. Please, make yourself at home.

Interaction

I like to put the following here:

→ I am here for you during your stay, but our level of interaction is up to you. I'm only a phone call/message away. You will be able to check yourself in upon arrival.

Or I'll replace 'but our level of interaction is up to you' with 'or I can be invisible. It's up to you.'

Other Things To Note

Here's what I say:

→ Please remember that you're staying in a house, not a hotel. Please treat the space with respect. If any problems arise, we will do our best to take action ASAP, but there is no one living on site 24/7.

You're giving yourself some leeway and helping the guest understand there are differences between a professionally-run hotel with a reception and you with a day job.

The Neighborhood

This and the next section are at the very bottom of the listing, and it requires another click to view this info. Needless to say, not many FPGs are reading this, but let's try and *optimize* this section as best we can. The biggest mistake I see is too much text here and too many activities. Instead highlight a few. Give the guest a taste of the recommendations they will receive. They're not just booking an accommodation; they're booking a local guide.

I simply put this: Click 'Show Host Guidebook' below for my personal and local recommendations.

This will open up the recommendations that you have filled in as part of your own guidebook.

You can also add here: All guests will receive a Custom Travel Itinerary for their stay. I will talk about this in the next section.

Getting Around

I suggest listing general things about your area's transit or travel options. What metro or bus lines are nearest? Do people catch tuk-tuks instead of taxis? Is there a bike rental shop down the street? In general, how do people get around? Is it a bad idea to rent a SUV Suburban due to parking issues? Tell the FPG here.

You can also include any discount codes to local ride-share companies or any other mode of transit. A lot of beach cities have organized bike/scooter rental stations.

You might even add another CTA here. If the FPG has read down this far, that means they're probably interested.

House Rules

This text box is usually somewhat hidden and low on P3, but a high percentage of FPGs look at it. We have a tricky little communication dance to do here balancing our rules and covering ourselves with potentially scaring away FPGs. Let's *optimize* this section!

Can you feel the energy!? Last section for text, let's go!

Most hosts deal with this in three ways:

1. They ignore it
2. They fill it out with a legal contract
3. They fill it out with the most important rules that the guest needs to know prior to making a reservation

By now, you certainly know the right answer is the third.

Using legalese (#2) is a personal choice. I know people who put in an entire legal contract, and I know people who put in more concise legalese like "We are not responsible or liable for any accidents, injuries, or illnesses that occur while at the premises or in or around the pool or fitness area." I know you want to cover your ass and you should, but organize the house rules into things the guest must read, then everything else.

Keep your house rules short and sweet and organized and relevant to the guest at the time of booking. Do not put check-out rules here. No obvious things. No parties, no drugs, lock the doors when you leave—these are all obvious. No repeating. No smoking, no events, no children, no pets are already visible on the listing.

You need to put all fees or fines the guest could incur here. But also consider whether you're actually going to collect that fee. A fee for losing the key is reasonable and most guests will pay it. But a fee for loud noise, extra guests, excessive mess, drug use are all going to be hard to prove and even harder to get reimbursement for if you're using an OTA. The house rules are best used as a deterrent. But the FPG has to read them for them to work as a deterrent. If you add too many rules here, or don't order them thoughtfully, the FPG will likely not read most of them, thus the main benefit they give you has been neutralized.

Some experienced Airbnb hosts are thinking that Airbnb won't honor the rule if it's not in the house rules. I even heard of one host whose guest stole things from their locked cabinet. The host told me that Airbnb didn't back their claim because it wasn't listed in the house rules. After all, it was an entire home listing, right? While I understand the sentiment, I think the response is just talk on the part of Airbnb. It's a professional and valid-sounding reason to turn down your request. It's like when investors tell unproven entrepreneurs to come back when they have a million dollars of revenue or 100,000 subscribers or some other large metric. Is this really *the* reason or is it a reason? It's a nice sounding reason with the goal of making you go away.

Always remember what the house rule section is for: to help us avoid problems and not to create them.

We just want the FPG focusing their little remaining attention on the things they must know for a pleasant stay or the things that will help them know it's not a good fit.

This means including just a few important rules:

If you don't allow visitors under any circumstances.

If you require total silence 24 hours a day.

If a plug must remain plugged in to avoid some type of damage.

If you are using any kind of noise recording devices or cameras.

You also need to prioritize the house rules, just as we do with all text. The most important rule at the top. This is the Hierarchy rule (refer to *iii. Terminology*)

If you have a basic listing and can't think of any additional rules, I still recommend you fill this in. Here are some generic examples.

- If you open it, close it; if you borrow it, return it; if you turn it on, turn it off; if you break it, fix it; if you use it, take care of it; if you make a mess, clean it up; if you move it, put it back.
- Recommended for all guests: travelers' insurance for the flight(s) and the duration of the reservation.

- Bookings within 24 hours of check-in will require a government ID prior to check-in.
- Local guests must contact me prior to booking.

There are two common mistakes I see in the house rules section. First is repeating information. If you say no pets or no smoking or no children, this is already in the listing. Don't repeat yourself unless you need to add some extra and relevant info.

Second, don't add too much text. If one in 20 guests smokes indoors, don't plaster 'NO SMOKING' throughout your listing and house rules. Even if you did, this guest would probably smoke in your home anyways. Unfortunately, it's a cost of doing business. Fortunately, it's not the end of the world.

If you can't help yourself, then please just remember to highlight the most important rules at top and include a separator (---) for the rules that don't actually matter to the guest, but you want to have in there to "CYA".

The last two generic house rules above are simply there to limit your risk. Last-minute bookings are high-risk because the majority of host/guest issues arise from them.

If you decide to add in a legal contract, I still recommend you add the most important, property-specific rules at the very top and separate the legalese. I understand you want to cover your ass, but the goal is still to attract the right guests and repel the wrong ones.

3.9 REVIEWS: WHY AND HOW TO RESPOND

Yesterday a Spanish couple asked me on a video call whether or not responding to reviews is really worth it. What a better time to write this chapter while it's fresh in my mind.

Short answer: Absolutely. It's a Level 3 activity. It's not going to make you a success, but it's one of dozens of choices that separates you from your competition in the eyes of the FPG.

I'm going to tell you when, why, and how to respond to both positive and negative reviews.

The concern of this couple was that it would just add another thing to their already full schedule. Fine. I understand this concern very well. But the information a review can give you is so important I advised them that they should, in fact, be reading their reviews no matter that it adds extra time.

You can imagine my surprise when they told me that they do read their reviews. If you are already reading your reviews, then responding to them takes seconds to do. Below I will give you some generic responses for generic positive reviews to speed the process even more.

If you are not reading your reviews, a goldmine of information, you need to start doing so right away. Shame on you.

Leverage the fact that your guests will tell you what's wrong (and right!) with your listing. Encourage them to do so.

Let's get started with the hot topic of responding to negative reviews. In the next chapter I will provide guidance on how to get a negative review removed, something I've done over a dozen times.

If you did what I did as a new host, then you didn't respond to any reviews. Mistake one. Then came your first negative review, a ghastly betrayal by the wicked guest the likes of which society has never seen before, and you felt that you must respond to it. And respond you did. At length. Mistake two.

What's worse is the added attention you brought to the one negative review in a sea of positive reviews because it's the only one with a response.

Don't you think an FPG will notice this difference and pay more attention as a result? And remember what added attention does? In this case, it's anti-persuasive. We want the least amount of focus on it. We want the guest to forget all about it like a bad dream.

Instead, the end result is the host making things worse than if they hadn't responded in the first place!

Unknowingly the host has forced their FPGs to pay more attention to their only negative review.

If you've ever been a guest on an OTA, you've seen it. Long, accusatory, negative review responses. They're so ugly.

In *Part 7: Bonus Content: Questions and Answers*, I will discuss strategies in avoiding bad guests and dealing with bad guest when problems arise. But for now, let's discuss how to optimally respond in the eventuality that you will get a negative review.

Do: Remove The Fluff

This first rule applies to both positive and negative review responses: be brief. It's Vacation Rental Commandment #2. The response should be no longer than your average response. Get in. Get out.

Don't: Respond To Private Feedback Publicly

NEVER respond publicly to private feedback.

The guest typically has two options when reviewing the listing. They may leave *private* feedback, but they must leave *public* feedback.

I've seen hosts respond to a positively-worded public reviews as if it were negative. FPGs cannot see the star rating, only the text. If you're not sure which text to respond to, go to your public, live listing and scroll down to the review section to see what your FPGs see.

Do: Address Issues Head-On

Whenever possible, address issues head-on. How was it resolved? That's the only thing the FPG cares about.

Complaint: bad smell
Solution: extra cleaning added, candles, new A/C, replacing bad pipes, unclogging toilet

Complaint: Dirty
Solution: Updated cleaning procedures, new cleaning team,
      re-clean of the space

Complaint: missing amenities
Solution: purchase them or explain why not

Complaint: Slow Wi-Fi
Solution: Router replace/temporary Wi-Fi issue resolved.

Don't: Be Accusatory

We're all humans. When we're attacked, we feel an urge to attack. Resist this urge. The guest is always right. Respond briefly, neutrally, and professionally. It's never the guests' fault. Add in statistics if possible. For example, if it's a cleaning comment, point to your 4.9 cleaning rating over 100 reservations.

Another favorite of mine is when the response starts off with 'Had you told us...' Well, they didn't, so address how it was resolved and seek out feedback next time rather than relying on the guest to communicate. For a guest to bring some deficiency to your attention feels confrontational for many. This is why you should be asking your guest for feedback mid-stay. I'll cover how to optimally do this in *Chapter 4.3 How To Message Your Guest*.

Sometimes: Ignore Negative Feedback

When the review contains both negative and positive feedback, sometimes you can completely ignore the negative feedback in your response. If the negative feedback is inconsequential or insignificant, ignore it. If the negative feedback is very specific, ignore it.

If both negative and positive feedback is provided, the guest will almost always start with the positives. In this case, if the negative feedback is something that you have no control over—the neighbor's barking dog, ignore it.

Additionally, sometimes the negative feedback is 'below the fold' or the FPG has to click 'Read more' to even see the negative portion of the review. Following the strategy, you can usually ignore it and respond to the positive.

As it relates to negative reviews, bury your pride.

The things that separate the good from the great hosts are these outlier situations. When things are going well, most everyone is a good host. But what do you do when you encounter adversity with one out of 20 guests?

Often, a negative review can be predicted. In other words, the guest will let you know if they're unhappy. How do you handle the guest complaint? We'll go over that in *Chapter 7.2 How To Deal With Problem Guests and Avoid Bad Reviews.*

In the bonus items, I highlight examples of good responses for real negative reviews in each of the categories above. I also have a game for you to play where I'll test you on what you learned here. I will give you a negative review, ask you how you would respond, then show you how I responded.

Bonus Item – Responding to negative reviews game

SCAN ME

Ok. Great work!

Let's move on to the art of responding to a positive review.

How To Respond To Positive Reviews

We know FPGs are reading reviews, well, skimming them, so let's *optimize* this section of our online listing.

Why do I recommend responding to about half of positive reviews?

1. Shows host engagement
2. Allows host to summarize a long review
3. Makes responses to negative reviews less noticeable

It surprises me how few hosts actively respond to their guest reviews. The above three reasons are why I recommend all hosts respond to reviews. But, there is a bit of science to it. I've told you the 'why'. Now, let me explain the 'how'.

To maintain our 50% response rate for reviews while *optimizing* the way in which we respond, use the following two review responses for short positive reviews that don't say much.

- Be sure to ❤ my listing to your Wish List so you can find me easily next time!
- Thank you for the ★★★★★ review!

Use the generic responses sparingly. If every response is the same, that defeats the purpose.

I want to further explain the three best practices in responding to positive reviews.

First, responding to reviews shows FPGs that you're an engaged host who reads and cares about feedback. This bodes well for you as the host. It's one of a hundred things that set you apart from your competition. The FPG notices.

As a guest who has spent more than 2,000 nights in STRs in more than 100 cities and 36 countries, I can tell you that most online listings appear very similar. So how do I choose where to stay? Often, it comes down to these small variables. I think, "Well, the host responded to their guest reviews, and I've never seen that before. I have to assume they care a little bit more than other hosts so I think I will give them a try." Whether or not it's a conscious thought, it's happening.

Second, we know that guests don't read, right? Right. At the same time, some guests like to leave long reviews. In this case, cherry-pick one aspect of the review to highlight in your response to assist the FPG in skimming the reviews. You should pick whatever your FPGs care most about.

Did they mention that really nice view or how central your location is? How useful your garage was? How relaxing the sun room was? This is your opportunity to review yourself based on a guest review.

You can also focus on things that are hard to depict in photos.

Did they mention how family-friendly your space is? This is something hard to depict in your photos and gives you a golden opportunity to sell FPGs with families!

The FPG is more likely to read your response and synopsis than the entire review. It's like the PS section on emails, it draws the eyes. This is really powerful when the review starts positive and then lists a few negatives, as we mentioned above.

The FPG will likely scan the first line for negative words, not find any and go down to read your succinct response, therefore, missing the slight negative altogether!

The bonus items for this chapter also include examples of this "mixed bag" review and how I responded to them.

Third, as discussed above, it's necessary to respond to negative reviews to briefly address the issue and how it was resolved. Now, since you're already responding to positive reviews, you won't call added attention to it.

Remember, all of your responses should be short, both the positive and the negative ones. The rule of thumb is **no more than two short sentences or half the guest review**, whichever is shorter!

3.10 HOW TO REMOVE A NEGATIVE REVIEW

It's Saturday afternoon, and the current reservation is set to check out the next day at 10am. The booking guest expresses interest in extending a night. I confirm the date is available, but the day ends with no payment confirming the extra night. I go to bed. While I'm asleep, I get an instant booking for check-in that Sunday. It's not uncommon for me as a quarter of my reservations come with fewer than five days lead time. I wake up at 6am the next morning and send the current guest a text that the date is no longer available, and he must check-out today.

An hour later, I receive a message from the guest who's supposed to check out in a few hours saying that he can't extend. I'm a few hours ahead of him in a different time zone, and I learn that they are still partying from the night before. It's 4am where they are. Confused, I message the guest repeating what I already said. The guest thinks that his verbal confirmation in extending was sufficient for me to block the dates. He's very upset.

I'm shocked. Is the guest playing dumb? This is not how things work in the real world. I was trying to reason with the man who my concierge confirmed was intoxicated. The guest thought I was doing the wrong thing by making his group leave at the last minute without time to find another accommodation. I tried to explain my side to no avail. Lots of wasted time ensued. After more than 50 five-star reviews on this property and his initial intention to extend his reservation, I believe he left a 1-star review.

I say 'believe' because I had it removed.

Ratings, especially on Airbnb, are cutthroat, so learning the art and science of getting a negative review removed will lead directly to increased revenue. There is a big difference between 4.89 and 4.95, both to the FPG and the search algorithm.

While the *number* of reviews is more important to the OTAs, closely followed by the review rating, to FPGs it's the opposite. As long as you have more than 10 reviews, most care about your rating more than the number of reviews. If your listing has between 10 and 99 reviews, the following applies to you:

- 5.0, congratulations
- 4.95, you're in the top 10%
- 4.90, you're in the top 25%
- 4.80, you're in the top 50%

Does it surprise you? I'm assuming you want to be one of the best listings in your market, and so I'm comparing you to your true competition and not to the sum of available listings in your market. You'll never hear Kobe Bryant or Lionel Messi compared to anyone other their peers.

But neither am I saying you're a bad listing with a 4.80. You're doing very well! But I don't want you complacent. I'm only trying to communicate that there *is* room for improvement. There *is* a difference between a 4.80 and a 4.90. It's a point of potential *optimization*.

FPGs subconsciously piece the above information together simply by observing how scarce each review rating is. There's a whole bunch of listings in the 4.7s and 4.8s. Fewer in the 4.9's. Fewer and fewer as you go up...4.96, 4.97, 4.98...the FPG can visually see this and understands what it means.

On to the good stuff! So how did I get that and a dozen other reviews removed for myself and my managed properties over the years?

It all comes down to the Airbnb customer service representative that you deal with and your knowledge of *both* the content and review policies, plus some hacks we'll cover at the end. Often, you will have to train the rep on the policy. Don't by whiny in your communication. In fact, be very pleasant. After all, they can remove a review "for any...reason at [their] sole discretion." [4] It doesn't have to violate a policy.

The overall point to keep in mind is that **you want to make their job easy**.

The other day, a friend conveniently asked me how to get a negative review removed as I was writing this chapter. I gave him the same advice I'm about to give you. After he explained the situation to me, I told him about a few of the policies that he might be able to use to get the review removed and the communication strategy he should employ to do it.

Days later, he told me his review removal request was denied. I was surprised as his explanation provided legitimate grounds for the platform to act. But there is a random element to this

---

[4] https://www.airbnb.com/help/article/546

strategy as is the case when dealing with humans. I asked him to explain to me what happened in detail. He told me that he listed seven reasons why the review should be removed. I can imagine how lengthy his request was.

While this is a common reaction, wanting to provide all potentially relevant information, avoid doing it. List one reason. All my friend did for this rep was make their job a little more difficult. The rep doesn't care if there are a dozen reasons because they only need *one*. Part of these reps' performance review is based on how many tickets they answer and how quickly.

Make their job easy and list the one reason you think gives you the best chance of getting a bad review removed. Make it very cut and dry for the rep. State the policy, point to the part of the review which violates the policy.

Let's find out the most common reasons why my negative reviews have been removed.

The most common way is by getting the guest to write that they will not leave a review or will only leave a positive review in exchange for a refund. On Airbnb, it is not permissible to coerce, intimidate, extort, threaten, incentivize or manipulate another person in an attempt to influence a review. Ideally, you want the guest to say it, but I've had one review removed where I asked the guest to confirm that if I send this refund they will not leave a negative review, and the guest affirmed it. (There's a module in the course dedicated to documenting effective strategies from the community in removing negative reviews.)

Another surprisingly common way is if a guest mentions a house rule they broke in the negative review. Reviews cannot be used as a form of retaliation for enforcement of a rule or policy. I charge $75 per guest after the fourth. Once the guest complained in his negative review about this policy as if I was trying to scam him.

Another common rule guests break is checking out late and incurring the late check-out charge. The more ridiculous the charge is, the more likely the guest will mention it in their review creating a way to get it removed. And just because you say the late check-out fee is $150, doesn't mean you have to charge that amount. It also gives you leverage to offer it for free if you think the reservation didn't go perfectly but you want to ensure the positive review.

By the way, let me stop right here and say I hate that I have to write this chapter. But I know from experience and talking with hundreds of hosts all over the world that many negative reviews are simply the result of a bad guest. Often the decision for the host is something like, let the guest throw a party and risk your business? (Airbnb does not permit parties, and parties tend to piss off other residents who then complain to the platform.) Or do I take the negative review? That's a shitty decision to have to make.

Because of the cutthroat nature of reviews on Airbnb, one negative review, especially for a new listing, can be absolutely devastating. If you get four 5-stars and one 4-star review in your first five reviews that equals a 4.75 overall rating. And this after many of these hosts put so much time and effort into their space and hospitality. Airbnb, if you're reading and I think you are, I recommend you take into consideration the existing reviews and the review rate. If a listing has months of 5-star reviews, the chance of getting a justified 1-star review is miniscule.

Ok, let's continue.

If the guest mentions any private, confidential, or personally identifying information, the review should be removed due to your privacy rights. I have my full name listed on my profile (I put both first and last name in the first name box): Daniel Rusteen. If the guest mentions my full name in their negative review, then I change it on my profile to only my first name and call Airbnb. I got one review removed for this reason.

Of course, if the guest didn't stay at the property, the review should be removed. You'll just need proof that they didn't, and this can be from texts or messages, not necessarily from video. A lot of this goes back to how clever you are in wording your conversation with the guest to trap them into helping you get the negative review removed.

By the way, both of the deleted negative reviews I reference in this chapter were not removed on my first attempt. They were removed on my second attempt. Call back a couple weeks later, on a different day of the week, and different time of the day until you get a rep who sounds like they work for Airbnb and not a call center because official employees have more flexibility in making decisions.

Let's end with some additional hacks. If you think you will get a negative review, be sure to write a negative review for the guest. Airbnb will often remove both out of fairness. If the guest ends up leaving you a positive review, you should feel bad and then call Airbnb who will happily and easily delete your negative review of the guest.

Similarly, submitting a damage claim against the guest increases the chance of getting a negative review removed.

Go forth and be great hosts, but also be armed to get unfair negative reviews removed!

3.11 VALUE OF AUTOMATED LISTING UPDATES

None. Zero. Let's move on. Please.

I hope to put this urban legend to rest once and for all. I'm going to tell you where it came from, why it still persists today, and why it is no longer relevant.

If you'd rather save your time, know that updating one day on your calendar by $1, flipping the last two photos in your listing, or adding a word or period to your text has zero effect on your listing.

There was and is a balance between the OTA trying to offer the browsing guest the best possible experience via an accurate search rank and hosts trying to game the system to rank as high as they can in search.

This is no different than Google search. People with websites are trying to get as high as they can in the search, even if that means trying something useless, while Google is trying to filter out the trash and show the most relevant results.

Back when Airbnb was a new company, one of the search rank factors was the last time the calendar or the listing was updated. To Airbnb, this seemed to be a reliable indicator of a good and up-to-date listing, and they promoted these listings. After all, before automation, is was a common guest complaint to inquire with a listing only to find out the dates weren't actually available.

They still show that metric in your hosting dashboard which is probably part of the reason for the confusion.

A lot of gurus sell tools with tips on how to rank high in search, and one of them is to change something meaningless on your listing to help you rank high. If your existing tool has this feature, or if the tool that you were already going to use has this feature, then go ahead and use it.

It's not going to hurt you, but it's also not going to help you. Do not let this silly idea sell you at all on whether or not you should buy a new tool, service, or software.

Today, this is no longer a reliable search rank booster. If you're an active host, you are going to naturally update your listing every few months anyway, if not sooner.

Airbnb's search algorithm has gotten smarter, and it's highly, highly unlikely that such a weak attempt at gaming the system still works. No one knows for sure, which is why I say to use the free tool if offered, but I don't want you spending any of your valuable time on this.

Now that we have that out of the way, let's learn how you can actually make a meaningful difference in your search rank with about 10 minutes of your time. Along the way, you'll also learn how I really got started in picking up the search patterns that lead to what I'm doing now professionally.

3.12 HOW TO RE-OPTIMIZE YOUR LISTING

I discovered this strategy while working for a vacation rental property management company in San Francisco.

My bonus was based on total listing revenue. I started to go in and re-optimize poor listings on a regular basis once I noticed a pattern between doing it and getting a reservation or inquiry within 24 hours.

Please note the following before getting started as this chapter is not relevant to every host at the same time:

- If your occupancy is adequate, skip this chapter until you need it.
- If your bookings suddenly stop after a certain future date, you probably need a price adjustment.
- A low-occupancy upcoming calendar is a great indication of a needed re-optimization.

What Is a Re-Optimization?

It's a manual refresh of your online listing. It's a tool in your arsenal. In fact, remember, it's the first line of defense when troubleshooting problems.

It's an opportunity to view your listing with a critical eye and make needed updates and revisions.

It also is a signal to the search algorithm that you are making a concerted effort to be a good host with an accurate listing, thus improving the guest experience and probably the OTA's bottom line.

Do You Need To Re-Optimize Your Listing?

First of all, if it ain't broke, don't fix it. If you have sufficient calendar occupancy, then just let it be and spend your time improving another aspect of your business or personal life.

Second, you already know to ignore your search rank. The position you see your listing does not correlate to how other guests will see it. **The metric that matters is your occupancy level.**

Third, ignore listing views. Again, it's about occupancy. With that said, OTAs do take into consideration conversion rate. If you have a low conversion rate, this would be a reason to re-optimize your listing to appeal more to your ideal FPG.

One more time: Focus on occupancy. It is extremely measurable. If you do not have occupancy goals, you need to pay special attention to *Part 5: Pricing.* For most listings and during high season, you want to have about 50% of days booked within the next month and every night within the next 7 to 10 days.

If your occupancy is fine, then you do not and should not do a thing to your listing as it relates to a re-optimization. However, you still want to be updating new settings that the platform adds and you still want to be replacing irrelevant information in your listing when appropriate.

If your calendar has a high occupancy rate and then suddenly there are no more bookings after one day, then you may just need a price adjustment. Maybe you are moving into low season?

On the other hand, if your listing has a booking here and there with many unbooked days in between (i.e. a healthy calendar with low occupancy. We'll cover this in *Chapter 5.5 Common Calendar Occupancies)*, then you very well may need a re-optimization. It happens to the best of us. The good news is that it doesn't take more than 10 minutes and should only happen two to three times per year at most.

How To Re-Optimize Your Listing

In no particular order, but doing no less than five of the below re-optimizations, here are the elements of re-optimization:

Update your title. Try highlighting some different amenities or features, or reorder the current title focusing on the left half.

Revise your description. If you have not read your listing in six months, I bet you will be able to write it more succinctly while being more informative. Additionally, some information may no longer be relevant. Ask for feedback from another STR host you know.

Change your cover photo. Your cover photo is the most important aspect of your listing after location and price. Choose something clear and simple. Have a look at your competition to see what colors show up most in their cover photos and do the opposite to draw more eyeballs.

Update the photo order. This is partly an art so it requires testing and measurement. You already know the best practices here so re-examine how well you know your FPG and what they're looking for and switch up the order.

Edit your photo captions.

Update your review photo.

Go through the entire listing's settings. Make sure the platform hasn't added something that needs to be filled in. OTAs do this often, and you want to show the system that you are an engaged host by filling these in. The sooner the better.

Add places of interest to your Airbnb guidebook. If you haven't already, add some popular tourist destinations to your guidebook because these locations are searchable within Airbnb. You'll also show up on the location's individual webpage on Airbnb. That's a link pointing to your Airbnb listing from Airbnb. Does it matter? Honestly, not much, but it most definitely doesn't hurt. There's a small chance it may lead to an extra booking. After all, if an FPG is looking at local recommendations, maybe they want to stay in the neighborhood.

Add all home safety features. OTAs want to mitigate their risk and liability as much as possible. As such, it would make sense for them to give a search boost to listings with all available safety features installed.

Appear in more search results. Refer back to *The Flexibility Concept*. Do any of the following to appear in more search results:

- Lower your minimum nights
- Increase your booking window

- Relax your cancelation policy
- Add another language to your profile
- Accept last-minute bookings later in the day
- Be an event-ready, pet-friendly listing or allow smoking

Featured Product Discount - Custom Guest Map

It's like the map on Airbnb, except better because you can add your brand name, identify nearby hotspots, and exclude some of your competition by marking off no-go zones. Notice the legend-identified 'not walkable' grey areas in my map below. If the FPG wasn't familiar with the area and one of their final listings were in the no-go zone, that might convince them to book with me.

Featured Product Discount – Custom Guest Map

SCAN ME

Find your 15% discount code in the 'Featured Product Discounts' PDF of the bonus items.

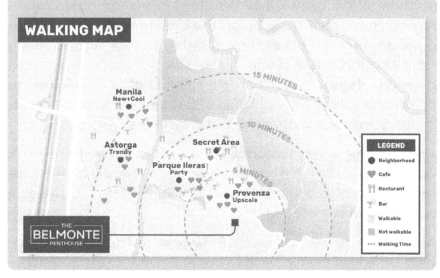

Every host will need to re-optimize their listing eventually. It's part of a healthy listing strategy.

Part 4

ELEVATE YOUR HOSPITALITY

4.1 SETTING EXPECTATIONS

Negative reviews are the result of mismanaged expectations.

Just as the FPG doesn't know exactly what they're booking, as we learned in the last section, they also don't know exactly what to expect upon arrival. We will continue to set and reset expectations through the entirety of the reservation, all the way until the guest leaves a review. That's what this section is all about. We'll be looking at various facets of your business and the guest experience and *optimizing* every single one of them.

How could you not be one of the best in your market after giving so much thought to your operation?

There are some bare minimum expectations the guest will have that you should be aware of and which are especially important if you've never been a prior STR guest.

A smooth, seamless check-in experience just like a hotel. In *Chapter 4.7 Check-in/Check-out*, you'll learn about all the nuances and how to *optimize* this process.

Consistent Wi-Fi, hot water, a comfortable and quiet place to sleep, and all amenities in working order. We'll get into the weeds here with *Chapter 4.6 Amenities*.

A clean space. This is super important for so many reasons, and I find many hosts are still misled by other experts preaching cost cutting here. Bad idea. Very bad idea. I'll smooth things out in *Chapter 4.5 Cleaning Process*.

But those are just the bare minimums. We're going to fine-tune our messaging plus allow ourselves to exceed the guest expectations with guidebooks, surprise and delight features, and more goodies. Oh, this topic is an important one and I feel proud right now that you've made it this far. Please accept my encouragement to continue forward. There's plenty of success just ahead.

Before we jump in, I want to take a moment to discuss the other part of the business often forgotten. And that's setting expectations with your staff—cleaners, maintenance, concierges, hospitality, live check-in persons, anyone who is working to make your business a success.

Just like you are setting expectations with the guest, don't forget to set expectations with your staff, who are now hospitality professionals! They need to know what you expect in order to fulfill those expectations. Also, *you* need to know what you expect. When we talk about cleaners, which nearly everyone will use, I talk about not doing their job for them. Let them be autonomous in the cleaning role, but that doesn't mean not setting standards and expectations.

Barring any specific cleaning rules for your home, the way they clean the house should be up to them and their judgment as long as it's resulting in 5-star cleaning reviews. But their punctuality, the way they fold towels, when to refill consumables, how to interact with guests, that's up to you to convey to them and should be communicated clearly and, sometimes, repeatedly. Pay them well, but make your expectations known. Your staff cannot, I repeat, cannot, be causing additional problems for you. Low paid staff causes problems.

They are there to solve problems. But they also might be new to the hospitality game. There was more than one instance when my cleaner showed up late after confirming a time she'd arrive to either cook breakfast, do the laundry, or clean the space. For my American guests (and myself), who expect timeliness, this is not acceptable. The expectations were re-set, and we moved on.

She is receptive to feedback, which happens the same day. She already knows my expectations. We've been over them, and they're written down. By the way, always write them down, maybe make a checklist. There's something special about the written word. Writing something down increases adherence to the rules and expectations.

When staff stray from your expectations, correct them. Explain why the rule exists and how it affects both your business and the guest experience. In this case, showing up late might mean the guests leave late for their day trip, thus setting off in rush hour traffic. This could add another hour on to their transit time. An hour lost on a three-day vacation is a long time. It could affect the review, which could affect the number of cleaning jobs. It could affect the tip given to the cleaner. And remember these magic words. "When you know my expectations, *and* you don't follow them *or* reset the guest expectation, I lose confidence (or trust) in you." I find this statement works exceedingly well to communicate your seriousness. You don't need to explain yourself here because the point is always understood. You should be providing training to your staff, especially on how to reset the guest expectations in advance. Life happens.

When I say reset the guest expectations, I simply mean that the staff is communicative with the guests when plans change. If new towels are to be delivered at 10am, but won't arrive until the evening, the staff needs to inform the guest. Anything, really. Will water or electricity be cut for a few hours in the afternoon one day? The guest original expectation is to have these for the duration of their trip. Communicating this information to the guests is setting expectations, and it avoids many problems. My cleaning staff does most of this, and as we'll learn soon, the cleaner is a natural property manager.

Do you know why my feedback is so effective? Because I'm paying my staff well, and I treat them like family. A staff member lost a close relative recently, and I paid for her to go back to her home country for a week. Treat people well, and all else seems to work out. We are more open to feedback when we feel valued and appreciated. I make a special note to call out good behavior and my appreciation whenever possible.

This goes for everyone, even maintenance folks who may need to come out on a Saturday or Sunday. Negotiate a fair rate with them, and in exchange for that, be very clear about your expectations. "I agree to pay you double on Sunday emergencies, and you or your backup agree to respond and resolve the problem within five hours." Be clear about your agreement. You might also explain the hospitality part in your business to maintenance folks and handymen. Changes in their schedules may require you to reset guest expectations. I'm over-emphasizing this point because I find it takes care of so many issues when you communicate something up front.

4.2 HOW TO PREPARE FOR YOUR FIRST GUEST ARRIVAL

You always remember your first.

I still remember my first guest from Airbnb in August 2013, Niklas, the doctor from Germany. I was nervous.

– *What am I missing?*
– *What would he want that I don't have?*
– *Does he want to interact with me?*
– *Will he think I'm cool?*
– *What might he not like about the space?*

Looking back on that experience, I was such a rookie, but Niklas was nice:

Niklas Paulus

Had a great time crashing on the couch with Daniel and the others. Although i contacted Daniel at last minutes notice he replied within minutes and was very helpful with everything. Less than an hour later i had found a place to stay on the border of chinatown and little italy, meaning cheap chinese shops where you can get almost everything including fresh fruit on one side, and nice (though more expensive) italian restaurants on the other. Downtown police department is just next door by the way, few homeless people on the streets at night, so you can feel a lot safer here than in some "downtown" areas. The house is very well located, the bus takes you downtown in a few minutes, cable cars pass just a few blocks away and there are a lot of bars in this neighboorhood. The guys are really laid-back, very friendly and even though they work a lot they took me to one of the bars almost every evening. Also, washing clothes was very convenient, with an easy to use washing and drying machine. They also have an amazing rooftop with a great view of the city. All in all, i had a great stay!

August 2013

Off to a great start!

My hosting evolved over the next decade until I perfected interacting with every type of guest. I also learned how to deal with some uncomfortable situations.

By the end of this chapter, you should have full confidence in welcoming your first guest, or improving your existing process.

The first question your guest will have is: what's the Wi-Fi password?

Don't wait for this question. Communicate this in the digital guidebook (covered in *Chapter 4.4 Digital Guidebook*). You may also consider posting it on the modem and even a third place like on the refrigerator or on bedside tables. Go above and beyond by testing your internet speed at www.fast.com in all areas of the house. In the Airbnb I'm at now, the Wi-Fi doesn't work in the office. Kinda crazy, huh?

You have control of this, so get it figured out right away. Potentially, you'll need to purchase a Wi-Fi extender. This is especially important if you require an application to unlock the front door where the guest needs an internet connection. Ensure they can connect just outside your front door in case they don't have cellular data, which they may not have, especially if they're foreigners.

Before Arrival

Before arrival, let the guest know who they are to contact for general questions and emergencies whether that be through the Airbnb application, a messaging service, or a phone call. Do not give the guest more than two contacts; ideally one.

Communicate this a few days before check-in and before the guest starts to feel nervous. If the guest does not hear from you around three days before check-in, I find they often message.

Help your guest avoid scammers and enable your guest to start their vacation quickly by telling them the best ways to get to your home from the airport or rail station. Include both cheap and expensive options, and be detailed. Ideally, you can get a discount code to your guest for a local taxi service or ride-share company. Sometimes the local ride-share applications have a referral code where both you and the guest get a small bonus. People love discounts.

If your house is particularly hard to find for whatever reason, ensure your directions to your front door are rock solid crystal clear. We do this by having a friend unfamiliar with the property do a check-in as if they were a guest and providing detailed feedback. If we don't have this, then we ask the first few guest arrivals about how easy it was to find the building, the front door, and to enter.

Providing the address sometimes is not enough. When I was in Almaty, Kazakhstan the host gave me the address, but not directions to the front door. The address they gave me was easy to find, but it had a shopping mall on the ground floor, and I could not figure out how to get in. I have to share this photo because I think it is kind of ridiculous. How was I supposed to know I needed to go through this dark and sketchy alleyway? I specifically remember thinking, there's *no way* this could be how I enter.

The entrance to my Airbnb in Kazakhstan that I debated walking into at 10pm at night upon check-in day.

If your guests may drive, provide parking instructions whether that's to the dedicated parking spot or to the nearest, recommended parking garage. Remind your guest to never leave valuables in their car! I learned this the hard way as a property manager in San Francisco, California where car robberies are rampant, and the police don't do anything about it. **Your guests' problem becomes your problem.** If severe weather effects on-street parking, like in winter resort areas, give them the link to the municipal website for alerts and tell them where they can park after dropping off their bags.

If you need or prefer to use physical keys, ensure you have one set per guest. If there is a gate that requires a remote, ensure you have at least two if you have anything more than a 1-bedroom home. I recommend you not put your address on the keys in case the guest loses them.

If you insist on a live check-in, use the guest's digital interactions as a guide to your live interaction with the guest. If the guest instant-booked and did not send any messages, they probably don't want a live check-in. If you must do this, make it quick. On the other hand, if the guest has asked some questions about the area (what subway station to get off at, local recommendations, parking info, etc.) then they would probably welcome a live check-in, and you can take a bit of extra time providing more recommendations or details of the area.

During The Guest's Stay

Especially if you are a new host, you need to be more familiar with your home than your guest. Know how to answer all of the following questions in as straightforward a way as possible:

- The location of the fuse box/breaker panel for electrical issues
- How to operate all appliances (TV, washer/dryer, coffee maker, oven, sound system, A/C, fireplace, etc.)
- How to get hot water from the shower (sometimes it's not very straightforward)

- How to connect to and reset the internet (where is the router?)
- How to dispose of garbage and recycling correctly

Better yet is to include this information in your digital guide-book (more proactive anticipation of needs...) so that your guest doesn't even have to reach out to you and wait for you to respond.

In summary, learn how to solve all of your guests' potential problems and work towards fixing them in the future.

Upon Check-out

If you have messed up during a reservation, luckily, you can redeem yourself with a good live check-out. Reviews are largely based on the final experiences a guest had in your space so ensure you make the check-out pleasant and leave them with a last impression of how personable and pleasant you are.

At the same time, if things went fine, don't insist on coming over for check-out. The guest is stressed on this day and probably running late. Leaving things behind is more common when the host goes over and interrupts the packing process. The last thing your guest wants is a pleasant chat with you when they're rushing to the airport. It's a delicate balance with what I said in the last paragraph. It's even worse when the host wants to do an inventory check of everything to ensure their guest didn't steal or break anything. Don't do this.

Instead, send the guest a message 18 hours before check-out (around 5pm the day prior) reminding the guest of the check-out time and adding any specific check-out instructions.

I recommend not asking the guest to do much upon check-out. Do not make them empty the trash, do the washer or dishwasher, add chlorine to the pool, don't make them turn off the gas or water valves or really anything unless absolutely necessary. I tell my guest to refill the ice cube trays and clean the lint tray in the dyer if they used it. And, to leave the keys on the counter near the door. That's it.

You might consider offering directions to the airport and telling the guest how long the trip will take at which times of the day and which days of the week.

After Check-out

This is the easy part. Assuming the guest didn't forget or break anything, all you should do is send a message to them. Two days later, we'll send a sort-of indirect review reminder via an automated message. In the next chapter, we'll learn how to do this with automation.

If the guest left something non-illegal, non-dangerous, and non-embarrassing behind (I have stories!), send it back to them. I normally do not charge the guest if it costs less than $25 to send, but this depends on your nightly rate and how much it would affect your bottom line. This is my personal preference as I consider it a cost of doing business and hope for an extra positive review instead. Or maybe I ask them to leave me a secondary review on another platform like Google if I'm accepting direct bookings.

If the guest broke something and did not tell you about it, I apply a $50 threshold to this as I prefer 5-star reviews over collecting small fees. Work these expected costs into your nightly rate and investment analysis. If the item was major, depending on the seriousness, try to wait until after the review to make a claim if you think the guest will hit you with a negative review because of it.

Conclusion

To be a good host, you need to be a guest. If you didn't notice, a lot of the above is us, as hosts, trying to put ourselves in the shoes of our guest. I suggest you stay as a guest at least a couple times per year as this will prove invaluable to you.

Maybe even do a staycation in your own neighborhood to scout the competition!

The whole idea is to get your guest acclimated as quickly as possible to your space so they can start enjoying their time in your city. And, when things go wrong, give your guest the tools to troubleshoot on their own as they would often prefer to fix the problem rather than wait on someone else.

The very last step after your guest has left is...*cleaning your rental yourself.* Remember, it's my recommendation to manage and clean your own rental for as long as possible to learn how things are done.

4.3 HOW TO MESSAGE YOUR GUEST

As you know from *Chapter 1.5 The Reservation Flow*, each reservation follows a predictable path in terms of when certain information needs to be communicated to be most useful and relevant to your guest. This also makes it more likely the guest will actually read what you're sending.

After understanding this natural flow, I created and *optimized* as set of messages for nearly complete message automation. When I talk about automation, I am referring to manually setting up a rule-based system once and afterwards a process takes place automatically based on those rules.

These messages are powerful because I've leveraged certain behavioral psychology techniques to increase both the number of 5-star reviews you get and the percentage of reviewing guests. Getting more of your reservations to review you means that, when you get a negative review, it will affect you less.

All negative reviewers leave a review so when I say getting more of your reservations to review their stay, I'm referring to the would-be positive reviewers who don't initially leave a review.

In this chapter I provide nine messages and how/when to use them effectively.

First, some general rules to keep in mind when you're sending *any* message:

- Short and sweet (be succinct, no more than 100 words or as short as possible)
- Send relevant info at relevant time (i.e. send check-out info only at check-out time)
- Don't repeat yourself

When you see the percentage sign (%) it simply means this is to be customized in your chosen PMS provider so it can be personalized to each guest and reservation. Both of my recommended PMS providers allow for this customization.

Inquiry Only

➤ When To Send: Immediately

You will send this message when the FPG wants to contact you *without* an intention (at least not yet!) to make a reservation:

Hi, %guest_first_name% -

Thanks a lot for your interest in my home for your trip in %listing_city%!

It would be a pleasure to host you from %check_in% to %check_out% (%guests% for %nights%).

P.S. This is an automated message, but I do read every message. I'll address any questions shortly.

Sometimes the FPG is just checking if it's an active listing and if they'll get a response. This is more common with newer listings. And, sometimes they have a question. This automated message is especially important to send if you receive inquiries when you're busy or asleep. We want to acknowledge receipt and let the guest know this is an active, professional listing which will get a response. If the FPG likes your listing but is in a rush to book, maybe the message gives you an extra few hours to respond and secure the booking.

Some guests will ask for a discount with the inquiry. If it is the slow season, I usually accommodate if it's reasonable. Otherwise, I suggest they reach out to me a week before the requested check-in date. If the calendar is still available, I will honor their requested discount. I find this is the most efficient way to respond to discount requests which potentially offers me a safety net with a last-minute booking if the guests wait it out (and some do!).

Request To Book

➤ When To Send: Immediately

You will send this message when either the OTA doesn't allow instant reservations or you have chosen to not allow instant reservations on your listing. When the FPG sends this message, they have intent to make a reservation, but you have to take an action, like accept or decline.

Hi, %guest_first_name%, and thanks for your interest in my home!

I want to confirm right away that I have received your request to book my home from %check_in%, with %guests% for %nights%.

I will review your request and come up with an answer as soon as possible so that you can prepare your trip accordingly.

P.S. This is an automated message, but I do read every message. I'll address any questions shortly.

You'll notice in the last two messages I call attention to the message being automated. I like to do this so that my other, also automated messages seem genuine. I've received zero negative feedback to date about this.

Additionally, if the guest asks a question, a canned response which ignores that question seems impersonal and annoying.

A large portion of guests are booking for the first time. They've heard that STRs are more personal than hotels. I want to foster this idea.

Booking Confirmation

➢ When To Send: Immediately

If a guest is ready to book and the listing/OTA allows instant reservations, you should send the following message to the guest:

Hi, %guest_first_name%, and thanks for your reservation!

I will contact you three days before your arrival to make sure that everything is okay on your side, and give you some additional instructions for a smooth check-in.

If you're a planner, here are some of my local recommendations: [url to digital guidebook or Custom Guest Itinerary]

P.S. This is an automated message, but I do read every message. I'll address any questions shortly.

We are sending local recommendations at this point because upon booking is when the guest is most likely to do a little research on the area. Also, great recommendations introduce the guest to the usefulness of the digital guidebook whose contents are covered in the next chapter.

Check-in Message

➢ When To Send: four days prior to arrival

The soon-to-be guest will receive this message just prior to their check-in date with relevant information about the day of arrival. If you noticed in the prior message, I told the guest that I would next reach out three days before check-in, but I'm actually sending this on the fourth day. Why? To account for any time differences and to avoid unnecessary questions. I find that around the second to third day before check-in, if I don't send a message, they will often send me one anyway. Here's what it looks like:

> Hi, %guest_first_name%!
>
> I've created a house manual for your viewing pleasure: [url to digital house manual]
>
> It has all the info you'd want like check-in info, address, Wi-Fi, etc.
>
> IMPORTANT: Please call [emergency contact] at [phone number] for anything urgent. Anything that is not urgent, please send a message through Airbnb or text the number listed on the account.
>
> P.S. If your arrival time has changed, please let me know.

As you can see, this message is extremely short with no repeated information and a link to a guidebook. The only time I would repeat information directly in this message is when it is of extreme importance (quiet hours, no smoking, and other generic house rules are not of extreme importance). An example of extreme importance is something that can seriously interrupt your hosting or the guest's having a good time.

Check Up Message

➢ When To Send: 18 hours after check-in

Send this message around 11am the day after check-in to all reservations longer than a single night:

> Good morning, %guest_first_name%,
>
> I hope that you have settled in alright and that you are experiencing a 5-star stay :) Please let me know if there is anything you need or if I can assist you in any way!

All the best and enjoy your stay!

This message allows me to address any problems real time to ensure a 5-star review. About three-quarters of all guests do not respond to this message.

You may also choose to send this message a few hours after check-in as this is the time the guest is getting used to your house and will have the most questions. I send it the next day because I do not know when the guest will check-in, and I want to let the guest figure out the small stuff for themselves rather than encourage them to first ask.

You'll notice I specifically mention 5-star stay. This is the first of three times I mention this. I want to communicate my expectations that the guest is having a 5-star stay and if not, that they should let me know, that I want to know. Keeping the lines of communication open is crucial.

Pre-Check-out Message

➢ When To Send: 18 hours before check-out

Send this message in the evening the day before check-out for all reservations longer than a single night:

Hi, %guest_first_name%! -

I hope that you have had a 5-star stay so far! I would like to remind you that the normal check-out time is by 11am, unless agreed otherwise.

Before leaving, please:

- *Leave used linens and towels on the beds, floors, or counters*
- *If you've used a lot of dishes, it would be great if you could start a dishwasher load before you leave. Dishwasher soap pods are under the sink.*
- *Turn off all lights*
- *Turn heat off*
- *Refill ice cube tray in freezer*

- *Clean lint tray in dryer*
- *Sign the guest book – we love feedback!*

Safe travels!

You will notice that I have bookended the reservation with the words '5-star'. Here is where you should be reminding the guest of any specific and necessary check-out requests. This is a good opportunity to repeat yourself (this info is already in the guidebook) as you are saving the guest time in opening the guidebook and finding the check-out instructions. Of course, replace the above bullet points with your own and no more than a few.

Regarding the last bullet point, think about leaving a beautifully-bound guest book and fountain pen to encourage guests to leave a note about their experience. If you rent to groups, this gives them all a chance to share feedback. And, some guests don't want to tell you directly, so I find this option resonates with some. Plus, guests love to read others' comments and share their own.

You can also let them know that late check-out is available, even if just 30 minutes or an hour later. Most guests won't take you up on this due to their pre-existing flight schedule, but just offering the option I notice gives me some extra goodwill at a very important point in the reservation flow.

Post-Check-out Message

➢ When To Send: around three hours after check-out

Send this to the guest just after check-out, but prior to them catching their flight, ideally. It acts as a sort of review reminder when the stay is still fresh in their minds, and they have nothing better to do while waiting for their flight than leave a nice, long review:

Hi, %guest_first_name%!

Thanks for leaving the place in good shape! If you have anything to share about your stay, pros or cons, I'm very interested to hear as I like to improve the guest experience. I'll be leaving you a 5-star review.

This is the most important message and the cause of the many extra 5-star reviews I have received. Three to five hours after their scheduled check-out time, I send this final message related to the actual reservation.

This message goes out regardless of how the guest actually left the place. This is because regardless of that, *I* still want a 5-star review. I don't charge the guest an extra cleaning fee except in the most egregious scenarios. With this message I am setting the expectations that I am happy with the guest, and they will be getting a 5-star review.

The message is sent before the guest can leave a review in the hope that if they were planning to leave a negative review, they feel bad as I have just told them I am sending them a positive review and open to feedback.

Friends and Family Discount

➢ When To Send: 48 hours after check-out

%guest_first_name%,

One last message...I would like to extend a Friends + Family discount to you. If you, or your friends and family, return to %city% then please have them reference your name and I will honor an extra 15% discount for any stays between November and March.

To increase occupancy during slow season, I extend an offer proactively to prior guests and their friends and family to stay at my listing for a discount. Just remember to turn this message off if the guest was not pleasant.

If your area does not have a clear busy versus slow season, then you may consider offering the discount for midweek stays or stays lasting a day or two longer than your average stay length.

For my property-managed clients with cheaper nightly rates (less than $250 per night average) I prefer a 15% discount because I prefer repeat, good guests at a slight discount to avoid potential problems that new guests bring with them. If I offer a percentage discount, then all reservations count. They are associating any trip to my location with a discount, not trips of four or five days or trips on certain months or days of the week.

You can also offer a fixed dollar amount. My average night at *The Belmonte Penthouse* is $500 so offering a 15% discount could be $600+ per reservation, but offering 5% off seems puny. Instead, I offer $200 off. And that's good for any reader of this book, all you'll have to do is show me your proof of review!

Thank you for reviewing my book!

SCAN ME

Review Reminder

➢ When To Send: 5-10 days after check-out

This message is optional, but if you choose to send it, remind the guest you left them a 5-star review.

Hi, %guest_first_name% -

Since you were a terrific guest, I left you a positive 5-star review last week. This should help you secure future reservations.

As a host, reviews are extremely important for my future success and online reputation. I hope you can make time to leave me a review and share your experience with my future guests. Either way I hope to see you again and remember the Friends + Family discount I sent you with my last message!

Daniel Rusteen 9:00 AM
Hi, Taylor!

Since you were a terrific guest, I left you a positive 5-sat review last week. This should help you secure future reservations.

As a host, reviews are extremely important for my continued success. It's literally all that actually matters. I hope you can make time to leave me a review and share your experience with my future guests. Either way, I hope to see you again and remember the 'Friends + Family' discount I sent you with my last message!

From @BelmontePenthouse in Medellin, Colombia.

 Taylor 8:41 AM
Sorry for the delay! Just left a review. Thanks for everything!

This goes out only if the guest has not already left a review. PMS tools are smart enough to recognize that and not send the message in these cases. According to Airbnb, 72% of reservations leave a review so this message mostly never goes out.

Keep in mind that if the reservation was not positive, you will not want to pester the guest about leaving a review which might not be five stars. Five stars (5.0) is an A+, four stars (4.0) is an F-. Depending on the listing, I may or may not send this message out. Sometimes, I find if the guest does not leave a review, they are doing so because they do not want to leave a negative review. Be cognizant of this.

Conclusion

Following this strategy has cut down on my manual messages by 85%. You will still get questions from guests about things already covered in your listing as that is just part of the game. Airbnb encourages guests to message numerous hosts each trip. If you have ever been a guest before, it is exciting to see all these homes available for you to rent and sometimes at very cheap prices, especially for international trips.

If you have a website, social media account, Facebook group, anything outside of the OTAs where the guest can contact you, feel free to sprinkle these throughout your automated messages. Sometimes I sign the message @BelmontePenthouse, and most people will understand this is an Instagram username. But remember not to add any phone numbers or website links before a reservation is accepted or after the check-out as the message will be flagged and the link/number will be removed.

Featured Product Discount – Automated Messages

This chapter is a downloadable product sold on my website included here for free. It's up-to-date at the time of writing.

For an updated copy/paste document with PMS-specific short codes (the % above) and other PMS-specific functionality built in to the message templates, you can download it with a 50% off code located in the 'Featured Product Discounts' PDF of the bonus items.

Featured Product Discount - Automated Messages

SCAN ME

4.4 DIGITAL GUIDEBOOK

Mission failed.

I've been talking about digital guidebooks for years. I dedicated two full chapters to the subject in my last book. I've produced enough content to fill its own book of what they are, why you need them, what to put in them, and when to send them to the guest. I've mentioned them whenever the subject came up on many podcasts and even when it didn't. Yet, years later, I can report as a guest and as a host that the adoption of digital guidebooks is pathetically low.

I've received a digital guidebook in all of my travels in over 100 cities exactly zero times. Not a single damn time. It's upsetting. But I'm not upset at you. I'm upset at myself. I could have done more, could have explained the benefits more clearly, I could have told you that it's totally free, I could have told you that it only takes about 30 minutes to set up and after you may never need to touch it again. I'll do better. Let's jump in.

What Is a Guidebook?

A guidebook, also referred to as a house manual, is for your guest. It can be digital or physical. It's a place to store and organize basic information that you know your guest will need or could use like local recommendations and how to use certain things in the rental. Ultimately, it's to elevate your hosting.

Why Do You Need It?

The guidebook accomplishes two things:

1. Decreases your time investment
2. Increases guest satisfaction

The guidebook saves you time in answering basic or standard questions by getting relevant answers in front of your guest at the right time. **You want to automate when your involvement doesn't add any value.**

On the flip side, it increases guest satisfaction because you're thinking about the guest journey and how you can make it as pleasant as possible. By providing a guidebook with relevant answers, the guest no longer needs to call or send you a message (and then wait for you to answer) and can instead refer to the guidebook for a quick answer to a basic or standard question.

There's a third bonus thing it can accomplish. Believe it or not, the experience the guest has in your neighborhood or city, as well as inside your home, affects your review. So, you say, 'why don't we *optimize* it then?' I agree, let's!

Types of Guidebooks

Your guidebook will fall into one of three categories: physical, digital, non-existent.

My preferred type of guidebook is digital for two reasons. First, it's easier to update. Second, I can send it to the guest prior to their arrival or send them a link to it when they contact me with an issue.

When creating a digital guidebook, you can use one of the many tools that will help you with design and organization. Or, you could create one on your computer. If you use something like Google Documents, please ensure it is viewable by the guest even if they don't have an account.

The best practice, similar with digital locks, is to allow your guest access without having them take another step by creating an account or downloading an app. Said differently, if your chosen application requires the guest to download their app to view the guidebook, it's not your best option.

If you decide to use a printed guidebook located in the home, this is okay, and much better than no guidebook. Just remember to update it when it starts to look old or when the information in it changes. You will want to verify periodically, for example, that the restaurants are still open and all website URLs work.

How Much Does It Cost?

Some cost money. Some are freemium which means it's free with paid upgrades. You will find my freemium recommendation in the Deal Sheet, and the majority of hosts will not need to upgrade to the paid version.

How To Create An Optimized Guidebook?

There are some best practices to *optimize* the creation and presentation of a guidebook.

Organization is key. No matter where you create your guidebook, it should be highly organized and easily readable. The challenge is getting the guest to actually open it that first time. To do that, try to force the guest to open it for the Wi-Fi access code ("Click here for Wi-Fi password.") But if that doesn't work and the guest asks you a question already answered in the digital guidebook, you should send the guest a link or URL to the answer in the guidebook (each section should have a unique shareable URL) instead of answering it directly. Remember, the guest has never seen a digital guidebook before and doesn't know what it is or how useful you've made it. You only have to do this once because the guest will realize they didn't have to ask. *When* the guest opens it up, we want them it to have an immediate 'this is useful' impact.

The second way we accomplish this is by not being wordy. This is not the time to sell or describe your home. It's for answering questions and providing additional value. The guest should already know your bathroom has a tub or that the master bedroom is located at the end of the hallway and has an ensuite bathroom. The average guest, if seeking additional blankets, will know to open the obvious drawers or closets to locate them.

The final thing to keep in mind is hierarchy. This is more relevant if you're creating your own guidebook. The information at top should be the most important information. One-hundred percent of guests will be seeking the Wi-Fi credentials, and it's probably the first thing they'll do so this should be the first bit of info.

What Do I Put In The Guidebook?

You should include any of the following information, but not necessarily all, in your guidebook:

- Directions
- Check-in

- Parking
- Host and emergency contact
- Wi-Fi and router info
- Instructions for amenities
- Trash and recycling
- Local recommendations and apps
- Check-out

Let's go over each one now.

Directions. This is where you tell the guest how to get to the rental from the most common points of arrival (airport, train or bus hubs). Only put information that a reasonable guest needs to know. For example, if your rental is a single-family home in a city, providing an address and a photo of the home is sufficient. The guest will be able to find your property with any map application.

However, if you live in the middle of nowhere, in a gated community, or many guests get lost going to your property, then clarify the directions.

Take your hosting to Level 3 status by recommending the most efficient route, bus, or taxi service. If bus, tell the guest the line number and where to catch it. If taxi, tell them how much the ride should cost. If it's your preferred shuttle, tell the guest how to reach the counter, and try to get a discount for your guests.

Know your FPG and know your space. If you're renting a $500 per night luxury penthouse on the outskirts of the city, you can probably skip public transit directions.

Check-in. On Airbnb, 'check-in' is one of the six categories you'll be rated on so be sure to get this right. This is where you communicate how to get to and open the front door. Be extremely specific if it's any less than completely straightforward. This is a HUGE pain point for guests, so please make it easy for them. Ideally, have someone unfamiliar with the property follow your check-in instructions to verify their effectiveness. You may need to add more information, text, or images, to clarify any confusion.

Similar to my stay in Kazakhstan, while I was in Miami Beach, my Airbnb host gave me the full address to an easily findable building. However, my front door was actually located in a connected building showing a different numbered address. This was extremely confusing for me until a neighbor helped me out. This is a common problem and within your control to avoid.

Be sure to also provide the floor, if necessary. In Chiang Mai, the host created three homes out of one. They all had the same physical address, but the front door was on a different floor for each unit causing some confusion upon arrival.

'Check-in' is where you can identify your luggage storage policies for early arrivals and late departures. If you are not equipped to offer luggage storage, I recommend you offer an alternative like setting up a deal with a local store or laundromat. Remember our levels:

Level 1: No luggage store and no alternative
Level 2: No luggage store with alternative
Level 3: Convenient luggage storage

Also remember Level 1 doesn't mean bad and Level 3 good. It depends on your offer (reference from *Chapter 3.3 Know Your Space*).

This is the one area it's okay to over-explain. Include a link to a private YouTube video showing how to operate your digital lock or add a photo of the lockbox location. Just in case.

Parking Information. If you provide parking, explain where to find the parking spot. It could be as easy as clarifying that parking in the driveway is acceptable. Or, you'll need to explain how to register your car, where to get the parking garage key fob, how to use it, and/or how to get to parking spot #94. Label the spot if appropriate.

Then, how do you find the elevator to your rental, if not obvious. Some garages have various elevators accessing different buildings.

If the parking space is small, be sure to identify the maximum size of the car that fits in your space or driveway.

If you live in a big metro city which has street sweeping, parking time limits, frequent car thefts, and different parking rules per side of the street, you'll want to make your guest aware of these oddities.

If you don't provide parking, identify your preferred nearby paid parking lot and its cost.

Host and Emergency Contact Information. Let the guest know who they should contact for both non-urgent and urgent situations. If it's the same person, even better. If you are writing your own manual, this should come right after the Wi-Fi code.

Tell the guest the best way to contact you. If at all possible, you should request the guest contact you via the platform's app if any bad situations arise. If you provide a phone number, include the country code and dialing instructions.

If there is space to introduce yourself or your property management company to the guest, do so. Additionally, take this opportunity to set your guests' expectations. Here's what I say:

> *Hi! I'm Danny and I own Belo: Airbnb Property Management who will be responsible for your stay. The best way to reach me is through Airbnb. Welcome!*

> *You have selected a 5-star Airbnb (mine!). Please tell me if at any point your experience is below 5-stars so I can remedy the situation.*

Wi-Fi Information and Router Location. Provide the network name and password. If your Wi-Fi cuts out often, get it fixed. In the meantime, tell the guest where the router is located and how to reset it.

All of my managed rentals have Wi-Fi network passwords like "PleaseLeave5*Review". Besides the obvious purpose, it's easy to remember and pass along. It's extremely annoying for a party of eight people with two devices each to share a password like "8Hfy^hbv936Gjts".

While we're at it, here are some creative Wi-Fi network names:

- Mom this is my Wi-Fi
- Tell My Wi-Fi Love Her
- Pretty Fly for a Wi-Fi

If you're branding your rental, the brand name should be the network name.

Amenities Guide. Any amenities that you have *might* need instructions. A common amenity needing instructions is the TV, especially if you have more than one remote. In one rental, I had a remote for the surround sound, the TV, the cable box, plus one I never figured out with no instructions. Did you know there are 20 buttons per remote!?! Poor, Danny boy.

Another common amenity needing instructions is the washer and dryer. They're so simple to operate if you know what you're doing or read the local language. But if not, these things have a lot of options—and people's clothes are precious to them. Provide a photo and highlight the two buttons to push. Press "1" to turn the machine on and press "2" to start the wash. Pre-set what you can, and tell them what the pre-set is: i.e., cold water, high spin, 1-hour wash cycle.

Other potential amenities that might need explaining are the thermostat, air conditioning, stovetop, or coffee machine, in short, anything with a digital control interface.

If you have any non-standard amenities, almost always you'll want to explain how they work. These could be heated flooring, security system, hot tub, or café-style patio heater.

While staying at an Airbnb in Mumbai, India, I came upon a unique stovetop that I was unfamiliar with at the time. I needed to use a tool that I was unfamiliar with, a spark maker, to light it. The host did not have a guidebook, and so the delay was hours when I was trying to cook dinner and ended up fasting that night. It all could have been solved with that central repository of instruction called a guidebook.

You'll even want to mention oddities with your common amenities. Will the guest know they need to hold down the toilet flusher for five seconds in the downstairs bathroom? Or that the back-door knob needs to be pulled up and wiggled to the left a bit to close properly? These also could be cards placed strategically in the house with a QR code leading to the guidebook. "Need help using the jacuzzi?" with a QR code sending the guest to the relevant spot in the guidebook.

Trash and Recycling Information. Especially important for medium- and long-term stays, tell the guest about any specific garbage rules, bin locations if no pick-up, and where to take the kitchen trash in a larger building or complex.

If you live in a city with trash days, tell the guest what days and time they are to bring the trash to the curb. In New York City, one of my managed properties gets a fine if the guest brings trash to the curb on the wrong days or leaves it outside too long. Some cities with restrictive STR laws even threaten to cancel your license. It's okay to ask the guest to do this, though they may need a reminder.

Local Recommendations. Your guidebook should include a section of a few awesome, local recommendations. I repeat: awesome, few. Remember, **the enjoyment the guest receives in your city affects your review.**

Avoid generic recommendations like common coffee chains unless you have a unique tip to go along with it. A host in Mill Valley, California recommends a popular national park hike, *and* they provide a trick on how to get free parking and entrance.

Start with providing the following local recommendation:

- 1-2 coffee shops
- 2-3 restaurants
- 1-2 nightlife venues
- 1-2 grocery stores
- 1 park
- 1 nearby convenience store

The point of the guidebook is to get your guest acclimated quickly both to your home and to your immediate neighborhood. If you don't have a washer or dryer, then you may want to recommend a nearby, trusted laundromat, especially for long-term stays. Long-term guests will also require a grocery store, so recommend both a conventional grocery store and a specialty store selling organic goods, depending on your guests' needs.

If your city is known for something like deep-dish pizza in Chicago, khachapuri in Georgia or khao soi in Thailand, you should provide a recommendation to the best or most unique place. But don't overdo it!

Trust me, if your three restaurant recommendations were solid, the guest will ask for more. If enough guests ask for more, then add another dining recommendation.

As part of my Airbnb property management company mission, I encourage my hosts to think about how they can improve their guests' trip. I want you to do the same. My Los Angeles host came up with the following: "I highly recommend 'The Infatuation' for the best of restaurant reviews in Los Angeles." Great recommendation. Los Angeles is known for world-renowned food. Now your guest feels a little bit more like a local.

Check-out Information. Along with the pre-check-out message reminding the guest of your check-out process, you'll want to include this information in your guidebook.

If you're charging a cleaning fee, I recommend against having the guest do any arduous check-out day cleaning tasks. The check-out day is already stressful, and everyone is always running late anyway. Don't add to the stress by requiring that your guest complete a time-consuming check-out list.

Instead, ask them to do anything essential or super important. Also let them know if they can store their luggage upon check-out, whether that's inside or in a breezeway and for how long.

Recommended Local Apps. Almost every region of the world has its local Uber-copycat. Beat in Colombia. Didi in China. Grab in Thailand. Yandex in Russia.

Same thing for messaging apps like WhatsApp, Viber, and Line.

Food delivery is another common useful app. Rappi serves the majority of Latin America.

In Rio de Janeiro, I found out about this super-awesome mobile app that listed free yoga, dance, volleyball, and exercise classes on the beach. It would have been great to hear about it from my host on arrival!

In Joshua Tree, California, one host provided an app all about star-gazing, and it helped them spot the different constellations. So cool!

Why not tell *your* guest about these! Remember, the guest's experience in your city affects your review. If you have a new user promotion code, tell your guest about it so they save and you earn.

A recent host in Colombia came up with the following: "Recommended Local Phone Apps: Bolt (on-demand driver) or Rappi (food delivery). Call #8294 for 24-hour taxi service." That's great! Again, don't overdo it. Just a few recommendations.

Other Information To Include In Your Guidebook

Always tell the guest if the water from the faucet is safe to drink. After a full day of traveling, and late arrival, to the guest this is just being kind. If the water is not safe, always make sure there is one large bottle of mineral water per guest—this is empathizing with the guests needs. This is Level 3!

Is there anything unique to know about the neighborhood or the neighbors? There's always that one odd neighbor. Does he hate it when someone parks even a single inch over his driveway? Tell the guest this. You always want to respect the neighbors. Even the quirky ones. Personal note: make someone feel respected, and you become more persuasive. Keep on good terms with neighbors.

(Digital) Guidebooks To The Rescue

Do you see how useful these things are now?

Trust me, the guest doesn't want to have to reach out to you when they can't figure out how to operate the wireless Bluetooth speaker or some other amenity. All that does is cause a delay in them taking advantage of your awesome rental.

Okay. I can tell you're on board with the usefulness of the guidebook. Did I mention it's free? In the Deal Sheet, you'll find my recommended tool.

4.5 CLEANING PROCESS

I'm gonna do it! I'm gonna say it again!

Do not hire budget cleaners. Hire local cleaners who own the cleaning company. Generally, you'll have a poor experience when you go with one of the larger cleaning companies with many employees who rotate through your home and have high turnover. If you do use a large company, the same employee should clean your home as often as possible. This lets the employee get in a groove with your space so that they will notice if something is broken or missing. It reduces your risk of theft by having fewer random cleaners in your home.

This is important. I've dealt with some serious issues directly or indirectly due to bad cleaners, including theft by cleaners who had been fired but who still had access to the home or knew how to get in.

I'll take it a step further, especially if you want to remotely manage your property, and say that your cleaner is a natural property manager. They're already at the home anyway. Leverage them.

This chapter is not being written for me to tell you to tell your cleaner how to clean. As we'll see, that's the least of our concerns. The cleaner knows how to clean. Let them be the expert there. If they don't, then you're hiring the wrong cleaner to being with. We'll solve that. This chapter is about bonuses, hacks, and tricks in *optimizing* the cleaning process, dealing with cleaning issues, and creating an environment to allow them to thrive.

What Are The Cleaner's Job Responsibilities?

In addition to cleaning the space, the cleaner can be an essential tool in your hospitality arsenal. That's because a quality, well-paid cleaner will help you with the following:

- Checking for lost, stolen, and/or damaged items
- Coordinating necessary monthly and annual maintenance
- Staging the space for each check-in
- Detail work like cleaning below or above big appliances, cleaning the skylights, etc.
- Replenishing consumables
- Putting a cute fold in the toilet paper or folding the towels in a cool shape on the bed

I could go on and on. They are potentially the only human contact your guest has with you and your business. This is important when a potential negative review pops up.

As it relates to replenishing consumables if you have your cleaner do it, ensure they are buying from the affordable locations in bulk rather than the convenient, expensive stores near your STR one at a time.

If you offer a welcome gift or departing goody bag (we'll talk about this soon), they can do that on your behalf.

And, don't neglect the outdoor space often forgotten by cheap cleaners! Water all the plants! Sweep every corner of the patio or terrace!

Then come the monthly tasks like checking lightbulbs, cleaning A/C filters, moving the fridge, stove, and couch to clean those hard-to-reach spots.

How To Find a Good Cleaner

You have a few ways to reach a quality cleaner. If you're in the US, you can use Craigslist which is like the classifieds section of a newspaper. You post what you need, or they post what they're selling. You could approach a local hotel or hostel and ask for their best cleaner.

You can search out relevant forums. In *Chapter 7.7 How Can I Connect With Other Rental Owners In My Area?* I'll talk about the Airbnb Facebook groups in hundreds of cities across the globe. Plus, there's the Airbnb Community Center. There are other digital marketplaces for exactly this. Just type in 'vacation rental cleaner + your city' to see what appears.

You could always stay with your competition with stellar reviews and ask their cleaners if they have open slots to help you. Maybe they don't want to work for you, but someone they know does and can be trained by the stellar cleaner. Or maybe they have a falling out with their prior boss who probably isn't paying them enough. Give yourself options. Give them options. Or, if you want to find a cleaner from your armchair, in the Deal Sheet you'll find my preferred marketplace under 'Cleaning Tools' that has become quite popular in many places across the globe.

You can also reach out to your local real estate agents for recommendations.

Best Practices

You often hear complaints of cleaners forgetting to do things. The reason is because they're being paid nothing, and so they cut corners. Cleaning wages are very transparent nowadays. They know the market rate, and they know their rate.

My cleaners are paid well and rarely forget things. And when I ask them to clean the outside of the windows once per month or to present the cooking utensils in an organized way or to open the blinds, turn on music, or put the fireplace channel on the TV for the guest check-in, they are very willing to do so.

I believe this is one of my greatest hacks. Overpaying great cleaners, especially if you self-manage and are not local.

Changing gears here, one of my favorite practices is to put a "seal" on the door that the guest has to break to get inside. Just like breaking the seal to a new package. It lets the guest know that no one has been in that home since the cleaner. Or, a thin, paper banner over the toilet seat that the guest will break open the first time they use it.

Always leave cleaning supplies for the guest. Believe it or not, sometimes they do want to clean up after themselves, and you should not stop them from doing so!

Managing Cleaners and Turnovers

Part of the reason you're paying the cleaner a premium is to remove any and all headaches and extra work from your schedule (refer back to Chapter 1.3 My Philosophy). You need to communicate your expectations up front, and one of those expectations should be that the cleaner is running their own business which will get its own reviews. They are there to problem solve. You give them the tools needed to receive 5-star reviews. Make it very clear how important their job is. How it affects their revenue, and yours. A clean home is one factor that affects reviews which then affects occupancy and revenue. A better listing means a fuller calendar and more cleanings. But you really cannot emphasize enough how truly important the cleaner's job is. Make them feel special and important because they are! And pay them like you mean it!

Share feedback. When a guest messages you or leaves a comment about the cleaner or the clean home in their review, send a screenshot to the cleaner and express your gratitude.

I will be sending a text and or email to the cleaner for three critical events:

- New reservation
- Cancellation
- Alteration of existing reservation

The cleaner is to manage their own calendar. There will be no reminder from me. There will also be no work for them if they miss a cleaning job. Tell that to them after you let them know how crucial they are to the success of your business.

Cleaners should not be limiting your calendar. Sometimes a cleaner does not want to work on a Sunday or requests a day blocked on the calendar before/after a reservation. If this is just a passive investment for you and the money doesn't matter, well, I don't think you'd be reading this book, but that's the only situation where it's okay. Otherwise, the cleaner has no say in that whatsoever. The reservation comes in, they're responsible to getting the place cleaned. Even if there is no same-day booking, the cleaner is still required to go that day and clean and ready the space as if there was a check-in at the earliest possible time. That said, it's a good idea to have a backup plan in place when life gets in the way.

Every now and then there will be cleaning issues. It may be due to the cleaner or the guest. You first need to know if you properly set your expectations with your cleaner. If you didn't, do so. If you think it's obvious, but you didn't communicate it, communicate it. Whatever it may be. And there will be various "issues" that come up. If the cleaner promises something to the guest—maybe that they'll come back to reclean something or change something out and they don't do it, or don't do it on time—you need to ensure proper expectations have been communicated. Maybe the cleaner thinks by the end of the day, but you think within one hour. Communicate your expectations.

The cleaner gets one redo with these issues. Remember, you're paying them a competitive rate. They are there to be giving you some of your time back, not the opposite. You are giving them an autonomous role and not micro-managing, but that requires they take full responsibility for their important role.

How Much To Charge For The Cleaning Fee?

Generally, charge whatever it costs. This is going to be good advice for 90% of all listings. I personally don't charge for cleaning on top of the nightly rental fee, and I provide daily cleaning. It works for me because I know it's a valuable offer for the FPG. And super memorable. Who doesn't charge for cleaning *and* provides it daily? On top of that, the cost to me is less because of where my property is located. However, even if you're in a developed market like the US or Europe, removing your cleaning fee and working it into your nightly rate can be an effective strategy without the daily cleans.

Don't try to make money on this. It doesn't make sense. Take your average nightly stay and nightly minimum into play. If you're a monthly rental, the cleaning fee hardly matters. In comparison to the cost, it's nothing. If you accept single night bookings and get them often, now the cleaning fee may represent a significant portion of the total cost. In this special case, I might negotiate something with my cleaner for single-night reservations if the normal cleaning fee seems to be hurting my occupancy.

You can go on to Airbnb or use a data analytics tool to find out what your competition is charging in your market. As long as you're within 20% of the average for your size home, nothing to worry about, especially, if you have the best offer.

Featured Product Discount – Cleaning Team Checklist

A general checklist of best practices for new STR hosts including per room, final check instructions, tips, and recommended cleaning supplies and software. Plus, monthly, quarterly, and yearly maintenance and cleaning task reminders.

Find your 50% discount code in the 'Featured Product Discounts' PDF of the bonus items.

Featured Product Discount - Vacation Rental Cleaning Team Checklist

SCAN ME

4.6 AMENITIES

Amenities are broader than you think. It's not just hand soap and hangers. That's Level 1. An amenity represents the overall pleasantness of your space. It represents an additional benefit to the location, somehow contributes to its enjoyment, and (this is the most important part) thereby increases its value.[5] More amenities equal more value.

Amenities are your chance to continue your guests' positive online experience with you into the offline real world. And I'm going to help you optimize this part of the experience, including some hacks and tricks.

Amenities can be fixed assets (washing machine, wine glasses, water filter), consumables (toilet paper, tissue, trash bags), or features like soundproof windows. As such, please start thinking about amenities not only for your current rental but also for new construction projects and remodel jobs.

No matter your price point, **providing a wide array of non-standard amenities to your guests is one of the easiest ways to improve your listing and obtain 5-star reviews**. Most guests expect basic amenities they would commonly find in a hotel, but there are many easy ways to exceed their expectations.

Amenities could be your competitive advantage! Whether you have a basic home, private bedroom, or luxurious penthouse, you can offer more amenities than your competition. This is within your control.

Think of it this way: What items do you commonly forget to pack on your travels? What 'extras' would make your stay more comfortable or convenient? Turn your answers into amenities that you can offer your guests, and you're halfway done!

Consider the following two questions when planning what amenities you'll provide:

- What am I offering in terms of my space? (Know Your Listing)
- Who is my FPG? (Know Your FPG)

---

[5] https://en.wikipedia.org/wiki/Amenity

What are you offering? If it's a no-frills space, then purchasing a waterbed probably doesn't make sense as an investment. There would be no return-on-investment and it probably would require extra maintenance which your budget doesn't allow for.

On the other hand, a luxurious space with no artwork on the wall and cheap, old mattresses, and mismatched furniture is an equally poor decision. I was recently invited to make a video of a penthouse with a heavenly view. When I arrived, I walked into utter madness in terms of design. The view was stunning and the floor-to-ceiling windows that opened fully only enhanced that experience. There was a waterfall in the bathroom. This is meant to be a high-end, luxurious space! But the furniture was not coordinated and of low quality. This host didn't understand what they were offering and what a guest booking this space would likely want.

Unless there was no other competition, there's no way I would pay the $1000 per night price tag they were asking and, even if I did, after I would probably not leave a stellar review.

Next, you need to consider your FPG. What do they expect? Better yet, what would they appreciate—the unexpected? Are they budget travelers likely to cook and happy with a few pots and pans? Adding some salt and pepper might be a worthy investment. Or, are they likely to appreciate high-end, sharp knives and cookware? Would they appreciate a comfy armchair to relax in the morning with a coffee? Does it make sense to upgrade that coffee maker or provide a coffee grinder? How about a half pound of local coffee?

"Do certain guests prefer different amenities?" I'm glad you asked! This is a Level 3 question. You're off to a great start. You're getting detailed about the guest experience. The short answer is yes and no. Argh! Let me explain. Some guests from some regions of the world sometimes prefer certain amenities, but rarely is it a make-it-or-break-it factor. Some, but not all guests might appreciate a rice cooker. Americans prefer both a washer *and* dryer. But it's unlikely to have a meaningful

impact on your revenue or occupancy if you don't have that cooker or dryer.

If you have a no-frills space, then adding a dryer probably doesn't make sense. If you have a more luxurious space rented by those dryer-loving Americans, then it probably does make sense to invest in one.

"How do I know what amenities bring the biggest bang?" Another mighty fine question indeed! If you know your listing and know your FPG, you will have a good, but not perfect answer to this question.

Based on my own experience as a guest in dozens of different cities around the globe, there are some amenities that are or should be universal. I think the lowest hanging fruit for all listings is to upgrade the shower head. Typically, you can purchase these inexpensively and install without any tools. Buy the largest or most unique looking shower head you can find. Guests take showers often. Typically, it's the first thing they do upon arrival and the last thing they do before departure. Talk about creating a great first impression and lasting final impression! Don't forget about the towels. The softer, the better.

Seating is another often overlooked amenity. Most listings can upgrade their seating and, depending on what you're offering, there are comfy seating options at all price ranges. You should have at least two seating options in your home, but the more you have the better. Your guest is seated or sleeping most of the day, so it makes sense to optimize these amenities.

In the current Airbnb I rented, I have two seating options. The original chair at the desk has a flimsy upper back support so I'd have to engage my abs to not fall backwards or write this book at a 35-degree angle. Luckily, the host provided different chairs on the patio, one of which I'm using at the desk. Everyone is different, and many suffer from back pain, so allow them to opt for their preferred seating option.

Here's another: cups and glasses and wine glasses. And a decent corkscrew! They are cheap. All rentals need them. All guests use them. Most guests are okay paying for breaking them. Upgrade your offerings.

Cooking utensils or cookware are often forgotten. Salad spinners, tongs, spatulas, pots. They last for a while, but be sure to update them occasionally and opt for high-end options if it makes sense. As a guest who cooks, we notice, and its bonus points because of how infrequently nice cookware is provided (and IKEA is not nice cookware).

Now that we know some amenity best practices, I want to go by room and identify the absolute bare minimum you need plus some easy upgrades.

Bedroom

When selecting bedding and linens, be sure to choose quality linens that are easily washed and replaced. Hotels choose white linens because they 'feel' clean. However, they stain easily so weigh your options. Every bed should have a hypoallergenic and waterproof mattress cover as a final barrier to cover your mattress from all unwanted liquids. Just don't let this amenity make your guest feel like they're sleeping on a hospital bed. Some options feel plasticky and stiff.

The Basics: comfortable mattress, linens, and two pillows plus pillow protectors per guest, silence, no lights, hangers, iron with full-size ironing board (extra-wide iron board for bonus points).

Regarding the lights, I'm not talking about light entering through the windows, but instead any lights inside the bedroom. This is especially true for studios. Does the microwave have a bright light? A/C sometimes has flashing lights; smoke alarms, TVs, or routers all have blinking lights. Even outlets sometimes have a small, bright green light. Any light inside the bedroom should be extinguishable and/or easily turned off or covered by the guest. In one Madrid short-term rental, the bedroom had a bright smoke detector light out of reach on the ceiling. These often get missed because you and the cleaner are working in the home during daylight hours. Another reason to sleep at least one night in your own STR (and use all the other amenities).

The Upgrades: blackout curtains or shades, upgraded mattress, linens, or pillows (both firm and soft), bedside lamps, eye covers, individually-wrapped earplugs, full-length mirror, suitcase stand, safe.

Level 3 Alert! Ensure that any bedside lamps or lights are easy to turn off from the bed. It's not ideal after you've read a chapter of a book or watched some TV, feeling sleepy and ready to close your eyes, to have to first get up, walk to the bedroom door and turn off the light. Then walk back to the mattress in darkness, step on something or slam your knee of the bed post, and then try to go to sleep. Details matter!

By the way, do you have cloth hangers? Throw them out or give them away. It takes four times as long hanging up a cloth shirt on a cloth hanger. Details matter! I feel maybe now is a good time to remind you about the One-of-a-Hundred concept. None of these decisions individually are going to make you a supercharged host, but cumulatively, *they* will. Control what is controllable.

Bathroom

The bathroom is used various times per day by all guests. This space is also used by visitors. Its high-foot-traffic attribute makes it an obvious choice for experiential *optimization*. How about a nice scent in there?

The Basics: consistent hot water, decent water pressure, toilet paper, First Aid Kid, hair dryer, one towel per guest.

If you don't have hot water, even if it's not selected in your listing, it's a smart idea to mention this in your listing to avoid those negative reviews due to mismanaged expectations. I was once in Panama City, in a new apartment building and without hot water. Upon review, the listing didn't select it as an amenity, just as my Hong Kong rental didn't select Wi-Fi as an amenity, but these are both so expected nowadays that your FPG won't be double checking them as offered amenities.

The Upgrades: ventilation fan, optimal mirror lighting, nice shower head, high-end soaps/shampoos/creams/hand soaps, shower shelving, replacement toothbrushes and toiletries in unopened packaging.

The fan is to keep the mirror clear from steam with hot showers and evacuate bad odors. A light above the mirror allows you to make better use of it. It's very common for bathroom lights to be located behind the mirror (more so over your head), thus your face is in shadows when close to the mirror. Details matter! The "high-end" soaps don't even necessarily need to be high-end, just not cheap looking. If providing shampoo and conditioner, I wouldn't purchase the big box store giant-sized shampoo bottles. Find the bottles that *look* high-end, but don't cost it. There's plenty of them. Again, it depends on what you're offering and what the guest expects. If you're a budget listing, offering a Kirkland Signature shampoo probably exceeds expectations whereas a luxurious bathroom with this brand would disappoint.

If you have a bathtub, bath bubbles or salts are a true luxury.

I should add a shower shelf in The Basics because they're often absent. They're so cheap, so useful, last so long, and are easy to install. It could be a tiny competitive advantage. It all goes back to making the guest feel at home. At home, do you think the guest bends over in the shower to get their soaps, shaver, etc.? Well, no one should be doing such a barbaric thing...I digress.

Kitchen

Available in most rentals, lots of STR kitchens often lack quality amenities. Even in those fully-equipped kitchens, the amenities often get forgotten and are old and unpleasant to use. Any kitchen supply store will offer you a plethora of items for your rental. The kitchen is one of those things that separate vacation rentals from hotels. Some guests don't cook, but those who do highly appreciate a thoughtful and fully-equipped kitchen.

The Basics: basic silverware, glassware, dishware, cookware, microwave, a place to eat, scissors, can/bottle/wine opener, cutting board, blender, sharp knives, strainer, coffeemaker.

Many of the required items in the kitchen are not only for convenience but for safety. If you provide a pot, you can assume the guest will boil water. But if you don't provide a strainer, you're putting them at risk of a burn when draining the scalding water from their cooked pasta or rice. Or, if you have a sharp knife but no scissors, any time the guest needs to open something, you're forcing them to use a sharp knife and putting them at risk of injury. Any injury the guest has on your property becomes your problem.

Regarding the reuse of opened condiments, there are no strict rules. Things like olive oil, seasonings, balsamic, ketchup I save for future guests. Anything that maintains a good presentation. But a half-used stick of butter and liquids like soda or milk are thrown out.

The Upgrades: upgraded silverware, dishware, and cookware including lids to pots and pans, oven and oven-safe cookware, coffee and tea, soaps, dish towels, cheese grater, any specialty items like peeler, lemon lime squeezer, electric kettle, etc.

Living and Dining Rooms

The bare minimums for your living room include a Smart TV (yes, that's required now), a remote, and a couch. You can upgrade the size or quality of the TV and/or seating arrangements. If your dining room doubles as the office space, then sound becomes a factor. If you're near a busy road or otherwise noisy area, consider sound-proofing your windows.

A cheaper alternative is to purchase a white noise machine which will help with the noise. An often-forgotten amenity here is a coat rack or some wall hooks to hang things like hats, bags, etc. Put that near the front door along with a mirror for any last-minute wardrobe and hair checks. The guest will thank you. Details matter.

Entryway

The only requirement is to have an easily enterable doorway and sufficient keys or clickers.

An easy upgrade here is a digital lock. No more keys for the guest to fetch or to lose. If you go with a digital lock, pay attention to the keypad layout, and make sure the code you choose is in some kind of pattern for easier memorization and not more than six digits. Some digital locks come with the buttons so small that many men and elderly will have trouble.

Once I was staying in a somewhat dangerous neighborhood, and the front digital lock was eight digits, totally random, the keypad unlit, and the buttons tiny. It also got dark at 6pm in this city. So, here's this obvious foreigner fumbling outside with his expensive phone out, light on, trying to pay attention to pressing the correct numbers, hoping he doesn't get robbed. On top of that, if I mistyped, I had to wait a full minute. Details matter.

There's no need to get a fancy digital lock either. These tend to break down more often and require more maintenance.

If your home requires a clicker or keyless entry remote to open a gate, ideally you should be providing one per guest. At a minimum, be reasonable. Once, with a group of others, I rented a 4-bedroom home with a private gate which was required to be closed for security. That would have been fine if the owners provided more than a single key fob for the gate. It became inconvenient to organize this one annoying feature so we tended to leave the gate slightly open. The security staff was annoyed, and so were the neighbors, I'm sure. We were also annoyed for having to be annoying! From our perspective, it was preferable to leave the gate open than to having someone caught outside in the rain.

Outdoor Space

I once helped a host, Veronika, I met in Tallinn, Estonia who needed help with her Airbnb. One of the things I still remember is her long, graceful balcony with absolutely nothing on it.

A slender, long, and sad-looking balcony with so much potential.

Whether you have a balcony, a patio, or a backyard, you should do something with it. The bare minimum amenity that you should add is seating. A level up from simple seating are lights at night, an umbrella for shade, a Bluetooth speaker, a hammock, some durable games like cornhole, and/or a BBQ if permissible and safe. If providing a BBQ, be sure to provide grilling utensils, an extra gas canister, and clean it after every use.

Extra WOW Factor

Guests booking vacation rentals appreciate and notice when hosts go the "extra mile" when providing unique amenities. A space heater, extra blankets, and even laundry detergent can make you stand out to your guest as extra hospitable. Welcoming guests with local baked goods or a bottle of local wine is a great way to start off their reservation. A budget-friendly welcome gift can be a hand-written note. Or, sending off departing guests with a goody bag. We'll talk about why this can be a better idea than a welcome gift in *Chapter 4.8 Surprise and Delight.*

The best WOW factor amenities are whatever your FPG would most appreciate.

Here are some ideas for business travelers:

- Desk supplies (staples, post-it notes, tape, highlighter, etc.)
- Printer/scanner
- International power adapter
- Ether cable
- Lint roller
- Hanging luggage scale
- Steam cleaner (for suits)

Here are some additional bonus items:

- Additional power cables
- Pre-loaded transit cards
- Local maps or guides
- Custom Guest Travel Itinerary
- Universal charging station with USB, USB-C, and outlet charging docks
- Umbrella
- Makeup remover facial towels (black)

Here are some ideas for listings near a beach or pool or nature:

- Mountain or beach cruiser bikes with helmets and locks
- Beach towels
- Beach chairs and umbrellas
- Cooler
- Pool toys

Here are some additional amenities for families:

- Board games
- Highchair
- Pack 'n' Play
- Cribs
- On-call, trusted babysitter or chef

When To Replace Amenities?

There are no hard-and-fast rules here. Even for stains on bed linens, how big is the stain? Can you flip the linen so the guest doesn't see it? Are you running a budget listing where you can't afford to replace linens every few months?

It all goes back to knowing your listing and knowing your FPG to ultimately know what might result in a negative review. This is the bare minimum standard. Ideally, we're going for powerfully positive reviews.

Some of the items that I find whose replacement is most neglected are pillows and cookware. If your pillows are deflated and/or having a brown/grey tinge, time to replace. If your pots and pans—especially nonstick—have many scratches and dents on them, time to replace.

Don't forget your A/C and other items with internal filters. The A/C filter should be cleaned monthly and occasionally replaced, as should the stove fan filter, if it has one.

A Final Note

Amenities can also be leveraged to smooth over any guest issues that arise during your stay. It's common for hosts to provide a bottle of wine in these instances. That's fine. The comment I want to make is that you should be, as with our high-end looking bottles of shampoo, doing the same thing here. In fact, this strategy can be applied to a lot of amenities. Get the fanciest, most expensive *looking* bottle of wine, bag of coffee, bar of chocolate, bottle of hand soap that you can find. That way, the guest is equating a higher value to the gift and/or amenity. Also, it just sets you apart in a positive light.

These examples are the perfect way to raise your standard of hosting and add an extra WOW factor to your guests' experience. Regardless of your budget, you can incorporate many of these ideas, or use them as a springboard to come up with your own unique and unforgettable amenities. Always remember that hospitality starts and ends with YOU and your interactions, whether live or digital, with your guests. Your demeanor, decor, and provisions will go a long way to ensuring that each guest has an amazing experience with you and your rental.

4.7 CHECK-IN/CHECK-OUT

The check-in and check-out processes of *The Reservation Flow* are very important (first and last impression) and often go ignored. By the end of this chapter, you'll learn how to master these processes and in the process increase your review rate by a quarter.

Buffer

The buffer consists of two features that take into account natural human tendencies (like being late).

First, I suggest you put your check-in time at 4pm or 5pm. And put your check-out time earlier at 10am. My data shows that early check-out and late check-in times don't negatively affect your rental occupancy.

On top of that, I tell my cleaner to not arrive until 11am and to finish before 4pm.

This allows for two things. First, if the guest asks for a late check-out or early check-in, I can immediately accept one hour without any further coordination. This takes care of half of those requests.

Second, the one-hour buffer upon check-out means the cleaner isn't waiting nor is she entering when the guests are still inside. You don't want the cleaner entering when the guests are packing because it increases their chance of forgetting something (personal experience) and unnecessarily increases your liability for the guest losing items that all-of-a-sudden must've been stolen by the cleaner.

Late Check-out and Early Check-in Requests

If you don't use the buffer strategy or prefer not to accommodate these requests, you can say this:

"Normally I would, but this time the next/current guest has already requested an early check-in/late check-out, and my cleaners can't accommodate it."

Notice I'm subtly removing myself as decision-make from the situation.

Generally, I don't charge for adjusting check-in or check-out. Typically, the guest doesn't want to pay no matter the amount. You should also consider what your main business is and what it is not. If you rent for $200 per night and charge an extra $25 for early check-ins, you're not going to move the needle, even a little bit, on your rental success.

Recently, in an Airbnb in Madrid for which I paid $2500 for the month, I was asked to pay $10 for an early check-in. While this wouldn't result in a negative review, I found it odd. An *optimized* version of this is to not charge and instead ask the guest to remember it during their review. You can also mention that the length of the review matters to Airbnb's search algorithm. I also mention that they shouldn't say I allowed an early check-in in the review because they're special, and I normally don't allow it. This also serves as a review reminder upon check-out when it's review time. "Hey, I just wanted to remind you that I prefer you not mention your early check-in in your review. Any feedback you have, positive or negative, I'm very open to it, especially the negative parts!" You're assuming the review here.

As you may have noticed, I prefer to not coordinate a bunch of early check-ins and late check-outs, but I do have an alternative—as should you. In my case, I allow the guests to store luggage in the building all day long. The building has a security guard there all day and all night so it works in my case. If you can't allow luggage storage, the Level 3 Host would make an alternate suggestion. There are some luggage storage options in many larger cities. Alternatively, you could suggest a nearby hotel. Most hotels will take in luggage without proof of a reservation. Just tip the bellboy, and you're good to go.

But whatever you do, don't allow the guest early access to the unit unless it's fully cleaned. If you do that, the guest will have a bad first impression, whether consciously or subconsciously. They'll also probably notice some things that your cleaner will not. Upon return, they'll check to see if that super specific thing they noticed was cleaned and if it wasn't, why not? And what else wasn't cleaned? And what was cleaned, was it actually cleaned? Did they wash the comforter? Did they use soap on the dishes or just rinse them? Normally this won't happen, but now you'll avoid it potentially happening ever.

Live Check-in Process

This is the first 10 minutes upon finding your front door. We've already gone over how to ensure this process is as smooth as possible for the automated check-in. Here I want to talk a bit about when and why to do a live check-in and how to *optimize* it.

There are three reasons to do a live check-in:

- There are important things the guest must know about your home
- You're unsure about the guest
- You want to offer added service

If you have custom features in your home (nonstandard windows, surround sound system, smart home devices, etc.) that are important your guest know how to operate whether that be for safety or damage, you might want to do a live check-in.

In *The Belmonte Penthouse*, I have both a custom security door and *had* custom super-awesome bay windows that fully opened to the sound of the river in front of my building. The windows were very complicated for the guests to open and close, and they were always breaking the locks. That is, until one day when the entire window fell to the ground. I kid you not. At 4am, my building security sent me a photo of an indent in the ground next to the windows on the ground floor. Now we're getting into another topic about making your rental as dummy proof as possible which is ideal. Anything that can be broken, will get broken.

This cost me an extra $50 because even though I informed the next same-day check-in guest about the damaged window, he still complained to Airbnb upon check-out who issued a partial refund. Well, that was frusteratin'!

If you are unsure about the guest, you should do a live check-in. You may even be waiting for the guest upon arrival. Maybe their messages seem sketchy, maybe you have Instant Book turned on, maybe they had a recent bad review, maybe they're local and not answering your question about the reason for their trip. Whatever it is, you can get a really good idea of whether the guest is up to no good by welcoming them with a smile to meet them and give them a 5-minute check-in. You are allowed to verify their identification matches that of the reservation as it's not within policy to make a reservation for someone else.

If your guest is asking a lot of questions through the OTA platform, you may want to ask if they would like you to meet them at the property upon arrival. Alternatively, if the guest doesn't ask anything, you may want to abandon your live check-in or shorten it to the bare minimum.

One thing you should always do on a live check-in is highlight how much you are open to feedback, both positive and negative, *and* to encourage the guest to advise you of any damage. Guests have a knack for hiding damage until the host or another guest notices months later. Would you rather have that, or learn about any damage in a timely manner, no matter how small it is, by reassuring them you'd rather know and will not nickel-and-dime them?

If you do a live check-in, keep it brief. And understand the guest isn't going to remember much so have everything in a guidebook. Upon checking into my first Airbnb Plus experience in Buenos Aires, Argentina, the host took 45 minutes at 9pm at night to thoroughly explain everything about the neighborhood and wrote things on a map. It was all for naught because I didn't remember much, nor was my brain fully functional after flying, and I was hungry. The live check-in should be 10 minutes or less.

Check-out

The check-out is the lasting impression the guest will have fresh in their mind when the OTA asks them to review their stay. So why is the check-out the butt of so many viral online videos about the ridiculous rules guests are supposed to, and almost never, follow? Well, because most STR owners aren't going to read this book.

Or, maybe because of this:

"Turn off water; valve is under the bathroom sink, and drain any remaining water by leaving the cold water faucet in the ON position and flush the toilets. Also leave cabinet doors under both the kitchen and bathroom sinks open."

That's a real-world check-out instruction. It's too much. I'm not going to go so far as to say no check-out rules, but let's *optimize* this process.

You already know when to send and what to put in the pre-check-out message the day before check-out. Let's go over what not to do.

Avoid onerous and unnecessary check-out tasks like sorting recycling. If anything, make them suggestions: "If you have time, doing any of the following would help us prepare for the next arrival." Keep the instructions as short as possible. Check-out rules should apply to the majority or be very important.

One of my favorites is when a host reminds the guest not to leave anything behind. Don't do this. Trust me, as a guest, we're not trying to leave anything behind. It's a hassle for us, too.

Remember, guests will have this final, most recent, portion of their stay in their memory, sometimes, more than anything else when they're asked to leave a review. If you had a bad reservation for whatever reason, you should do a live check-out. It's a lot easier to leave a negative review to a digital screen than to an actual, pleasant human who you met and who apologized for whatever it was that made you upset. This is a powerful technique and how I personally avoided a few potentially negative reviews.

This stuff is what separates good from great hosts.

4.8 SURPRISE AND DELIGHT

Some features can't properly be advertised before the guest arrives for a variety of reasons.

One common example is a sunset. A guest probably isn't booking your home because of a great sunset, no matter how great it is. A great sunset also doesn't photograph well when you compare it to real life. Neither is it a terrible photo. But this type of feature is simply better experienced in real life.

A subtle consideration is the constant and delicate balance between selling your rental via the listing description and the amount of time given to your listing by an FPG (which is not very much). Your rental may be loaded with cool amenities, but is the neat bedside lamp with wireless charging going to put the guest over the edge? It depends on your offer, but probably not. Will they be pleasantly surprised when they discover this amenity upon arrival? We hope so. Just as you don't photograph every angle or room in your home, you also don't advertise all amenities.

This chapter is about knowing what to advertise and what to let the guest discover upon check-in and throughout their reservation. Think of it as under promising and overdelivering.

What Is It?

Your Surprise and Delight feature and/or amenity is what sets you apart from your competition. It's not something you advertise, instead it's a treat the guest discovers upon entering your rental. It's something that shows the guest you've thought about their experience, not just your profit. It's that extra buffer you give yourself when things go wrong, and yet, the guest still leaves a 5-star review.

The Surprise and Delight feature is a Level 3 Host strategy.

Examples of Surprise and Delight Features

An S+D feature doesn't necessarily need to be a physical item. It can be the service or hospitality that you provide. When I was staying in Saigon, Vietnam, the host informed me about a local holiday, what it meant, and what I could expect on this day. That is a S+D feature.

How you handle guest complaints is also a S+D feature. At this same Airbnb in Saigon, there were problems with the router. The host got me a second router. Another time I was in Medellin, Colombia with similar Wi-Fi problems, and the host brought me some complicated mobile device that needed to be charged and that didn't work but still cost me an hour of time. Same situation, different hosts, only one got a benefit.

The most common S+D feature is a welcome gift, and it's a great idea! Common welcome gifts include wine, baked goods, or a fruit or breakfast basket--but no need to stop there. Get creative! If you host a bachelorette party, maybe provide a little gift bag with a clay facial mask, scrubs, lotions, or a moisturizer. I recommend buying from local vendors as it adds additional value to the welcome gift. The downside of a welcome gift is that it's at the beginning of the reservation. This means that by the time the guest needs to leave a review, all the initial goodwill has probably evaporated. I prefer goody bags upon departure. Yes, I'm referring to those things you got as a little kid as a reward for being social? At least that's what I thought of them.

Right now, I gift my departing guests a full bag of Colombian coffee and a bar of Colombian chocolate. Both are not only local products, but they also look the part. A bonus is that sometimes a guest wants to purchase another for a family or friend. I mark the cost up 2x which almost fully covers the cost of these goody bags. It works for my situation. What works for yours?

If you rent to families at a beach destination, maybe inform them that you will rent some beach chairs and an umbrella for them on the day of their choosing.

I was once in Chiang Mai during "burning season" when the air quality is so bad many are wearing masks. I thought a great idea would be to include an indoor air filter so the guest was assured that at least their indoor environment was safe.

If you don't have the budget to purchase additional gifts, then don't. Luckily, you have options. How about a personal note with the guest's name on it? "Welcome to Puerta Vallarta, Danny!" I've seen large chalk boards in rentals with such greetings as well as timely local attractions ("Don't miss Applefest in the park down the street on Saturday!") and recommended spots. Pretty cool! How about folding the towels in some unique and cool way on the bed with some reusable flowers? Anything that will have an impact on the guest. High value. Low cost.

Here's some more low cost or free S+D features:

- Slippers
- Reusable grocery bags and grocery caddy
- Umbrellas
- Ice cube trays already filled up
- Extra phone chargers
- Local souvenirs
- Gift card to a local café
- Discounted or free mid-stay cleaning

You could create a deal with a nearby bar for a welcome drink or a discount. Few guests will take you up on this, but a little goodwill is gained by offering it.

Or, do the majority of your guests rent cars or scooters while at your location? Then why not secure a discount for your guest with a local provider? If not a discount, how about a guarantee that they'll save a rental for your incoming guest?

Featured Product Discount - Custom Guest Travel Itinerary

A thoughtfully-designed one-page PDF of unique recommendations, a fun fact, your branding, and other cool features about your city. Created once, used for the life of the rental. I send it to all of my guests. "Oh, hey, I recently made this for your trip. I hope you enjoy it!" I also had a few more designed for two-, three-, four-, and five-night reservations which makes it seem even more customized to each guest.

Featured Product Discount - Custom Guest Travel Itinerary

SCAN ME

Find your 10% discount code in the 'Featured Product Discounts' PDF of the bonus items.

The Surprise and Delight strategy gives the guest something additional to mention in their 5-star review. And, as we'll learn in *Part 8: How To Rank #1 On Airbnb*, the review length seems correlated with level of search placement.

4.9 DO YOU NEED A PROPERTY MANAGER?

Whether or not you need a property manager comes down to one question: Do you want or need to be 100% hands-off?

There's a caveat to that question because choosing a bad property manager means you will not be 100% hands off.

There are all sorts of property managers out there from full-service to remote to à-la-carte providers offering only check-in, guest messaging, or revenue management. This chapter assumes you are interested in full-service property management.

When Should You Hire a Property Manager?

If you already know that you want to be 100% hands-off, then you should hire a property manager. It's that simple: If you do not want to spend any time managing any aspect of your rental, then you need a property manager. There's no shame in that, especially if you have no choice. In fact, it's money well spent if you don't believe you can offer the guest an amazing experience. You can move to the next chapter.

But let me assume, if I may be so bold, that you are not yet sure if you need a property management company for your STR. What do these companies offer that you can't or won't do yourself? (Okay, I admit it. I am biased against property managers. Especially these days when you can do so much remotely or with one or two initial site visits to get things off the ground, check over the cleaner's work, and make any changes or recommendations necessary.)

First, let's figure out what a good property manager can do for you. Then, we'll find out how much time each activity requires if you were to do it yourself.

What Does a Property Management Company Do?

A good, full-service STR property management company will perform the following tasks on your behalf:

- Create your profile and listing
- Respond to every initial guest inquiry within minutes
- Provide a 24/7 local emergency contact for the guest
- Coordinate all maintenance issues
- Be the main point of contact for the guest
- Monitor your calendar and nightly rates
- Handle any issues, including damage or insurance claims
- Coordinate with the cleaners
- Coordinate late check-in/out requests
- Continually optimize the listing for high search placement
- Create a digital guidebook for your guest
- Replenish consumables (toilet paper, tissues, soaps, garbage bags, etc.)
- Manage keys (if applicable)
- Create a seamless check-in experience
- Be your main point of contact for all issues
- Be responsible for accounting and tax remittance (if applicable)
- Provide guidance on interior design and amenities
- Give continual suggestions for improvement
- Monitor and respond to guest reviews

This seems like a lot! And, it is. Most property management companies do not offer all of the above. Some advertise it but don't deliver. With some planning and initial setup, you may be able to do all of this for not much time each week.

So, the real question becomes: Do you want to be totally hands-off assuming you find a good property manager in exchange for 15-25% of your revenue or do you want to automate where you can and set up your hosting in such a way that it requires one hour of your time per week?

Again, I'm not that keen on property management companies. It might be a surprise to learn that I own a property management company. What might surprise you even more is that I do it all remotely, oftentimes from different countries. Some of the properties I manage, I have never even seen in person. I'm not pitching my company, and I'm usually not accepting new properties as I only manage up to five at the same time, but if you'd like to learn more scan the QR code.

The process I've developed and use for my own property management company has been bundled up into my most premium product on my website called "Optimized Host". Again, this is no sales pitch. Instead, I'm going to tell you how to implement it on your own. Essentially, if you have some time to devote to your rental each week and don't mind the initial setup, then I want you to consider doing so.

We've covered a lot of the process already in this section with one more big topic to cover in *Part 5: Pricing*, but I'm going to package it all up nicely for you here.

Optimized Host: A "Do It Yourself" Property Management Alternative

If you are willing and able to do a bit of work (one hour per week per listing) then you do not need a property manager and can save the monthly commission charge.

If you rent your space out for $150 per night with an 80% yearly occupancy and your property manager takes 20%, you are paying them $8,760 per year. Alternatively, if you spend one hour per week managing, then your hourly rate comes to $168 ($8,760 savings / 52 hours of work) for the time you're spending here. If you think that's worth it, then let's do this!

In no particular order, you will:

- Connect to a dynamic pricing tool
- Learn how to manage your nightly rates based on your occupancy (in *Part 5: Pricing*)
- Create a digital guidebook
- Create a highly-converting online listing
- Set up message automation including cleaner communication via a PMS
- Find a reliable cleaning company who will replenish your consumables
- Find a reliable emergency contact
- Find a general handyman for water, gas, electricity, internet, cable, and any other amenities you offer like a pool or hot tub

The above is meant to both decrease your ongoing time investment (message automation, repairmen, cleaners) and increase guest satisfaction (digital guidebook, emergency contact, targeted listing) while increasing your monthly income (pricing tool and calendar management strategy).

Regarding the handyman or repairmen and similar to how we pick cleaners, start with your local company. I find when I'm able to create a connection with another small business in my area, everything works out better. Of course, you still need to vet this person and give them a trial before you put all your trust and money in them. Creating redundancies with a backup is also wise.

If you go with a larger, cheaper organization, then you're dealing with an employee or employees who probably don't have the motivation to go above and beyond to facilitate a long-term business relationship. Also, the charges for odd hours (when most of the guest issues happen) will be high. If you go with a smaller, local company, you will often be interacting with the business owner who will understand your situation and make him- or herself available at odd times and not always at a premium.

You always need a reliable, local emergency contact who ideally is your cleaner. This is why cleaners are so important and my secret weapon. If you have one local, reliable person, then you can manage your rental from anywhere, as I do.

A Note On Cleaners

As part of my property management experience, I started out trying to get the cheapest cleaner. Sure, I'd vet them and even spot check their cleanings in the beginning, but sooner or later (and never that much later) I'd have problems.

- No shows.
- Missing or stained linens.
- Poor quality cleaning jobs.
- Guest complaints.

These all result in refunds, re-cleans, negative reviews, and countless wasted hours.

Nowadays, I hire the quality option, and I get nearly zero headaches and 5-star cleaning reviews after every reservation. And the price difference between the mid-tier and high-end cleaner isn't even that much.

If it's down to two listings, yours at $500 for a weekend and your competitors at $470, both of these listings are in the same price range. The guest would be using other factors unrelated to price.

Trust me, **opt for the expensive and reliable cleaner**. You'll thank me in the long run. Make this one of your competitive advantages.

So, self-manage or hire a property manager?

4.10 HOW TO CHOOSE A GOOD PROPERTY MANAGER

I recognize that some people are not cut out to be a vacation rental host for any number of reasons. There's nothing wrong with that. In fact, I salute you for knowing yourself and being realistic. But knowing yourself is just half the battle. Now, you need to actually find a good vacation rental property management company.

Many people and companies can and do promote themselves as "the best". I'm living in downtown Medellín, Colombia at the moment. It's not glamorous, so when I saw "the best hot dog in town" sign at a nearby restaurant, I had to chuckle. That can't possibly be true. But they put it there because it brings people to the storefront.

On top of having a few of "the best" property managers to choose from, it's hard to understand truly what separates them from each other. This chapter will help you sift through the madness and find the right one. The right one rarely finds you because they have more than enough work to keep them busy.

Choosing the wrong property management company will cost you time and money.

Choosing the right company will save you time *and* earn you more money.

Pros of Hiring a Good Property Management Company

- More "you" time!
- Year-round impeccably clean home
- Professionals handling home maintenance, repairs, and upgrades
- Home in perpetual sellable condition
- Faster response times to guests (increases conversion rate from inquiry to reservation)
- Round the clock on-call emergency contact
- STR Knowledge (how the OTA and industry works, handling insurance claims, recommendations for common amenities like smart locks, etc.)
- Connections (established and trained cleaners, maintenance staff, etc.)
- Increased occupancy and nightly rate
- With a bad property manager, all you get is none of the above plus headaches, less revenue, and lower reviews.

Small vs. Large Property Management Company

I recommend you seek out a smaller property management company local to your market. This doesn't mean they're automatically your best option, but I suggest you start here. Any one individual listing is more important to smaller companies while you might get less attention from larger companies.

In larger companies, they have a one-size-fits-all system which may not be optimal for your listing. This usually becomes clear when occupancy drops and complaints rise, but the company won't devote resources to figure out why. I receive weekly inquiries from hosts who have hired a property management company and are unhappy or know they can do better. They're very frustrated!

This leads some hosts who are trying to be helpful to purchase an optimization report from me for their listing to send to their property management company. Only problem is, the host is doubly frustrated when the company doesn't want to or has no resources to implement the changes.

One well-known YouTuber Airbnb expert who runs a property management company with over 100 listings boasts, "we don't have 5-star reviews on our ten thousand reservations... we don't have a perfect score, and it's not important to have a perfect score."

And for his business, as a large property manager, this strategy makes sense as long as he onboards more vacation rentals each week than those who cancel their contract. This becomes a winning business model for them, not for you.

However, if there are reasons you must hire a property manager, let's explore how you can find a good one.

Consult Online Reviews

The company must have a robust online presence, even if they're small. Why? Maintenance of an online presence is essential for your listing.

An online presence whether it be a website or page on an online review site gives you peace of mind and allows them to demonstrate to future hosts (like you) that they have prior hosts who are very happy with them.

Many property management compa-
nies encourage hosts to leave reviews early and/or without earning them. Look for reviews that say how long the host had been using the manager before writing the review. Anything longer than a year is good. If a review is unprompted, it's likely to be long as the host is pas-sionate about the good job this com-pany has done. If you want to see what truly authentic reviews look like for my property management company, scan the QR code.

Yelp Reviews For My Property Management Company

SCAN ME

If you were to contact any of these hosts, even if they no longer use my services, I bet many would be willing to talk to you about the great job I did for them. Why? Because I made them a ton of money while taking very little of their time. I also taught them how Airbnb works.

I encourage you to contact some of the reviewers for the manager that you're considering. If they don't respond or aren't very forthcoming in telling you how great the company is, then it could be a fake or incentivized review. You can also directly ask if they were asked to leave the review or given any compensation in return.

Similarly, don't take all negative reviews at face value. Just as some guests leave unfair negative reviews of listings, the property management company could be the recipient of an unfair review from an unruly host or even other local man-agement companies. The reviewer could also be a guest who stayed in one of their properties and was upset that the property management company enforced a house rule and collected additional money. This could be a positive signal. Luckily, the reviewer is more than happy to talk to you about their bad experience. Ask them a few questions to understand the cause of the negative review and judge for yourself if it was earned by the company or not.

Best not to ask the company for their reviews as they can use this as a point of influence in your decision. Instead, do a simple search on Google or Facebook. Here are some additional review platforms in the USA: Trustpilot, Yelp, Better Business Bureau, Angie's List, Foursquare. You might catch some negative reviews on some of the less well-known review platforms as the company is less likely to monitor them.

In addition to online reviews, consult their website. Is it maintained and professional or full of typos, outdated, and hard to navigate? This gives you a view into how this company operates.

After working at Airbnb, I went to work for a local Airbnb property management company, and one of the first things I did was rebuild their website—a website they still use today. This led to more credibility when we sold the hosts and brought us more organic business. If a company is not willing to do this, you have to wonder why not.

Maintain Control of Your Listing

It's your rental, and the listing should be on your hosting profile on any OTA for one simple reason: you don't want to have to start all over if/when you decide to move on. It happens all too frequently that the property management company encourages the host to allow them to list the property on the PM account because it's a "strong account" with many positive reviews and the Superhost badge. While this is a legitimate argument, you can get to just as strong a profile within three months.

How To Locate a Property Manager

Worst case scenario first: It's possible that there are no property managers in your area. If this happens to be you, then you're out of luck. Unless you want to start your own....

I don't recommend you hire a traditional long-term property rental company for your vacation rental. In this case, go back to the previous chapter which will automate much of your work allowing you to manage your rental in about an hour per week.

However, most areas either have companies or individuals providing these services. You can probably find a few of them with a quick Google search 'Airbnb/vacation rental/short term rental property management [your city]'.

Otherwise, check out *Chapter 7.7 How Can I Connect With Other Rental Owners In My Area?* for additional ways to get in touch with a potential property manager.

OptimizeMyBnb.com Instagram Account

SCAN ME

If you are having trouble finding one, send me a message on Instagram with the property location, and I'll try my best to help you out.

Questions To Ask Your Potential Property Manager

The above strategies should narrow down your options to just two or three. Usually, they will want to talk to you on the phone or meet in-person. Accept this offer. This is your opportunity to ambush them with questions they won't hear from other unprepared hosts and thus for which they won't have a canned response.

Choose a few of the questions below to ask based on what's important to you or what's lacking from the information you gathered from your online research. Always dig for more. Ask 'why' and 'how' often.

Question: **Do you monitor guest reviews?**

There's only one right answer: yes. You can also ask if they respond to guest reviews. Or, more generally, you can ask about their general process in review management. Ask for examples.

Question: **What is the biggest issue you have with managing all of your properties?**

The only wrong answer is if they say none. There is always room for improvement. This answer should be rather thoughtful and quickly determined. They shouldn't be trying to sell you. Instead, they should be trying to ensure you're a good fit for them. If you sense they're hiding information, kindly let them know that you're both trying to decide if this is a good fit. If you happen to be talking with a larger property manager, you probably have an entry-level employee who is not privy to the overall business and won't have an answer. Another reason to go local.

Question: **What percentage of their existing hosts are Superhosts?**

It's not easy to achieve and maintain Superhost status. The reason you ask this is to see if they start defending why their clients are not. It's okay not to be a Superhost, but if they place the blame on the guest, the host, or the property, then you probably want to avoid this company.

Question: **How do you handle early check-in and late check-out requests?**

They should be able to accommodate this when possible, most of the time.

Question: **How do you hire cleaners?**

Bad cleaners will cost you money. It's the number one complaint of guests. The company should have a process in hiring cleaners. They should send the same cleaners to the same properties whenever possible. Ask about their cleaner turnover. You do not want a constant flow of new cleaners into your home as it's a security risk and inefficient. Do they quality check cleanings? Do their cleaners or the company have insurance?

Question: **How will you price my calendar?**

They should have a very specific answer here. They should not use Airbnb's Smart Pricing. Manually is okay if they actively do this. However, active management on a dynamic pricing tool is ideal. You can ask to see all of their listings on an OTA. You don't have to see 100% of them, but ask to see a few more than are shown. If they only show you a few, it might be because most calendars are not well occupied. If they don't want to send them for privacy concerns, even though they're publicly available, then ask to view them during your meeting.

Question: **How long does the average host stay with your company?**

If a new host leaves after six months on average, this is a red flag. Anything more than one year is good. You can verify this by noting the average number of reviews on the listings you see from the prior question.

Question: **Who would the guest contact at 11pm on a Friday night? Or 6am the morning of Christmas Day?**

Here you will understand how they deal with emergencies. If they answer something generic like 'we take care of the issue no matter when the guest reaches out', you can assume they do not.

Question: **Do they use a message automation service or any other tools?**

> They should say yes. Quick host responses via message automation get more reservations. They could also be using noise monitoring devices, guest data collection services, digital guidebooks, etc.

You should also bring up any criticisms you found in their existing reviews and ask what they've done to fix those issues.

What Does a Property Management Company Charge?

Most full-service companies will charge a commission between 15-25% of the nightly rate, excluding cleaning fees. If your rental is a high-end property, you may be able to negotiate a lower percentage commission.

PRO TIP: ————————————————————————

Shady property managers will overcharge on the cleaning fee and make a profit on that portion. The cleaning fee should be at cost.

If you are more risk averse, some companies will guarantee to pay you a fixed rate each month no matter how much it is rented and at what price. Generally, I advise against this option as you will make much less in the long term.

For the amount of work they do (the good ones!), this is an absolute steal if you know you don't want to manage yourself.

All property management companies are not created equally. Far from it. Like anything else in life, it's best to spend some time figuring out what you want before you pursue. Understanding your needs and communicating your expectations to the property management company will save you time in the long run.

Part 5

PRICING

5.1 INTRODUCTION

The year was 2015. I was working both for Airbnb and a local property manager in the San Francisco Bay Area when Airbnb announced their dynamic pricing tool, Smart Pricing. These tools had already existed for years in the vacation rental space, and I was using the market leader at the time. I asked the founder of this competing tool if he were scared about the announcement by the behemoth of the industry. To my surprise, he wasn't at all, though I couldn't tell if his confidence was braggadocio or well-founded. Fast-forward only a few months later, and it was clear that the founder had been largely correct in that confidence. Airbnb's pricing tool was poorly received, almost a bust.

Simply, Airbnb isn't in the business of pricing. It's not their specialty. The overall intent of Airbnb's Smart Pricing tool did not align with that of the hosts' maximization of revenue. From the beginning Smart Pricing was implemented to increase bookings. Bookings. For Airbnb. Not increasing revenue. For hosts.

This was one of my first run-ins with dynamic pricing, and it's been a large part of what I do ever since then. Early on in my business I used to manage revenue for property managers. I'd charge 2.5% commission. The pricing tool charged 1%. The average listing earned around $5000 per month. I was making, on average, $125 per listing per month spending 30 seconds per week per listing. That's how in demand this service *was*, and it's only gotten more important. I no longer offer revenue management as a separate service, but I still personally manage the revenue for all the listings under my property management company.

In this section, you'll learn my strategy for occupancy management. I call it occupancy management, and not revenue management, because we'll be managing our occupancy. Revenue is the output, the last step in the process. It's like going to your dentist with a cavity, and not being told the *cause* of the cavity and how to prevent more in the future. If you don't fix what comes before revenue, you're always going to be unsatisfied and lost.

My assumption going into all this is that you want maximum occupancy at the highest rates. While this may sound obvious, there are some hosts who want the highest rates and occupancy is less important. Maybe they're doing it as a hobby or for side cash or do the cleaning themselves, and they would prefer a lower occupancy with premium rates. If that's you, it's okay. But in my experience, you represent a sliver of the market, and there will be some subtle differences between the strategies below. Namely, you will probably not change your prices very often, opting for only the premium, in-demand dates to get booked at premium rates.

But if that's not you, then I want to set the stage from the outset. **Occupancy determines your price**. In the short-term, the market will tell you what to charge through your occupancy. We'll cover this in *Chapter 5.4 Weekly Occupancy Management*, but remember that. Your current occupancy will set your current price. If you're not happy with your current occupancy, either, you can lower your price. You see how if you're not happy with your current price, you couldn't simply increase it *unless your occupancy was already high*. If you increased your price with a low occupancy, it'd result in even lower occupancy. Or, if you're not happy with your current price, you should increase the value of your offer (refer back to *Chapter 3.3 Know Your Space*) which will have the effect of raising your reviews, thus increasing your occupancy and, ultimately, your price. A consistent focus on improving your value is a best practice, regardless.

We adjust our nightly rates based on our occupancy.

As it relates to lowering your price, of course, we'd prefer not to do this. It is very effective in increasing our occupancy, but it's our last option. I have some tricks to share with you before you do that.

I'll share one with you now: Snooze your listing. It's been rumored that snoozing your listing for as long as you can, but at least a few days, can result in a temporary rise in search rank likely resulting in bonus reservations. Though this is not a 100% infallible trick, depending on your situation, it's worth a try.

Throughout this section I'll be referring to supply and demand. Supply is the number of listings available for a particular date and/or filter options (i.e. entire home rental on specific dates for two guests). The demand is the number of guests who will book a reservation for that same data/filter combination.

There are four kinds of owners as it relates to occupancy management:

1. Those who set one price all year-round
2. Those who make periodic manual adjustments
3. Those who use Airbnb's Smart Pricing
4. Those who use another proprietary dynamic pricing tool

The prior owner of *The Belmonte Penthouse* was in the first group. The same price, all year-round. This group is performing poorly at occupancy management and missing loads of opportunities for revenue maximization.

The manual adjustments group is better, but still not ideal. They're changing rates based on dates, typically weekends and local events. You don't want to be in this group either.

Airbnb's Smart Pricing tool is the dominant market leader, simply because it's easy and built directly into Airbnb. Many hosts think Airbnb must know what they're doing because they want to make more money. That's partially true. But from Airbnb's perspective, how they make more money—unlike how hosts make more money!—is mostly a result of more bookings and *not* getting you a slightly higher nightly rate. A quick aside: I find people have similar thoughts towards real estate agents. They are not there to help you get top dollar. To them, success looks like selling a lot of homes, not necessarily selling *every* home for the highest price. Keep this in mind when you sell or buy your next investment. Your individual result matters not to Airbnb or the real estate agent. Airbnb wants more heads in beds. More bookings, at cheap rates, is a recipe for success for Airbnb.

The fourth group is where you want to be, if you're not already there. Here, we are pricing based on occupancy. There's a variety of quality pricing tools out there.

Bonus Item - Deal Sheet

SCAN ME

In the Deal Sheet you can find my recommendation under 'Dynamic Pricing'. This chapter assumes that you are using a dynamic pricing tool that you can customize for your needs.

Pricing Levels

I break out pricing into two levels. The first month you will be at level one, learning the basic features and metrics. You'll need to learn and get familiar with a new tool, so let's start walking before we run. I'm here for you. Trust in me. Pricing is all about knowing your occupancy and your booking lead time. With these two important data metrics, you become the expert. Data is power in our world, and now you have two critical pieces of data that the guest does not. We're going to use them to our advantage.

Then, you will graduate to level two and learn all about the customizations. Customizations, like last-minute discounts, are used to tailor the dynamic pricing tool to your individual situation. We'll learn why and when to use the most popular options. The risk here is using too many customizations. Just because they're available doesn't mean you have to use them. Similarly, if you're making a lot of manual adjustments, you're probably not leveraging the tool.

Related to pricing, let's first look at your calendar availability. This is how many days in the future are available for reservations. On many OTAs, you can automatically choose to show 3, 6, 9, or 12 months on a rolling basis.

Always have your calendar open for bookings during the *next* slow season, but *never* the next busy season. Let's assume your slow season is November to April and busy season from May to October. If you're currently in your busy season, open up your calendar to six or nine months into the future, through April of next year. The goal is to have competitive prices months in advance to get some bonus bookings during that next slow season. Guests looking for deals tend to book far in advance, and we're happy to give them a deal during slow season.

Alternatively, when you're in the current slow season, limit your calendar as you don't need a booking months in advance during the upcoming busy season. If someone wants to book your calendar months in advance and during busy season, it's probably because your rates are too low. Sometimes, the guest knows something you don't. Perhaps a recent conference or music festival was just announced, and the pricing tools don't have the data yet to adjust.

5.2 LEVEL 1: THE BASICS

When you first sign up for a dynamic pricing tool, it can get overwhelming fast, so I'm going to ease you into it with some guidance. There's a lot going on with these tools. Many of them have a dashboard with a bunch of numbers, market analytics, and other bells and whistles. To start, we're going to take one month to get used to the tool's interface and to familiarize ourselves with just a few of the most important metrics. Don't worry about leaving money on the table. This is your training period. You're going to notice things, specifically booking patterns, which we discuss in the next section, that will help you speed up your learning curve to maximize revenue.

We're going to cover four topics:

- Booking lead time (BLT)
- Base price
- Minimum price
- Maximum price

Booking Lead Time (BLT). It is of the utmost importance. Without it, you're blind. It tells you the booking pattern of your specific listing. On average, booking lead time is about 30 days +/- five days. And you can think of booking lead time as a bell curve, the majority of your reservations are coming between 15 and 45 days into the future. This booking lead time is roughly accurate for all the major OTAs. There are exceptions. One of those exceptions is larger homes and big events which usually see a longer booking lead time. Regardless, you'll want to confirm what it is for each specific listing.

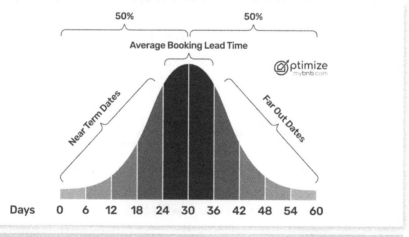

A normal booking lead time (BLT) curve where the majority of bookings come around the BLT, in this case 30 days.

The above is showing that if your booking lead time is 30 days, half of your reservations are confirmed from today until 30 days into the future and the other half confirmed more than 30 days from now. This concept is very important. If we know that 50% of our bookings come same-day to 30 days into the future and 50% come 31+ days into the future, we can calculate what our occupancy goals (a concept we'll explore shortly) are and, thus, peek into the future and make corrections in advance.

You should have an idea of your booking lead time if you've already had some reservations, but you can find it within the Airbnb hosting dashboard, using an analytics tool, on most PMS, or from your dynamic pricing provider.

Bonus Item: Google Sheet - Booking Lead Time

SCAN ME

You can also calculate it by keeping records of your prior reservations. In the bonus items, I've provided an Excel/Google worksheet that will automatically break down your booking lead times based on your reservations.

Base Price. This number affects all prices on your calendar. Each dynamic pricing tool will take this number, apply their logic based on your individual listing and market data, and assign a nightly rate to every available date on your calendar. On some dates, the price will be much higher and some much lower than your base price.

Think of the base price as your average rate on an average night in an average month. Usually, the dynamic pricing tool will suggest a base price. You can use it to start even though it is certain to change. Err on the lower side to start. It's better to get bookings coming in, even at a slightly lower rate, than going high and getting no action.

We want the base price to be slowly rising from year to year. From low to high season, you'll have to raise and lower it drastically, probably doubling it. In times of lower demand, you will have to lower it, even in busy season. We'll go over when and how to do this soon, but we also have strategies to implement before lowering our prices.

Minimum Price. The minimum price trips up a lot of hosts. It is not what you would like to charge, and it is not the base price. Instead, it is the price you would begrudgingly take if the alternative is no reservation.

More specifically, it will equal your fixed costs plus variable costs plus profit margin. Your fixed costs are things you'll pay regardless of the reservation like mortgage, taxes, building or community dues, cable TV, and pool maintenance. Your variable costs you only pay when you have a reservation like utilities, consumables, and if you provide things like a welcome gift, breakfast, or airport transit.

Most listings have a fixed minimum price which only comes into play during low demand times like slow season and weekdays. We'll learn how to adjust this, if needed, in the next section.

Maximum Price. You can usually ignore this except for under one specific set of circumstances. If you have a tremendously popular listing, you will be able to charge higher rates. Depending on what you're offering, there is some rate which is objectively unreasonable and will result in lower ratings. You'd only be able to charge this super-premium rate in the short term until your rating started to decline.

In the real world, here's how that happens: You're offering a basic listing, and you're in a micro-neighborhood with a lot of demand for your specific listing and not a lot of supply. I have personal experience with this. Remember the couch I was hosting? It was in the heart of San Francisco. My FPG was a budget traveler. Nearby hostels were often sold out or expensive. So, the budget traveler had an option to book my $100 couch or a $300 hotel room. I could get away with $100. Once I started getting to $125, I started to get poorer ratings because the value simply was not there. Nothing changed about my offer, and I was able to raise it really high, even for a couch, but eventually, it was just unreasonable. In this case, my max price was $110.

5.3 LEVEL 2: THE CUSTOMIZATIONS

Well done. You've successfully completed month one. You've eased yourself into the wonderful world of pricing. You now have a strong foundational knowledge of the basic metrics used by your dynamic pricing tool and how they connect to each other. Though you're not yet an expert, you're well on your way. You will soon be self-sufficient and able to troubleshoot all of your own pricing doubts. That will be a glorious day! Trust me, I know how confusing pricing can be because it's the most common topic I discuss in private consultation calls. I end up saying the same thing over and over again, and I'm being paid to repeat myself. What I say on those calls with individual hosts is now here for you, laid out, and organized.

Let's jump in.

During the past month, you may have noticed some booking patterns for your listing.

A booking pattern is simply a trend in your reservations. Are your weekends getting booked more often than your week-days? Have you lowered your price for the next 5 to 10 days in order to get a last-minute reservation? Or maybe you peeked into the metrics and noticed something a little more advanced like your booking lead time is twice as long as your market.

In this chapter, we will go over many common booking patterns and how to use pricing customizations to *optimize* the trend for a more profitable property.

Manual Adjustments. Sometimes you will want to change the prices on individual dates. This is the most common customization. While you shouldn't be doing this too often, it's an eventuality. I've noticed these tools don't do a good job at pricing extremely high-demand, one-off dates like yearly conferences, music festivals, college graduations, or other popular events like the Super Bowl. These will probably need a manual adjustment.

When you do, my advice is to change the price by percentage based on the recommended price instead of inputting a fixed price. For example, let's say you want to change the prices for an upcoming popular weekend, and your original price was $300 per night. You want it to show $500. You have two options.

First, you could manually adjust the dates by entering $500. I don't recommend you do this because you'll have to remember to come back and readjust the price every few days if the nights remain unbooked at that rate. If this popular weekend is two months away, maybe you initially reach for $500 per night. But as soon as the weekend is a few weeks away, should it still be $500? Probably not. The market demand and supply has shifted in this timeframe, so the price needs to be adjusted, too, probably downwards.

Your second option for date-specific manual pricing adjustments is to change the recommended price based on a percentage. In this case, to get from $300 to $500, we'd add 67% ($300 + *$200* = $500) to the recommended price. As the manually adjusted dates get closer without being booked, the recommended price will change, thus the final price adjustment will also change. When I say recommended price, I'm referring to the nightly rate suggested by the dynamic pricing tool. In two weeks using this option for manual adjustments, the price might be $400, but we don't need to remember to go in and change it.

As for how to price individual in-demand days, the best method I've found is using a data tool and looking at historical data. Specifically look at this in-demand date last year, look at the final market occupancy for your size rental (and, ideally, the top percentile of best performing listings) and keep an eye on that along with the current occupancy. The final data point you need to know is the average booking lead time for this in-demand date, last year. Super in-demand dates usually have an extended lead time.

Last-Minute Discount. Another very common customization. The best way to add last-minute discounts is via a gradual increase in the discount over a specified number of days. You should start your gradual last-minute discount based on your average booking lead time. If you recall with *The Belmonte Penthouse*, I initially set a gradual discount starting at 25 days into the future because that's what my average booking lead time is. The amount of your discount should get you down to your minimum or near it within the next week.

Example: Your average booking lead time is 25 days, and your minimum price is $175. You'd want to add a last-minute gradual discount of up to 40% percent within the next 25 days. Why 25 days? Because at this point we know the majority of reservations have already been booked based on our average booking lead time (remember, we expect about half of bookings to have been completed at 25 days in this example). There will always be unbooked listings (i.e. supply is higher than demand) as dates pass. We don't want to be one of them, so we're outsmarting the competition by lowering just a little bit more than them, a little bit sooner. Most listings apply a discount only within the next 5-10 days. We're already in big trouble if we're waiting until then. We'll talk more about that in the very last-minute pricing section below. We chose a 40% discount because our dynamic pricing tool showed our daily rates within the next seven days around our minimum price of $175. The discount will depend on your Base Price, but will generally be in the 30-50% range. Assuming we selected a 40%

gradual discount starting at 25 days out from target booking date, the discount customization would look like this. Let's assume it's September 1st today.

26 days from today (September 26th)...0% discount
25 days from today (September 25th)...1.6% discount
24 days from today (September 24th)...3.2% discount
1 day from today (September 2nd)...40% discount, but never lower than our minimum price.

POP QUIZ:

In what situation would we input a last-minute gradual discount?

Answer: As with all customizations, we add a last-minute gradual discount because we notice a booking pattern. Remember, we only use customizations *after* we notice and to counteract booking patterns. In this case, our occupancy was consistently low for dates closer than our average booking lead time, suggesting that we needed to lower near-term prices with a last-minute discount. We'll go over this with an example one more time in *Chapter 5.6 Common Calendar Occupancies*. Please note there are other last-minute discount options like a fixed rate discount percentage, but they are all inferior to the gradual discount.

Are you ready for your first wrinkle in the pricing game? I call it the "Weekday Wrinkle".

This wrinkle, this booking pattern, may have less to do with last-minute pricing and more to do with weekend versus weekday pricing. If your weekends are getting booked much faster than your weekdays, this is common and something to pay attention to. It would have the effect of showing you a low near-term occupancy rate, but the real reason for few weekday bookings is low demand. Once we notice a booking pattern, we need to think about customizations to counteract it.

Day of Week Pricing Adjustments. I highlighted the "Weekend Wrinkle" because it's a very common booking pattern, and I don't want it to go unnoticed. It's also easy to address with a common customization. If your listing is getting its weekends booked faster than its weekdays, you should apply one or both of the following pricing adjustments:

- Lower weekday recommended pricing
- Raise weekend recommended pricing

You should do this as a percentage of the recommended price and not a fixed number. Start small. Your weekdays are not getting booked so add a 10% price reduction for whatever your booking pattern tells you are your weekdays. At *The Belmonte Penthouse*, the lowest demand weekdays are Monday, Tuesday, and Wednesday (I noticed some reservations Thursday to Monday). Alternatively, your lower demand weekdays could be Sunday through Thursday.

At the same time, you may want to increase weekend prices following the same logic. Start low with a 10% increase. Let it roll for a couple weeks. If you're still seeing the booking pattern, then change the customization to 15% for weekend dates, and go up from there until your occupancy gets in line with your goals. I wouldn't implement both of these customizations at the same time. Again, we'll go over your occupancy goals in the next chapter.

Very Last-Minute Pricing. Very last-minute pricing includes same-day bookings up until five days into the future. This is when demand shrinks a lot yet there's the same amount of last-minute supply.

The remaining supply is not going to be the best value for the FPGs as better listings get reserved first and worse listings last if at all. Waiting to get bookings until the very-last minute is not a winning strategy because you'll only get bookings if you are offering the best value. That doesn't mean you're the cheapest listing necessarily, but your price will be your lowest or minimum price. You could have a high-end home that normally rents for $800 per night but last minute you give it away for $400. Any FPG who's looking at the last minute is going to know this is a killer deal, even though there might be lower-priced homes. Guests win in last-minute situations because they have the leverage. For the host receiving a last-minute inquiry, it's usually this reservation or no reservation. For the guest, it's this listing or dozens of others.

Remember our bell curve above? In the last few days there are a tiny portion of confirmed bookings, *maybe* 5% of the available listings get booked within the final few days.

You'll know you are offering a high-value home if you are getting last-minute bookings, including same-day bookings. This is not where you want to maximize profit. This is where you want to maximize occupancy. I'd rather get a few bonus bookings throughout the year at my minimum of $150 rather than ask $175 and get no bookings.

How do we know what this minimum price should be? Again, the market will tell you. If your $150 last-minute minimum price is not getting any bookings after a month of data, then you should lower it to $135. Alternatively, if you're getting a good number of last-minute bookings at $150 (you're never going to get the majority of last-minute dates filled up, that's why we want to avoid this), then you can think about raising your minimum price to $165.

Last-minute reservations can be dangerous. Bad guests do not plan. Typically, the problem reservations are booked last-minute by new accounts or by local residents. Some markets have a plethora of bad guests. For many years, I managed a friend's listing located in the Bronx, New York. This is a problem market, full of headaches and bad guests to be avoided. Our minimum price was high to avoid these bad guests. This is not always the case, and really depends on your market. Proceed cautiously here. You'd rather lose a reservation than deal with a bad guest.

Minimum Stay. On your chosen OTA, you'll be allowed to select a minimum night stay for weekdays and weekends. In your dynamic pricing tool, they allow loads of customizations related to minimum stay. In general, I am a proponent of a single night minimum stay requirement as long as you have a popular listing, are getting fair prices, and have your cleaning process *optimized*.

You have the option here to get creative. You could set a general minimum night requirement of two, but any reservations further than 60 days out would require a 3-night minimum. You could then adjust that to be a single night minimum within the next 10 days for last-minute bookings.

Orphan Minimum Nights. Although not a pricing customization, this next strategy will help increase your occupancy and can be set within the dynamic pricing tool. If your listing has anything but a single night minimum, you'll want to consider this customization. The booking pattern here is very simple: inability to get a reservation below your minimum stay requirement *even if that is the only available option*. In the real world, let's say you have a two-night minimum, and you have a reservation ending on a Tuesday and another starting on Wednesday. That means your Tuesday night is impossible to book, thus orphaned, based on your current minimum night restrictions.

If you want to unblock that Tuesday night, you can create a customization that adjusts your minimum nights to any gap less than your general minimum night setting. In the example above the dynamic pricing tool would create a one-time single night minimum for this date allowing for a single night reservation on that Tuesday. If your minimum night setting was three nights, then you could create this customization for gaps of two nights.

Orphan Night Prices. Related to the above minimum night customization, this one has to do with the price on that day.

You could raise or lower it. You might want to raise orphan nights simply because you prefer not to have them though at a 20% premium, you'd happily accept them and avoid bad guests at the same time. Or, you could lower orphan nights because you understand the demand for this single night is very low and would prefer a booking.

Far-out Pricing. Far-out reservations are defined as two times your average booking lead time. You'll use this pricing customization if you notice you're getting too many or too few far-out bookings. In general, only about 10% of your bookings should be far-out. If your average booking lead time is 30 days, a far-out booking is anything further than 60 days from today.

Sometimes, the dynamic pricing tools raise your pricing too much for far-out bookings. In this case, I find the best customization is to lower the recommended price for these far-out dates until they have a premium of only about 5-10% over your normal rates.

Alternatively, if you're getting too many far-out reservations then your pricing *may* be too low. If those reservations are coming in your slow season, that's a good thing. In slow season, your goal is occupancy maximization, not profit maximization. But if you're currently in slow season and those reservations are coming during the busy season, when you don't need bonus reservations in advance and your goal is profit maximization, then you probably need to raise your recommended pricing. You'd know by comparing the rates you're getting on those far-out dates with the rates you get around your average booking lead time. If those reservations are coming with a slight premium, then there's probably nothing to change.

To me, you need a full year of data for your individual listing to know precisely what you can and cannot do with customizations. Dynamic pricing tools will assist you in a big way in navigating those situations you're not familiar with. But remember, these tools are not set-it-and-forget-it.

In the next section, I'll put it all together and explain my overall strategy to managing your occupancy and rates. It's the revenue management strategy that I've followed for years and years with success, and it's a large factor in how I quadrupled the revenue on my latest vacation rental investment.

5.4 WEEKLY OCCUPANCY MANAGEMENT

Goal: Learn how to manage your Airbnb business revenue effectively and efficiently by maximizing occupancy and nightly rates.

Tool: dynamic pricing software

Time Investment: 30 seconds per listing, per week, on average

I feel your plight with pricing. It can seem very complex and time consuming. It can feel like you don't know what to do in a sea of options and customizations. This all makes pricing overwhelming, and you feel lost. But it doesn't have to be that way. I'm going to share the same strategy that I use.

By the end of this section, you'll be managing your occupancy and revenue better than 95% of hosts. Let's get started.

Booking Lead Time and Occupancy Targets

You already know how important your booking lead time is for occupancy management. You know where to find and how to calculate it. Next, we need to set up our occupancy targets.

Remember that a booking lead time tells you how far in advance the average reservation is confirmed. If it is 30 days for your listing, a common BLT, then it tells us that half of our bookings are confirmed within the next month and the other half further than that 30 days into the future. With that information, we know that around 30 days, we want to be about 50% occupied.

This bears repeating because it needs to be understood: if 50% of my bookings come between today and day 30, and 50% of my bookings come at day 31 and further, then I should be about 50% occupied at 30 days into the future.

A quick clarification about occupancy. A lot of the time we associate occupancy with historical data, but I'm referring to your future occupancy. If we know what our future occupancy should be and what it currently is, we have a time buffer to make corrections in advance of last-minute vacancies.

Another note: I'm going to say 'about' and 'roughly' a lot in this section. That's because these are all estimates. The relationship between supply and demand is fluid. A single booking can take your occupancy from under-occupied to within your target.

Working off our BLT, we can then fill in the other occupancy targets for how much we want to be occupied at 7, 15, and 60 days into the future. It would look something like this:

Days From Today	Occupancy Target (Busy)	Occupancy Target (Slow)
7	100%	80%
15	75%	60%
30	50%	40%
60	30%	25%

Table 5.4.1 Occupancy Targets Based On 30-Day Booking Lead Time

As a host, you may feel more comfortable with higher occupancy targets. You may opt for 60% or even 80% occupied within the next 30 days. It's your choice. You'll be leaving money on the table, though, because the higher you want your occupancy above average, the lower you'll have to put your price to entice more FPGs to book your place early. Remember, early bookers are typically looking for a deal.

The middle column is based on a busy season where you're able to get to full occupancy.

If instead your maximum occupancy is 80%, say during slow season, your targets would look more like those shown in the right column.

Occupancy Management - Level 1

The first thing you have to understand is that these tools aren't one-and-done. You've got to monitor your future occupancy rates. With my strategy, you will do this once per week. Let's say Wednesday morning. That's when I do it.

I choose Wednesday morning because all weekends should be booked and in advance. If not, you'd better make sure they are. On a Wednesday, you've given yourself enough time to make any last-minute adjustments to increase your chances of getting a last-minute booking.

Ideally though, you're focused on the 30-day occupancy number most of the time because the next week or so is mostly reserved.

Most hosts are concerned with only their nightly rate and their minimum, but it doesn't matter what you think you can get or what you want your minimum to be. We've touched on this already, but it's an important concept. STRs are a true market in that the market will tell you what your listing is worth (by booking it consistently or not), not the other way around.

For example, if you want to charge $200 per night and you're at 20% occupancy, you're charging more than the market thinks your space is worth. It's the opposite if you're charging $100 per night and your occupancy is 95%.

Every Wednesday morning, you should log in to your dynamic pricing tool to monitor your future occupancy levels for each of your rentals individually.

If your true occupancy is above your target at your BLT, you should raise the base price by 10%. If your true occupancy is below that same target, lower your base price by the same margin.

Let's run through an example.

Your base price is $250.

Your average booking lead time is 35 days.

Your occupancy at 35 days (into the future) is 37%.

Assuming your occupancy targets are standard and you're in busy season, what will you do with your base price?

You will lower it by $25 which is 10%. Lowering your price makes your listing more competitive. It's also the most effective thing you can do to increase your search rank. OTAs *love* cheap listings because they represent good value. If you're in a pinch, lower your rates. It's an effective short-term strategy.

You should keep track of this change in a spreadsheet. I'll tell you what I do, and you can change it to fit your needs. I add the date in one cell of a Google document and just below it, I type $225 and fill in the cell light red to signal I'm below target.

Let's assume last week my occupancy was 52% and my base price was $250, before the change for this week. Last week I would have also put that date, one week ago, typed in $250 into the cell below that date and colored it green to represent that I'm on target.

Light red tells me I'm below target. Dark red tells me I'm significantly below target. No color tells me that I'm over-occupied.

Remember when I said I'd be saying about often? That's because my targets aren't fixed numbers as I showed above. They'd be ranges because all of these are approximations. My ranges would look like this:

0-20% = dark red
20-40% = light red
40-60% = green
60-100% = no color

This becomes really powerful as you start to get a record of your historical occupancy, along with your future occupancy. You'll be able to make changes in advance to maintain a healthy calendar occupancy. Let's say that two weeks ago, my occupancy was 61%, and my base price was still at $250. That cell would be clear.

So, I would have seen something like this on my Google document:

1/1/XX	1/8/XX	1/15/XX
250	250	225
Clear	Green	Light Red

Table 5.4.2 Example Weekly Base Price Adjustments Over a 3-Week Period

In this example, I can see that my occupancy has been dipping for three weeks in a row. In this case, even though 37% occupancy in the next 35 days isn't terrible, just below my target, when paired with the data that it's been falling for the past three weeks, it becomes worse. Maybe instead of dropping by $25, I drop my base price by $35.

It's just another booking pattern. We're noticing a booking pattern and making a change to our pricing to reverse that pattern. Whether it's under-occupied like above or over-occupied, it's a booking pattern. If we were over-occupied, we'd raise the base price until our true occupancy came in line with our target occupancy.

By the way, when I say true occupancy, I'm referring to your actual occupancy rate. If 20 of the next 35 days are actually booked, that would equal an occupancy of 57% over the next 35 days. The dynamic pricing tool will provide this information.

We have a couple strategies before we drop the price. You can re-optimize the listing. It's our first line of defense. We may have chosen to do that on the date 1/8/XX above. Refer to *Chapter 3.12 How To Re-Optimize Your Listing* for a refresher on this topic. When I do a re-optimization, I bold the number/base price in the cell on that date just to remind me in the future, if needed.

Or, you can make your listing more flexible (using *The Flexibility Concept*) by increasing the pool of FPGs.

If none of this is working for a prolonged period of time, then you may need to re-examine your market dynamic. It may have turned bad, and you should think about selling. Don't jump to this conclusion. This would be a big decision, and it's probably not the case. But if it is, I don't want you torturing yourself in an unprofitable market. Return to *Part 2: Vacation Rental Market Analysis* for a refresher on this topic and to re-examine the supply/demand relationships in your market.

Occupancy Management - Level 2

The final part of our occupancy management is for customizations, if needed.

The vast majority of Wednesdays, I'm not doing anything with my customizations, and the entire process takes me 30 seconds per listing unless I want to do a re-optimization which is two or three times per year.

The only time I will test a customization is if, what? I notice a booking trend.

I'm often testing and re-testing pricing customizations because the supply and demand dynamics are fluid, and everything can change in one month, three months, six months or a year from now.

In the last chapter we had addressed all the common booking trends and the relevant customizations to implement.

In summary, find your "Booking Lead Time". Create your occupancy targets. Choose a day per week to measure your occupancy targets to true occupancy, make any needed adjustments to base price, minimum price, and/or customizations, and keep records of prior adjustments and occupancy to spot your pricing trends.

The prior two chapters and the next will also be covered in the course with video explanations.

5.5 COMMON CALENDAR OCCUPANCIES

I have identified through the thousands of Super Host Optimizations I've done over the years, five common calendar occupancies, good and bad, and I'm going to tell you how to think about and *optimize* each situation, or how to avoid it in the future, if applicable.

As always, I'm assuming you're aiming for full occupancy. If you're in slow season and the top percentile of listings in your market are only at 75% occupancy then adjust the numbers. You also need to know what I consider over- and under-occupied. It all depends on your BLT. It doesn't matter if it's 30 days or 300 days. But let's take the more common 30 days. I would expect to see a calendar occupancy like this, and let's assume it's September 1st:

Within 7 days (to September 7th), 86-100% occupied (no more than one available day)

Within 15 days (to September 15th), 67-80% occupied (3-5 days of availability)

Within 30 days (to September 30th), 40-60% occupied (12-18 days of availability)

Within 60 days (to October 30th), 20-40% occupied (36-48 days of availability)

Here's what that looks like:

A healthy-looking STR calendar.

Under-occupied (represents about 60% of calendars). The most common calendar occupancy. This means one of two things, hopefully not both. Either your pricing is too high, or you're in slow season.

You have a few options to help you in the short term, namely to make your listing more flexible, re-optimize, or lower your pricing until your occupancy comes in line with expectations. Again, if you're not happy with that price, it doesn't matter, at least not in the short term because the market has spoken and told you what you're worth right now. In the long term you can increase your reviews, offer more value, or sell and start over in a market with more upside.

No Bookings (represents about 10% of calendars). Luckily, this isn't common and half could have been avoided with my New Listing Calendar Strategy (see *Chapter 7.22 What Is The New Listing Calendar Strategy?*). If you're an existing listing, then as above you have to increase your listing flexibility by lowering minimum stays, say, and/or lowering your price. I would lower all prices, including high-demand dates, to your minimum price for the first half of your booking lead time (so 15 days if your BLT is 30). Airbnb seems to be momentum-based. If you don't have any bookings, the algorithm has communicated something to you that you need to fix and urgently, and you'll only be able to fix it with more reservations which will have to come at your minimum price in this case. But, it should only be temporary.

I do want to make note of markets with drastic seasons where there can be four or five months with extremely low occupancy for everyone in the market. You have to be cognizant of your particular situation. If there are simply no guests booking, then there's nothing for you to do.

Over-occupied (represents about 15% of calendars). If this is by design and you prefer to be over-occupied by setting your occupancy targets higher, then pat yourself on the back. You're doing great!

Alternatively, if you'd rather not leave so much money on the table, then you should raise your base price in increments of 10%. Depending on your base price, here is how much you should be raising:

- $100 per night = $10-$15 increase
- $300 per night = $25 increase
- $1000 per night = $50-$100 increase

Good Occupancy, But Low Within 2-3 Weeks (represents about 15% of calendars). If you'll recall from earlier in this section, this means one of two things. Either your minimum price is too high, or your midweek days are priced too high. If you don't have a gradual last-minute discount, this would be step #1.

One Long Booking Then No/Low Occupancy. This is very rare situation with a very specific strategy to be applied. Let's say you have one long booking coming up or already in progress that ends around your BLT (to stay consistent with our examples, that would be a 30-day reservation). And that you have zero bookings afterwards. Here's what that looks like.

1	2	3	4	5	6	7
8	9	10	11	12	13	14
15	16	17	18	19	20	21
22	23	24	25	26	27	28
29	30	31				

1	2	3	4	5	6	7
8	9	10	11	12	13	14
15	16	17	18	19	20	21
22	23	24	25	26	27	28
29	30	31				

ptimize
mybnb.com

A calendar with one-long booking and no other reservations. Nothing to be overly worried about, but something to keep an eye on especially as you approach the middle of that reservation without any inquiries or bookings.

This could be a bad sign. You want to closely monitor this situation. Have you at least received some inquiries? If not,

I want you checking two times per week as we get to within the BLT, and I want you to start lowering your base price if no inquiry or booking comes in starting at three-quarters of the way through your BLT. That means, if your BLT is 30 days, then you should start lowering your base price in increments of 10% starting once we get to about 22 days from the end of that one, long reservation.

Now, if the actual booking is longer than your BLT, let's say it's for six weeks, then I want you to increase your base price by 25% as the long booking starts. We want to reset the algorithm and/or get some bonus bookings. Interestingly enough, the OTA doesn't really know what your listing is worth. They have an idea, but there are a lot of anomalies. One listing could typically get booked at $150 per night but also get some bookings at $450 per night. The OTA doesn't really know why, they just know what happened.

So, let's stick with that example and say you've been getting booked up around $125-$175 for the past couple months. Fine. Now you have a long 6-week reservation. You raise your price to $225 as that reservation starts. Ideally, you get a bonus booking at these higher rates within the next couple weeks. This is absolutely fantastic when it happens. Now you are communicating to the algorithm your new value because you have an increased base price, you are fully occupied, and you just got a booking at this increased price. You are resetting your pricing in the algorithm. Congrats! Even if you don't get a booking, in the future, when you lower your prices, the theory is that the algorithm is going to think you're on discount thus raise your search rank because the single most effective thing you can do to increase your search rank is lower your rates. I've used this very strategy numerous times with success.

When you get to your BLT (30 days out from the check-out of the long reservation), I want you to do the first lowering of your base price. If you raise it by 25%, then lower it by 15%. We're still in bonus booking territory. If the booking runs from January

1st to February 15th, then you'd lower 30 days before the end of the long reservation, or January 15th.

To the OTA, they are only going to make money if you get bookings. So, their option now is to get you a booking at your 15% discounted rate or make no money. In one week, if you don't get a booking, then lower your pricing another 10%. Continue to do this in line with the revenue management strategy in the prior chapter.

You will cycle through all of these calendar occupancies throughout the life of your rental business. It's a constant game. You have to make constant assumptions. Good luck, and, let me know what I can do to help further. I really want you to get this.

Part 6

DIRECT BOOKINGS

6.1 INTRODUCTION

As with most things in life, there are cycles. Pre-2010, direct booking in which the guest paid the host directly, or an approximation of it, was the norm. Airbnb was founded in 2008 and shifted things heavily in favor of the centralized OTAs who also collected guest data and handled payments as they became ever more popular. Airbnb revolutionized the short-term rental industry. But the pendulum must swing, and the direct booking movement has been gaining steam over the past few years as Airbnb has managed to upset both hosts and guests, repeatedly. They've even upset me, and I'm fan boy #1 of the company!

Years of poor management by Airbnb has created demand on both sides of the marketplace. Recently, I was talking to the founder of a popular PMS tool who was against creating a direct booking widget but is doing so anyway due to host demand. Hosts are ready, and I want you to be ready.

I think guest demand for direct booking is lacking partly due to the ease and trust of the OTAs. This will be a common theme discussed throughout this section. How do we, as direct-book hosts, create trust and ease for interested guests? What are our advantages? How can we leverage them?

Regardless, direct bookings are here to stay. That is my prediction. As to how far the pendulum swings back in favor of direct bookings over the coming years, this depends on many factors, not the least of which is continued and increasing guest demand. At the very end of this section, I have a stern public service announcement to all hosts starting down the direct book route to ensure the pendulum swings far and mightily.

In this section, I'll be sharing my journey with you in getting *The Belmonte Penthouse* online and able to attract and accept direct bookings. Let me tell you, it does feel good getting a reservation from the work I've put in getting my brand in front of FPGs outside of Airbnb! It feels like a more legit business. I don't need you, Airbnb! But also, don't go away, pretty please, because it's not right for everyone. Airbnb does make things easy due to their budget and economies-of-scale. Those come, as with everything, with their own advantages and disadvantages for the host.

By the way, it's not black or white. You can and should use both the OTAs and a direct booking strategy. Typically, you'll start on the OTAs first to start generating revenue, while you build up your direct booking presence.

You probably fall into one of three camps. If you know you want to do direct bookings for your rental, you can skip this and the next two chapters.

If you know that you're not interested, then you can skip this entire section and move on to the next section.

I figure most likely you are not sure. You've heard about it. It sounds like a lot of work and entails some risk. And you're not clear about what's required of you and the benefit of doing it. Maybe everything seems fine right now, and you're not concerned (bad mindset! Bad, bad, bad!). The next two chapters, where I'll lay out the pros and cons of getting direct bookings, are for you. It's not right for everyone, and I want you to know that up front.

All of my research and experience can be summed up in one simple question as to whether or not direct bookings are probably a good idea for you: if you lost the income related to your rental tomorrow, how much would your life be affected?

How might you lose all your rental income overnight, you ask? Not too long ago, Airbnb permanently banned the accounts of hosts who attended a political rally the company disagreed with. As a prior employee, I know this wasn't first or last time Airbnb removed hosts for suspect reasoning. Do a search online, and you'll find hordes of hosts banned from Airbnb without explanation (so much for hosts being partners!). Look, I understand the risk may be small, but it exists.

More importantly, it's not fully within your control, so you can't fully control it like you can much of your short-term rental business. That's the most frightening kind of risk. Add to that how they handled and communicated policy changes in the pandemic years ago (confirmation the company definitely doesn't consider their hosts partners in any way), and the time to start considering the above question is now.

If it's a pastime generating bonus money for life's extras or is otherwise nonessential, then the lost income probably won't affect your life much at all. And that's okay. That's the beauty of these OTAs.

But if you rely on the income generated from your rental, my guess is that it would affect your life, and possibly, significantly. I find that many hosts take their rental seriously and often aspire to expand, even if they didn't at the outset. If this is you, I want you to seriously consider starting on the journey of direct bookings. I'm not here to convince you. I simply want to give you clarity into the topic so you can decide whether or not direct bookings are right for you. If it turns out that you do want to attract direct bookings, that doesn't mean you have to dedicate 40 hours per week. Quite the contrary. I've discovered the most efficient strategies in securing direct bookings, and we'll get to them later.

If you already know that you want to do direct bookings, but haven't yet taken any action, there are some things I want you to know up front.

You will now be responsible for doing your own marketing, so you really need to know your FPG (*Chapter 3.2 Know Your FPG*) to able to know where they're hanging out online and how to reach them.

You will be in competition with the OTAs. Their job is to convince the FPG why it's better to book through them. Your job is to convince them why it's better to book directly with you. This will be a central theme throughout this section. That is, convincing the FPG why it's better to make a direct booking.

Direct bookings mean branding. You need a brand to represent you online. That's really what the OTA takes away from you when your brand is instead subsumed by a listing on their platforms, for better or worse.

It will take more time, especially up front, but how much is largely your decision. It's a whole wild new world out there where you could spend many hours per week learning about and implementing all the neat tools and strategies related to direct bookings. Or, you can softly enter the direct booking scene with a few hours every now and then. Personally, I've worked hundreds of hours on this over the past year and half, tried dozens of strategies. Partly to be informed as the author of this book and partly to have a more secure business. But I can't say the extra time matters to me in this case because I'm learning so much. I'm going to communicate all these learnings to you in this section.

The direct booking journey involves three phases. First, getting online and allowing yourself to be found by the FPG. Second, getting yourself in front of the FPG and creating traffic to where you are online (website, social media, etc.). Third, setting up your processes and automation just like you do on an OTA. The great news is that everything from screening the guest, collecting a security deposit, sending automated messages, and more—all can be automated now. If you decide to join the direct booking movement, this section will separate out the things you absolutely must do right away, and the things you can address over the coming months when you have time.

6.2 THE ARGUMENT AGAINST DIRECT BOOKING

The most common argument against direct bookings is that it takes extra time and costs extra money. And, it *will* take more time, and there *are* costs. Up front, you will need to set up your website, create social media accounts, and sign up for a Google My Business page at a minimum.

The website will need maintenance, and you'll need to post to your social media accounts and engage with the community on some kind of regular basis.

You'll need to reconfigure your systems so that as much as possible remains automated. Everything can be automated, but it will take time to set it up and learn the new system.

The main extra and required cost you need to pay for is a direct booking website, but there are other additional services that come with a cost like a credit card processing fees and many other optional expenses.

Additionally, your time has value, and you will need to spend your precious and finite time executing a direct booking strategy.

On top of that, there will be more time spent testing out strategies to get direct bookings. You will likely try a few different methods before you find the ones that work best.

You will now be responsible for charging, collecting, tracking, and remitting local taxes whereas on Airbnb this is automatically.

Maybe you want to create business cards with your logo and website on them. Maybe you want to start an affiliate program where you pay someone like a real estate agent to bring you direct reservations.

A direct booking website will not be able to take advantage of some things a mega-corporation can. For example, Airbnb's service is translated into 35 languages and accepts payment in over 70 currencies and has dozens of country-specific payment processors. How many languages will your direct book website be translated into? And how many countries will your payment processor service?

Direct booking can be thought of as a second platform. Listing on any secondary platform will disperse your reviews. As we will learn in *Part 8: How To Rank #1 On Airbnb*, the number of reviews is the single biggest factor in your search rank position.

You could be increasing your risk as you no longer can take advantage of Airbnb's included guest review system nor the insurance policies. It should be noted that these insurance policies are not really guaranteed insurance at all, and the policy is applied based on the whims of the agent you're dealing with.

These are all the main arguments that I can think of *against* direct bookings. Next, let's go over all the arguments *for* direct bookings.

6.3 ARGUMENTS FOR DIRECT BOOKINGS

It was a Sunday morning, and I got a call from my concierge. He sounded panicked. He told me the guests who just checked out hadn't paid the driver for the airport ride. On top of that, they also hadn't paid for the tour transportation the day before. Yesterday they told the driver they'd pay everything today. Today they told the driver that the concierge told them the payment was taken care of. All this after they spent a lot of time negotiating with my concierge for absolute rock bottom prices.

It wasn't a miscommunication. It was intentional. And it wasn't the end of the story.

I walked into *The Belmonte Penthouse* to learn that they also drank all the beverages in the fridge (value $102), decided the price was too high, gave my cleaner $12, and told her to not tell me as if they were doing her some kind of favor.

On top of all that, my lovely cleaner made them special kosher breakfast each morning to match their dietary restrictions. They gave her no tip. When asked if they'd come back, they told her that they wouldn't because it was too expensive.

The amount they stole from my concierge and the driver equaled a quarter of the average monthly wage in Colombia.

For them, this was a big deal. I felt sick to my stomach, especially after pouring so much into every operational detail including sending a free SUV to pick up their group from the airport at 1am upon arrival.

If you've been hosting for more than a year, you, too, probably have experienced bad guests. They come in a variety of forms. These bad guests owed me money. But they had their review to write. Because on Airbnb, it's 5-star or bust, I wasn't going to risk a negative review for this. I bit my tongue, paid the concierge and the driver, and replenished the beverages in the fridge.

They did end up leaving a lethargic 5-star review with only four stars in the value sub-category.

This experience helped push me towards direct bookings where I can collect a security deposit, not go through a middleman if I need to keep a portion of it, not be at the mercy of every review, and not have to accept every single reservation with no cancellations.

From their first message, I knew I didn't want to host this group. They wanted a discount, whined about the price when I declined, and ended up Instant Booking anyway. Cancelling the reservation, even though I knew I'd rebook those weekend dates anyway, was out of the question.

Direct bookings give the host more flexibility in terms of cancellations, refunds, and reviews.

That's nice and everything, but do you want to know what truly convinced me to get direct bookings?

Direct bookings represent another stream of guests to my rental. Translation: more demand. What happens when supply is fixed and demand rises? It means I can raise my prices. Today, I accept reservations from both the OTAs and direct. The talk of the direct booking town is saving commission fees, which range from 3-20%, but for me it's about increasing my demand which will increase my occupancy. Last year I was

93.5% occupied. That extra 6.5% represents $12,000. My goal is to get my rental running through my direct booking website, thus allowing me to treat Airbnb how we already treat Booking.com. Yes, I'll happily take a booking on Airbnb for a 20% premium nightly charge. That'll serve to increase my bottom line and boost me in Airbnb search because the algorithm knows my ADR (Average Daily Rate) is much higher than my competition which translates to more fees for Airbnb. It's the circle of life baby, the holy grail!

This is why Airbnb is working to eliminate any public platform fees shown to the guest. Their 12% fee sometimes is a few hundred dollars, providing more than enough incentive for many guests to book direct. Even though the final pricing is the same, the guest is less likely to venture off the Airbnb highway if the fees are invisible.

The guest funnel—every thing/every place that leads your guest to your listing—is the main factor determining success for direct booking websites. The website might look great (many of them do), but where are your future guests hanging out online, and how are you convincing them to go to your book direct website? We'll cover this in the following chapters.

You can make more money. Not only do you get the money up front with direct bookings, but you can charge more. Guests who book direct fall into two categories. They're money-motivated and saving any amount is valuable to them. Either that or they seem not to care at all about the price. Most of my highest rates have come via direct bookings without any hassle. And believe it or not, some guests simply prefer the privacy. They'd actually prefer to book outside of an OTA.

In fact, I just got a direct booking while writing this section! Let's examine the differences:

Potential Earnings on Airbnb: $1,382
Guest Price on Airbnb: $1,626
Guest Price/My Direct Book Website: $1,523

I made an extra $140, the guest saved $103, and I was paid four months before the check-in date. It's typical for OTAs to send payment for the reservation only upon check-in.

Think of how many FPGs visit your online OTA listing and never book. Having a direct booking website means you can capture some of their contact details and market to them in the future. After all, if they're looking at your listing, they're probably interested in visiting your city and may even have a reason to go there regularly. You then have potential access to everyone *they* know with strategies we'll cover below in *Chapter 6.12 Email and Text Marketing.*

Let's say in some hellish future one of the OTAs takes all market share, buys all the competitors and pushes up the commission to 60%. Sound crazy? Well, there's another company you're familiar with that has done just that for some products. You probably bought this book you're reading from them. Amazon has market dominance in book sales, and they charge for it. I have to pay Amazon up to a 60% commission per book sale.

Or, let's say your preferred OTA changes their algorithm, and your listing is shown less. This has already happened to varying degrees in the past, but I want to share a real-life example from a host who got in touch with me. He used to have a thriving vacation rental business on Airbnb and, one day, it all but disappeared. Why? Guests loved his rental and left stellar reviews. But Airbnb, in this case, changed the algorithm, and ever since this host has been struggling to get any reservations. He provided a loved rental, but the rental was in a somewhat isolated location where not many guests would have discovered it on their own and thus deemed less valuable by Airbnb.

In the past, when the FPG searched Airbnb for the nearest large city, in this case Seattle, his listing would appear as an option less than an hour away from the city center, out in the countryside. In the past, when an FPG searched Seattle, they would be shown not only listings in the city, but also a few popular destinations just outside the city limits. Now that same search only highlights the most popular neighborhoods within the city. He became nearly invisible overnight. What Airbnb bringeth, they can taketh away. Yes, the guests may be flowing today. If you're completely reliant on an OTA, however, they could change one of a million things, and your business could dry up.

And, finally, when you create a direct booking website, you are creating a more diversified business. Any business eventually realizes to diversify revenue streams is to limit risk. On top of that, making your rental more business-like has value when you go to sell. Having a website with 5,000 monthly visits, an email list of 1,000 prior guests, and a social media account with 10,000 followers has real-world value.

6.4 YOUR DIRECT BOOKING WEBSITE

Do you remember MySpace? I do. At first, I only heard the name over and over. I asked a friend, and his explanation was brilliantly simple and relatable. "It's like AIM but better." AIM was a simple computer messaging app created in 1997 by AOL. My first experiences with the internet was from AIM where I'd not speak a word to a girl at school out of shyness and go back home, log on, and talk to them all. Everybody used it.

Think of your direct booking website as your OTA listing but better. That means it has much more flexibility and customization of the guest journey as soon as they find it.

Remember: I said that I'd give you more than enough resources to succeed with a direct booking strategy, but I'd also call out the things you must do. Interestingly, this is *not* one of those requirements. If you're still not sure if you want to do this or how much you want to commit to it, then

I recommend you create an Instagram or Facebook account. Start there.

Don't get me wrong, a website *is* essential. It's where you'll accept payment and what will give the guest the confidence to send money to a stranger online. But it also takes time and money to manage, and I don't want you starting down that path until you are committed. Until you'll do it right.

After all, it's how I started. I created an Instagram, a Facebook, a YouTube, and a Twitter account assuming that I could drive interest to those social media accounts and then field inquiries from people who were interested. Boy, was I wrong about that! I'm in one of those moments where you look back at yourself in the past and think about how naive you were!

It's not that it wouldn't work. It's just hard and inefficient. I answered so many messages and had so many conversations with fake FPGs. These people had no intention of booking but started up a message anyway.

Is it available?

How much?

What's the cancellation policy?

The same questions, over and over. I've even had weeks-long text conversations leading to nothing.

Often the potential guest just wasn't sure if I was legit. And I want to emphasize that I had a professional and STR specific YouTube and an active Instagram. You could even search my name and find additional personal details on me, yet all of this still wasn't enough for some people to know that certainly I was not a scammer. And that's fair because everything I just told you is from my perspective. I know that I'm not a scammer, but I never once decided to put myself in the guests' shoes.

Quick aside: I'm about to go into specific details about my journey into the direct booking world. And, I'm going to do that because I know you are likely to follow a similar path as me, especially if I simply fast-forwarded to the end and told you to get a direct booking website. I want you to *feel* my pain and decide to avoid it by not doing exactly what I did. Let me explain.

In the back of my mind, I kinda always knew that I needed a direct booking website, but I delayed because I wanted to create the Picasso of such sites and didn't yet know how to execute it.

So, I took the easy way first, and I got a "dumb" website, dumb because it did not accept payment. My idea was to test the interest. I thought, to start, I could manually charge the guests who wanted to book. I did that for a period of time until I could no longer take it.

With my "dumb" website, some of those who did want to book ended up backing out once they learned my website didn't collect payment. "Oh, cool, you want to send me money? Just send it to my personal bank account, and I promise...." These prospective guests were not comfortable that I was so lax about everything. No contract, no booking confirmation, no nothing really besides the word of a stranger (me).

My—flawed—thinking was that I wanted to avoid unnecessary, extra work. A contract, syncing calendars, accepting payments, vetting guests, security deposits, ugh. I just want things to be simple! Little did I know that these systems already existed, that I didn't have to reinvent the wheel.

This all brings us to our first key point: **creating a feeling of trust on your direct booking website is paramount**. Throughout the website creation process and the overall direct booking strategy, keep front and center *why* the guest would book on the OTA versus book direct with you. The guest is incentivized to book on an OTA because it feels more secure and trustworthy, and their payment details are already stored there (so more convenient).

The realization that I needed a "smart" website set in rather quickly. I did my research about who makes the best direct booking websites and found a few good ones, but, yet again,

I decided to go it alone. First, because I wanted that Picasso. Second, because I wanted to learn things on my own.

The Belmonte Penthouse Direct Booking Website

SCAN ME

To sum up, I'm very happy with the end result, but I also used a lot of time learning things for which tried and tested solutions already existed. You don't have to reinvent the wheel, so let's explore that. Here, by the way, is what my "Picasso" looks like.

I learned that an FAQ section will decrease the amount of time you spend responding to inquiries because visitors have similar questions.

And direct booking websites come with a unique phenomenon: unlike the OTAs' listing page, visitors actually read the website.

I learned that you need to clearly and repeatedly communicate the benefits of booking direct in order to convince the visitor to book with you.

The benefits can be anything from an early check-in, free ride from the airport, guaranteed best rate, luggage storage, or free cancellation. Anything that sweetens the deal. You don't have to actually change anything. Maybe your check-in time is 3pm currently on the OTA. Change it to 5pm on the OTA and advertise a 3pm check-in on your direct booking website. Or maybe you already offer luggage storage. Simply advertise it as a benefit exclusively for direct bookings.

I learned about a plugin which automatically shows the most recent reviews gathered from the OTAs, review websites, and Google. Such content is an essential piece in building the trustworthiness of the direct booking website. I also learned that showing some 4-star reviews actually increases website credibility.

I learned that you should be highlighting any rewards your rental has won as it increases the trust factor and shows off that other people are looking and booking. Interestingly, on OTAs, this strategy is not necessary as the platform and how it was built acts as the trust factor.

I learned that you should be capturing emails from as many visitors as possible because almost no one is ready to make a booking immediately. With that email, you can market to them and their network in the future. We'll learn about 'lead magnets' which incentivize guests to give you their contact info in *Chapter 6.12 Email and Text Marketing.*

And, the black hole that gave me the biggest headache and wasted the most amount of time was solved in finding the right booking engine plugin that allows the guest to search for availability and complete the check-out process.

A smooth booking process, just like with the OTAs, is crucial to creating trust on your website, the trust that gives the guest the confidence to complete the booking. This is where I lost the most direct bookings because there's nothing that scares off a potential guest more than an unsecure-looking checkout process.

Everything from syncing the calendars to showing correct availability to collecting an initial deposit to charging for extra guests to a smooth and professional checkout experience—each step of the process created a new issue I had to fix.

And fix and learn, I did. It might come as no surprise to you that I also lost a lot of reservations in the meantime.

Probably not coincidentally, once my website was mostly bug-free (after months of trial and error), I started getting more direct bookings. I remember the first hands-free deposit I got for a reservation. Money just appeared in my account; it was magic! These days I'm over 50% direct booked.

If I could go back, would I have done it the same way? That's a resounding, hell no!

What would I do instead? I would have used one of the existing solutions and saved myself 100 hours of unnecessary work. It provided me no benefit to learn this on my own except for being able to more intelligibly write about my pain here. Did you feel my pain?

A proper existing solution is one built for vacation rental websites. This is important. You do not want to hire a random website developer without experience building a vacation rental website just as you wouldn't want to hire some random person off the street to babysit your kids. Doing this was the root of many, if not all, my problems...ahem, excuse me... my learnings.

There are two existing solutions. One solution is to go with the direct booking website included with your PMS provider. Many are decent, some should be avoided, and one I've found so far does a great job. Find them in the Deal Sheet. The benefit here is that the site-builder tool is included with the cost of the PMS subscription, and the booking plugin will work well. The downside is the actual website won't be as professionally *optimized* and, thus, will not convert as highly as a specially-built vacation rental website.

When I talk about conversion in terms of the website, I'm referring to the sum total power of the website's layout and features plus the information shown to the visitor to inspire interest in the property and confidence in completing the booking through payment.

When building a website, you want to leverage your advantages. Can you think of some of the advantages a direct booking website has over an OTA? One is more personalized communication. Your vacation rental website should have a live chat or direct to WhatsApp button for your visitors to ask any final questions before making a booking. Another leverageable advantage is video or 3D images. You'll want to incorporate one of these into your website when possible.

The other option you have is to go with a specialist who builds vacation rental websites for a living. You would then connect that website to your PMS. There are a few benefits here. First, the website is custom to your needs. A custom-built website has limitless features of your choosing. Second, it incorporates all of the elements needed to convert the visitor into a guest. Third, if you decide to change your PMS, you can take the website with you.

I don't want to underemphasize these points. Your direct booking website is where you'll point all your social media and web traffic to. Whether the guest first sees you on an OTA, social media, or Google, they will ultimately land on your website to learn more and complete the booking.

As mentioned above, there's nothing wrong with the website function included on your existing PMS, especially to start out. Or, maybe you've learned from my experience and want to skip to the finale which is the custom vacation rental website from an experienced developer.

In the Deal Sheet of the bonus items under "Direct Bookings" you will find my two recommendations, one PMS tool and one custom-built. If you decide to go with the custom-built website, you can book a free call to learn more. While they build you a real gem tailored to your needs, they also guide and teach you how to get those bookings coming in—and guarantee to refund your money plus

Bonus Item – Deal Sheet

SCAN ME

$200 (exclusive to readers) if you haven't made back your investment with them in the first year. If you decide to buy from them, they have doubled the standard discount if you mention "Profitable Properties".

6.5 SEARCH ENGINE OPTIMIZATION (SEO)

Although a separate strategy entirely, SEO is closely related to the website strategy.

SEO has to do with how well you rank on a search engine for the keyword that is being searched. It's *similar* to how well your listing ranks on an OTA.

If you were to type *The Belmonte Penthouse* into your favorite search engine, you would see my direct booking website, Google My Business page, and branded YouTube, Instagram, Facebook, Twitter accounts. "The Belmonte Penthouse" is the keyword, and I'm *optimized* to appear for it on Google.

SEO is broken down into two categories: on-page and off-page. On-page is further broken down into technical SEO like navigation and website load speed and non-technical SEO like the keywords and content. Off-page has to do with backlinks from social media, forums, and other websites that are pointing back—linking to—your website. Backlinks, especially from reputable websites, tell the search engine that you have a valuable website and should rank high when someone searches for a keyword that you're targeting. That's easier said than done, significantly easier.

And, you can probably forget about most of this already. Your website developer will do the basic on-page SEO so that search engines see your website. Today this is a basic service. Anything more than targeting your specific brand name will not be time wisely spent unless you have a very large portfolio of rentals where you may want to target broader keywords.

As you know, *The Belmonte Penthouse* is in Medellin, Colombia. If you were to search 'Medellin vacation rentals' I would not appear anywhere in the first dozen pages.

That's because as you get broader with a keyword, the competition increases, and you are less and less likely to rank on the first page without a finely-tuned strategy and healthy budget.

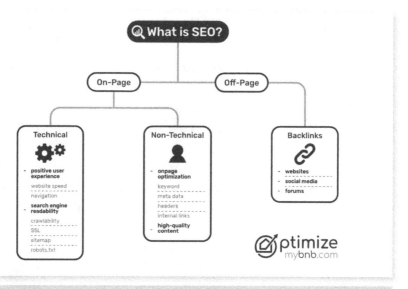

SEO is easy and hard at the same time. The above chart breaks it down into the three main parts.

You will be competing with the marketing budgets of Airbnb, Booking, VRBO, Kayak, and local hotels in the market who are all paying for ads. Paid ads are shown above organic, non-paid search results. Not a wise choice of our time or investment of our money.

I'm keeping this chapter short because I don't want you spending time trying to rank for broad keywords in your market if it's not going to yield any ROI. I want you focusing on the things that are most likely to get you direct bookings. Before I let you go, though, I can think of one wise use of your time where leveraging SEO is beneficial.

And that is writing blog posts. If someone is coming to your market, they probably will search something like 'things to do in [your market]', 'best restaurants in [your market]', 'is [your market] safe', etc. prior to looking for accommodation. Depending on your market, you may be able to rank for these keywords. I've written blogs about the best restaurants, best nightlife, best coffee shops, and best activities to do in Medellin. I also am able to send these to my guests who undoubtedly will ask about dining, nightlife, activities, etc. On top of that, I create a social media story, tag all the businesses I mentioned in the blog post, and about half of them repost my story. To be clear, this is not a highly converting strategy but instead a way to leverage something that you're already doing. This strategy falls into the optional category. If it doesn't sound like something you'd do, then don't.

6.6 SOCIAL MEDIA

Social media is interesting. Huge potential. One viral post could fill out your calendar for a year. And yet, it's unlikely to be a viable strategy because it's very, very competitive. It's not as simple as just showing up, posting some photos, then replying to comments.

You need to show up consistently for 30 to 60 days before the relevant social media platform algorithm starts to pay attention. That means posting at least daily. Why? You're not proven yet and, until you are, the platform would rather highlight their loyal creators. The last thing a social media platform wants to do is show you to a bunch of their users only for your account to go inactive in a month. And most accounts do go inactive within a month.

And let's face it. Is your space "Instagrammable"? It might be. But it probably isn't. That's not to say a social media strategy can't work for you, at least to some extent. Many FPGs will start their search for you here. But is it where our time is most wisely spent? Probably not. Nevertheless, we still need a social media presence, so let's figure out how to use those platforms most optimally.

It's easy and free to create a profile, and many tools allow you to send the same post to various platforms with the click of a button. Each platform adds a backlink to your website. But how much time you want to spend here depends on how serious you are about this strategy working for your situation. I am assuming for the purposes of this chapter that you want a social media presence, but do not want to make it a key focus of your direct booking strategy. That's how I do it.

To start, you should post consistently for a few weeks just to get some content up there so the profile doesn't look empty and brand new—and so you quickly learn what people do and do not respond to. After you have a dozen or so posts, posting monthly is sufficient. Our goal here is to show any guest landing on a social media platform that it's active and current.

Regarding content, you can post photos of your space and reviews. Photos communicating the experience are great, too. The sunsets, the firepit, the hammock, the wildlife you see in the backyard. If you get stuck, search for content ideas online in the tons of blogs and videos giving ideas. Search "social media content ideas."

One potentially worthwhile idea is to run a promotion with a local bar or restaurant that is also active on social media. Exchange a night or two free to their audience in exchange for an equivalently valued gift card. They will post to their social media channels pointing to you. This gives you exposure to a new audience for no cost.

All of your social media platforms should have a link pointing to your direct booking website. They should also highlight the benefits of booking direct. You should include a promo code to further incentivize direct bookings. This can be advertised in the profile text or in the profile banner or cover photo. "Use code *INSTAGRAM* when booking direct for 15% off." Of course, you can raise your prices to compensate. This 'promo' code should be everywhere so that most bookings are coming with the "discount".

Let's briefly examine the most popular social media channels.

Instagram. Younger audience between 18 and 40 years old. Open to inspiration for travel ideas. Shorter stays. More unique accommodations do better here.

TikTok. Similar to Instagram but claims an even younger crowd and specializes in short-form video content.

LinkedIn. Professionals. Not here for travel inspiration, but can be leveraged. More standard spaces are acceptable. More weekly stay interest or mid-week stay interest for business travel.

Facebook. Older crowd. Generally longer-term stays. Guests come here to find accommodations via the groups where you can directly post your website. Search for your city plus vacation rentals or Airbnb.

Twitter. Guests are not here looking for accommodation, but there is an active community of vacation rental experts and real estate investors of all varieties posting valuable insights and responsive to your comments on their tweets. In the bonus items, I will provide a list of the best vacation rental/real-estate Twitter accounts to follow. I'll update that regularly.

Pinterest. A hidden gem of mostly visual content. Visitors come here specifically looking for travel inspiration or information about a travel destination. Boasting 200 million users with nearly 80% of them female.

Let's talk about influencers. You can seek them out, or they will seek you out with a message asking for a discounted stay in exchange for content on their platforms. Beware. There is only one way to benefit from this, and many ways to waste your money. I have done this without success. I no longer exchange stays or discounts for mention and suggest that you do not unless you know what you're doing.

I gave a fitness influencer with 500,000 followers a 50% discounted stay which was $1,300 off in exchange for some content, but nothing more. That decision led to zero additional bookings, and the influencer didn't fulfill all promised duties.

If you decide to go this route, be sure to verify that the followers and engagements are real. Verify the demographics of the followers and how likely they are to have interest in your market for a vacation. Specify exactly what is required of the creator (how many posts, stories, videos, etc.) and that you own or can repost the original content on your own social media.

This is not where your time or money is going to be best spent. The best success stories I've heard of is when a real influencer makes an unsolicited video. After all, real influencers are very wealthy and probably not wasting their time asking for discounts. If you want content, pay for it, or encourage your guests to create some and tag you.

That is called user-generated content. It's when your existing guests create videos and other content to post to their social media accounts. You want to ensure your current guests know that you have an active social media account. I let them know upon check-in. I also leave business cards throughout the apartment.

6.7 YOUTUBE

YouTube is the second most-used search engine after Google. Similar to social media, huge potential, but unlikely to move the needle. Nevertheless, you should create an account with a couple video walkthroughs of your space. They can be professional or with your smartphone. You can get creative here if you wish. Who knows, maybe you realize that you enjoy making videos like I did.

One of my video ideas to show the space was me walking through the apartment turning off all the lights. Throughout the home I have dimmable and accent lighting. It looks great at night. I'm showing off an amenity while showing the space in a unique way. I thought it was a fun idea. I did it. The content can be used for all social media accounts.

Check out *The Belmonte Penthouse* YouTube channel for inspiration.

The Belmonte Penthouse YouTube Channel

SCAN ME

You can also film things unrelated to your actual space. How about the best views or trails in town? Anything the guest may be searching for prior to their trip to get your accommodation in front of them. Your videos might also show up on Google for those searches. Even if they don't, they'll show up when a user searches your brand name, taking up more value space in the search results.

On my personal YouTube, I film reviews of local hotels. During the video I slyly mention *The Belmonte Penthouse* which happens to be in the same city. It's just another strategy I'm trying out.

Again, always advertising the incentives for direct bookings and always with links back to your website.

6.8 GOOGLE GOOGLE GOOGLE

This is one of the must-dos! Create a Google My Business page. That way you will show up with a unique listing when someone searches for your brand name.

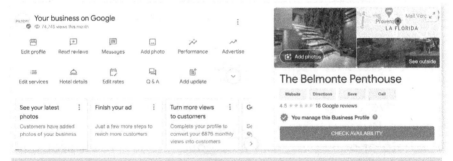

Note the amount of views I'm getting. I'll reveal why in this chapter.

Next, you want to get shown in the vacation rentals section of a Google map search. This comes up when a user is searching for vacation rentals in your city. You want to appear here, but you will not if you're only listed on the major OTAs.

To get listed on Google Vacation Rentals you will have to list on a vacation rental search engine. I use BluePillow, though there are many.

There's another unique strategy I want to share with you. I listed *The Belmonte Penthouse* as a hotel on Google. The strategy here was to be the elephant in the room. My listing has reviews, but the photos don't look like a hotel.

To be listed as a hotel, the website visitor must be able to complete the check-out process on your website, and so you need to have availability and pricing shown and updated, which you'll share with Google.

Check out the views I am getting from the above screenshot from Google. Lots!

Finally, you want to encourage guests to leave reviews for you on your Google listing. Offer them a perk like a free night stay on their next reservation or some kind of discount. Say that you run a promotion where you choose one reviewer each quarter for a free night stay. This isn't a bad strategy for the OTAs either. After all, positive reviewers are less likely to leave a review so the best practice is how to encourage more of them to leave a review any and every way you can.

6.9 PAID ADVERTISING

Paid advertising is interesting because it guarantees reservations. But you have to know what you're doing and without the help of an expert, who also costs money, you'll probably spend a lot of time and money here, too. This will probably not produce a meaningful ROI for your rental.

Nevertheless, in the name of completeness, I want to introduce you to this strategy.

First, keyword research is needed because you'll be targeting a keyword with your paid ad.

The title should start with something relevant to the search so the user immediately knows it's a relevant ad, followed by a benefit or two, followed with the brand name which ideally communicates something further than just a nice sounding name.

Medellin Rental | Daily Cleaning/Bfast | The Belmonte Penthouse

The description of the ad is where you list the additional benefits plus a CTA (call-to-action). You must suggest what you want the user to do. Book Now. Send message. Request more info.

Finally, be sure the link is trackable for extra data and insight into your campaign. I use a free website tool that does this at bit.ly.

The single best thing you can do when it comes to paid advertising is retargeting. When you pay for ads, you have two options. You can setup a 'lookalike' audience which are people who Google thinks are most likely to have interest in booking your rental. Or, you can pay to have your ad shown only to people who have already interacted in some way with your social media or website, which is called retargeting.

Retargeting will likely produce the highest ROI on your marketing dollars and makes sense because you can't expect someone to remember you after having visited your website once. There are various ways to setup a traditional retargeting campaign. For example, you can add a 'pixel' into your website that tracks the cell phone of anyone who came to your website. When they are browsing another eligible website, your ad will appear.

Traditional retargeting, though not super complex, is still somewhat involved.

However, there is a company that developed a hybrid retargeting tool that simplifies this process. The tool collects your guests' (and their visitors') data for later retargeting (with their permission) with an email or text campaign which we'll cover soon. For me, this is low-hanging fruit and a must for any direct booking strategy. You'll find them in the Deal Sheet listed under 'Retargeting'.

One more thing regarding paid ads before you decide to list on Booking.com.

When I did so, a paid advertisement started showing up at the top of search results for my brand name. Not cool because this paid result appears first and takes up a lot of the screen space.

You have two options. First is to not list on Booking.com, and thus they have no incentive to advertise for your brand name. If you list and unlist your property this will also remove the paid ad. Second, you can trademark your brand name. Upon doing this, anyone will be prevented from targeting that brand name via advertisements. You will have to submit a claim to Google against the paid ad and show proof of trademark, but it will get taken down, and it's not a cumbersome process.

Trademarking your name is not an intense process and is valid for 10 years.

After some additional research I learned another neat hack. Even if there was no competitor ad here, I might consider creating one anyway for my own brand name because organic results get 61% of clicks, but having an ad increases clicks to your brand by 27%.

6.10 LEVERAGING OTAS

The other day I got a reservation on Airbnb from a guest who told me they first tried to book direct. When I asked how, they told me that they sent a message to my Instagram. I was shocked because I check my Instagram messages often.

I didn't see it because this guest sent a message to my personal Instagram account which gets more activity, thus, more spam. His message was lost. I should have known better because my full name is visible on Airbnb.

I have the brand name *The Belmonte Penthouse* as the first words in the title, plus I have it in the first bit of text in the summary section with a CTA to check us out online.

I asked this guest, "did you read the text of the listing?"

"Yes."

I was shocked. How could this guest not have connected the dots? A learning opportunity, indeed.

> I was debating whether or not to include this section in the book or save it entirely for the course because it's a very powerful and efficient one. Everything I tell you here is allowed, at least today. But Airbnb pays attention to my content. It's been confirmed. Prior hosting hacks have been removed shortly after I published a video. Additional features appear in much the same way. Just last year, a multi-month pending resolution request was released days after I published a video. For good or bad, I'm on their radar. In 2019, Airbnb threatened to sue me related to my content.
>
> This is no gimmick. In order to preserve the most powerful hacks, as this one is, I will communicate them in a more private, targeted way to my audience.

The most efficient thing you can do to get direct bookings is to leverage the OTAs. They are just another source of traffic to your website. But you can't add in any links. This is not permitted.

What you can do is add in CTAs and your brand name. Your level of aggressiveness in terms of how you advertise your direct booking website is up to you. Even if the following strategies are allowed, you can understand the problem an OTA would have with them.

In no particular order, you can:

- Add brand name in the title, your profile photo, and/or in the text

- Brand your photos with your logo, but never contact information
- Add text in the summary portion or photo captions directing the viewer to video content you have on YouTube or your stellar reviews online

The savvy guest will figure it out.

Currently I say "Welcome to The Belmonte Penthouse by Daniel Rusteen. Check out our reviews online!" This gives the guest two ways to search me out as I have two active profiles. Will Airbnb disallow full names and brand names in the future? We'll see.

Never be pushy, either, both on the OTAs or when the guest is contacting you. If it feels like you have to convince the guest, throw in the towel. The guest either wants to book direct, or they don't. If they're unsure, they don't. There's nothing wrong with accepting a reservation on an OTA. If the guest is more comfortable doing that, tell them either way is fine with you. Then, go back to the drawing board and figure out why the guest was not comfortable booking with you. I, for one, understand that there will always be those guests who feel more comfortable using an OTA.

You can also leverage the OTAs in the review you leave for the guest. Be sure to mention your brand name and a little about it, including the city. "This review is from *The Belmonte Penthouse*, a luxury rental in Medellin." Or, "Thanks for staying with *The Belmonte Penthouse*, luxury rental in Medellin." You can also list your biggest incentive to book direct by saying, "Book direct for best rate guaranteed." Host reviews of guests are largely off the radar of OTAs, at least for now.

Here's a list of the large niche OTAS:

- Furnished Finders (30+ day STRs for traveling nurses & business professionals)
- Surf Holidays (world's leading surf holiday travel website)
- Bud and Breakfast (cannabis friendly)

- FlipKey (owned by TripAdvisor)
- HostelWorld (world's biggest budget accommodation provider)
- BringFido (dog-friendly rentals)
- Agoda (leading OTA for Asian markets, but pushing into USA and Europe)
- Despegar (leading OTA for Latin America)

The OTAs are now working for you.

6.11 ACTUALLY GETTING DIRECT BOOKINGS

The most efficient ways to get bookings are to leverage the OTAs, your network, your prior guests, and anyone who comes in contact with your brand. We've already talked about how to leverage the OTAs (profile, text, reviews, and photos) and your prior guests (retargeting tool). In the next chapter we'll talk about how to leverage anyone who encounters your brand.

In this chapter I'm going to share with you the most effective strategies besides the above to get additional direct bookings.

Leverage your existing network. I want you to think of family and friends and send them a message. Tell them about your rental. Even if they already know you have one—and don't assume they know, tell them. And call it a rental, not an Airbnb. Ask them if they know anyone who might need it. Ask them to keep your rental in mind. This is manual work, but it has the potential to get you direct bookings, especially as you're starting out.

If someone in your network mentions a good prospect, ask them to make an introduction or ask them for the contact information so that you can introduce yourself. Be sure to state up front how you got their number and why you are contacting the potential guest. Be very direct here.

When I did this, a friend who owns a medical company and had a client come down for a few days to receive treatment got in touch. Yesterday that client checked in to my rental for a 4-day reservation, Sunday to Wednesday, which are my slow nights.

This gave me the idea to reach out to other well-known medical facilities to offer my rental to those guests who prefer not to stay in a hotel. I'm making progress there, but it's already clear that leveraging my network led to a quicker conversion.

Always be specific about where you think your future guests are hanging out and concentrate your energies there. This is always better than generally spamming the internet and a better use of your time.

Let's get your creative juices flowing with some examples of how you can secure direct bookings.

Insurance Claims. When someone's home is damaged (fire, flood, storm, etc.), the homeowner makes an insurance claim and sometimes needs alternate accommodations during the repair process. Your time is better spent reaching out to smaller, boutique insurance companies.

Local sports leagues. Outside of professional sports, local sports welcome travelling teams, fans, and their families. There are various local and amateur sports leagues all year round.

Educational institutions. Not only schools and universities, but also adult education, language classes, culinary schools, private study programs, the list goes on. Colleges and universities, particularly, would love to be able to show off by putting up staff interviewees in quality accommodations and not your run-of-the-mill Best Western.

Religious institutions. Any nearby religious institution has people traveling to them for various reasons. You can also leverage their congregation to host incoming families. Talk about ideal guests!

Housing problems or transitions. If you sell your house, sometimes you cannot move into the next home right away. In this case a short-term accommodation is needed.

Construction sites. Be bold, and go up to someone onsite. The managers will normally be wearing something different than the construction workers. Or, be less bold and, look for the contractor name usually on the fence to get in touch directly with them.

Corporate housing. From local startups to big business, it's possible to offer your accommodation to employees visiting the offices nearby your rental. They may require additional insurance on your part, but these guests are generally a dream.

Medical staff. Hospitals, clinics, plastic surgery venues, dental specialists—they all have visiting patients, doctors, and staff in need of short-term accommodations. The great thing is, once one nurse has experienced your lovely STR, they recommend it to the next taking their place.

Hostels or boutique hotels. Even though they may be your competition, if they're full, why not offer your space which happens to be just down the street. Or maybe they have a larger group, but not enough accommodations. If your rental is nearby, especially within walking distance, this could be a feasible alternative over finding a new hotel. Ideally, you'll send them some business first.

Conferences. You can get in touch with the conference facilitator directly or keep your eye on the incoming conferences to offer up your suitable accommodation.

Travel companies, agents, or concierges. These local companies are servicing those who definitely need accommodations. They are likely to have an existing preferred accommodation list so you might need to sweeten the deal with a kickback. Money talks.

Real estate agents. Something that worked especially well for me was reaching out to real estate agents and offering them a referral fee. I know that many potential guests who would be interested in staying at my rental are coming to town for a few days to view real estate. As my space is high end, I searched out real estate agents who seem to be specializing in higher-end real estate. This also has the potential added bonus of generating interest for selling the apartment when the time comes.

Large Companies. Visiting employees or specialty consultants who stay for weeks or months are a staple of large companies. Contact the HR department who makes accommodation decisions.

For all of these, you need to find out who to get in contact with and ask to get on their preferred accommodations list. If that doesn't work so well, remember, money talks. Give whoever you're talking with an incentive like a commission.

6.12 EMAIL AND TEXT MARKETING

Before we jump in, let me touch on the "lead magnet" concept. A lead magnet is something you offer visitors to your website in exchange for their email so that you can stay in touch. These are typically called popups which you are familiar with as those sometimes-annoying boxes that pop up inviting you to share your email usually when you first visit a website. We're going to do the non-annoying version. You should try to entice visitors by offering them something of value like a special promotional discount code, a guide to the city, the Custom Guest Travel Itinerary, etc.

Or you could strategically place QR codes on-site offering something. On the fridge it could say "Don't want to cook?" When the guest scans the QR code, ask for their email/phone number and send them your blog post about the best restaurants in your neighborhood. Or send them a local foodie website or Instagram account.

Or, for local discounts on food delivery apps, "Scan me for $5 off [food delivery app]."

These applications usually offer a small discount for the new user and credit for you for referring new customers to the app.

Or, next to the front door, "Going out tonight?" The QR code can deliver a blog or video of your favorite nighttime venues. This allows you to get the contact information of the guests coming from the OTAs and any visitors.

On a personal note, I find it interesting how emails are the oldest and still the best piece of data for marketing. An email list is still so valuable.

And can be even more useful if you're a property manager or real estate agent where some of these prior guests may turn into future clients.

With that said, let's get into how best to leverage our emails and phone numbers.

This part is rather easy and just involves creating a series of *valuable* automated emails or text messages to be sent to people who have asked for you to contact them about your rental.

There are many software tools to help with this, some of them free. These tools are called CRM (customer relationship management) or email management/marketing software.

Email Marketing

If you decide to go with the custom-built vacation rental website partner, they will set you up with email management. The retargeting partner comes with this functionality built in, as well.

As for the content, let's cover that now. Here is a selection of emails you may choose to send to those website visitors who have expressed interest in staying in touch.

Subscription confirmation. Right away send out an email to this website visitor confirming their subscription to your email list. Say a little more about your accommodation, maybe link to a video on your YouTube. You can say a little more about your market or immediate neighborhood. You can attach the branded Custom Guest Travel Itinerary which they may even share, which you should encourage (it has your URL and branding on it). And don't forget to remind them of the benefits of booking direct.

Book direct. Not too far into the distant future send out an email reminding your guest that you still exist and of the benefits of booking direct. If providing a discount, it can be that same 15% discount you've been advertising on your social media channels. Even if this guest has already seen the discount, they've already forgotten or you can create a different promotion code. After two opened emails, their email provider will default your emails straight to their inbox (avoiding the spam or Google promotions folders).

Promotion. Offer the visitor a 'friends and family' discount. Again, it can be the same 15% we've been offering. Provide a promo code for use during the reservation check-out process. Include a couple photos of your space to remind the visitor of who you are.

Secret season. Everyone likes secrets. Whenever your low season is, send out an email a month or two before highlighting the benefits of booking your rental during low season. For example, if you're in a snowy destination, let the guest know about the all the additional activities they can do like snowshoeing, dog sledding, snowmobiling or ice fishing at discount rates and without the crowds.

Improvements. I recently bought a hand massager, remodeled the jacuzzi room, and made other improvements. I sent out an email to prior guests. When I added a Christmas tree, I let the email list know that I'm ready for the holidays. When I installed a whole home surround sound system, too. These are infrequent. Two or three times per year. Don't be annoying, but you want to create some kind of impression that lingers in the guest's mind whether they return or someone they know returns. If you haven't made any large improvements, how about a new blog or did you open a new social media channel with some cool videos? Did your city build out a new park or add something else you know your guests would be interested in? Maybe there's an upcoming music festival or event. All can be used for email material.

Send the following email to reserving guests:

Anniversary. A couple months before the one-year booking anniversary, send out this email reminding the guest of their trip last year. You can also remind them of the returning guest discount and the other book direct benefits. Also add in the improvements you've made over the past year.

With all emails, be careful about including too many graphics or using subjects with capital letters. This might land your email in the spam folder. Simple emails are fine and even more personal in these cases.

Text Marketing

Text messaging is only used with current and past guests and their visitors. We collect this information via the retargeting partner when they connect to the Wi-Fi or scan that QR code I mentioned above. Here are the texts you can send.

Upon signing up, send out a text with a link to your digital guidebook or to one of your social media channels. Always sign your text at the beginning or end.

Belmonte Penthouse: [text message content]
[text message content] – Belmonte Penthouse

Upon check-out, send a feedback text. One of the reasons I love the retargeting provider is because their software makes all negative feedback private. If the guest answers with anything less than five stars, they're asked why and this is sent to you. If the guest rates five stars, then they're provided a link to Google for the public review. This is all automated.

As with emails and texts, I urge you not to bombard your list with too many. Popular marketing advice recommends sending as many as one email every day. I suppose this is the best practice, but I'm at odds with this marketing tactic. And it's probably why open rates are only a few percentage points. Nearly half of all recipients open my emails. I send one email per month. You decide.

And that wraps up everything there is to know about direct booking! Ok. Well, definitely not everything, but it pretty much sums up my current understanding. At the very least, I hope I've given you a solid foundation to build on.

In summary, here are the must-do's:

- Build a direct booking website
- Sign up for a Google My Business map location
- Sign up for at least one social media channel
- Add your brand name into your OTA listing
- Contact your network to start generating direct bookings
- Setup a retargeting system (optional, but recommended)

As I end this section, I have a public service announcement for those who will go down the book direct route: make it just as, if not more, pleasurable for guests to book direct than to use an OTA. The great thing about OTAs is that they got rid of slum lords.

A slum lord is someone who offers the basics and creates bad experiences for guests. The only thing that will serve to do is create more demand for the OTAs. Banishing slum lords is probably one of the main reasons the big OTAs became so popular in the first place, to hold property owners account-able which they've done a fantastic job of. Even though a review on an OTA isn't at stake with a direct booking, and it will be easy to relax your hospitality standards, please don't do it. Don't be a slum lord with your direct bookings.

Part 7

BONUS CONTENT: QUESTIONS AND ANSWERS

This book has been quite fun to write,
Six months it took, it's been a delight.
But now it's time to get back to the grind,
Sipping coffee, hitting the gym to unwind,
Cooking my dinners, helping STRs shine,
These are my details, oh so fine.

But wait, there's more, I can't resist,
An 'extra' section, you get the gist.
I'm enjoying myself, that's for sure,
Sharing answers that are quick to lure.
I'm writing them down, 'cause I'm feelin' randy,
These questions are quick, they're very handy.
The most common and powerful to behold,
Answers that, I hope, will leave you feeling bold.

7.1 HOW CAN I IDENTIFY A PROBLEM GUEST IN ADVANCE?

Sometimes you can't. Let's just be honest. Don't beat yourself up about it. Many hosts don't leave reviews for bad guests, so that doesn't help. Airbnb is known to delete negative reviews from guest profiles, and many guests just create new profiles anyway. So, what do we do?

The highest risk reservations are those that come from guests with incomplete profiles who book with little notice. If you receive this type of reservation, you should ask questions and judge how the guest responds. If their profile is not complete, ask them to complete it because you like to know who you're renting to. These are not foolproof solutions. Instead, you're making inferences based on the available data. If the profile is lacking a photo, text, where they're from, verifications, and everything else, it means the guest did the bare minimum in filling it in. It's a warning sign and to be considered with the following points. By the way, if you want to see whether or not they have a profile photo (Airbnb blocks this data on inquiries), just copy the URL of the guest profile into an incognito window in your browser, and it will appear.

If the guest didn't verify their ID, ask them to. If they say they don't have time and are in a rush, I wouldn't accept. You can ask them why they're coming to town. The answers don't matter as much as their attitude towards the questions and the grammar of the sentence. Yes, I even pay attention to the grammar as another data point in my decision to accept the reservation, and it works very well. This is based on my experience, but be sure to differentiate if the guest doesn't speak English as a native. This is often easy to identify. My goal is to forego revenue in favor of avoiding bad guests.

If the content of the message is suspect, be on guard and ask a few extra questions. A suspect message is curt, contains spelling and grammar errors, or is overly wordy. If it sounds off, be wary.

Some example questions you can ask are:

- What brings you to town?
- Have you used Airbnb before?
- Are you already in X city?
- Where are you coming from?

If I'm uneasy about a reservation, I will mention to the booking guest that my next-door or downstairs neighbor keeps an eye on the rental and sometimes comes by to say hello to judge their reaction. This is all bad if you're a guest with bad intentions because this neighbor represents a risk for you. As a last resort, you can do a live check-in. If a different person shows up, if more people than stated on the reservation show up, or if they're acting sketchy, then you should be on standby for the reservation.

I screen guests on my own, but I recognize some hosts want extra protection, especially if they are taking direct bookings. If you want extra security, refer to the Deal Sheet under 'Guest Screening' for my recommendation.

7.2 HOW TO DEAL WITH PROBLEM GUESTS AND AVOID BAD REVIEWS?

There are two types of bad guests. The first type complains about the space. The second type breaks the rules by throwing a party, bringing pets or extra guests, or breaking something.

If it's the first type of bad guest, ask yourself: are *you* the problem? Seriously. To know if you're the problem, think back to the last issue, and ask yourself if you approached it as solvable or did you blame the guest?

I find that many of the bad guest issues are actually caused by bad hosts. Ask yourself honestly if the guest has a legitimate complaint. "The customer is always right" holds true in the STR space. In these instances, you should do three things. Express your understanding of the issue. Tell the guest your actions to solve it. Be overly communicative.

No matter how small the issue is from your perspective, the guest is telling you because they see it as a problem. You also want to keep the guest feeling like it's okay to share their feedback with you. It's truly a beautiful thing that a customer will so readily tell you what you need to do to improve. Never cut off feedback communication. And never, ever, ever tell the guest that, say, internet service has never been a problem *before*. It is now, and you need to solve it!

Empathize with the guest. "I'm so sorry, that's not acceptable!" Amplify the issue. That way the guest feels like they're being heard. And tell them what you're doing. "I have already talked with my cleaner, and we have a meeting set for tomorrow to review our cleaning process."

Bad guests are best vetted up front as discussed in the prior answer. If the same type of problem guest keeps reserving your home, highlight the relevant house rule in the summary text so the guest is more likely to see it prior to completing a reservation. If this happens to you, first, recommunicate the house rules to the guest via the platform so that there is a record. There's a 50% likelihood they didn't know and will correct their behavior. Second, record any and all proof that you can. Always leave the guest an honest, negative review. Airbnb is known to remove both negative reviews, guest's and host's, as a way to mediate issues.

A powerful tactic to avoid bad reviews is having a co-host (or someone who pretends to be) who can come in over the top to mediate. Sometimes the host and the guest just aren't getting along, or there's already too much bad blood. It's really powerful to have a third party come in, show empathy to the guest, and act as the voice of reason. This co-host is especially powerful if they have in-person contact with the guest. It's really hard for a guest to negatively review a human being, which is why I suggest you show up on check-out day, maybe even with a small gift, to briefly introduce yourself and apologize if needed. It's very easy to be mad at a digital screen, but meeting an actual, nice human is relatable and will decrease the likelihood of a negative review.

In my particular situation, I have various people who are in contact with the guest besides myself: the cleaner, the concierge, and the doorman. If I feel a negative review is coming, I will have one of them (whoever had the best connection with the guest) reach out so the guest knows that a negative review would hurt the business and, in turn, hurt them. This works phenomenally well.

7.3 HOW SHOULD I WRITE A NEGATIVE REVIEW FOR MY GUEST?

Neither host nor guest see the review until either both have written a review, or one has written a review *and* 14 days have passed since check-out (the maximum time allowed to leave a review). **If you write a review, and the guest does not, you actually have 48 hours to edit it.** The prior information is Airbnb specific. The following information is for all OTAs.

I recommend, in all cases, you write an honest, unemotional, and concise review. Stick to the facts and leave out anything biased. Just be honest! I hear from hosts that they feel bad writing a negative review, but you shouldn't feel bad about honesty. Don't be accusatory, don't be offensive, just be honest. If you really can't bring yourself to write an honest, negative review then a concise review works. A two-word review 'good guest' will give most hosts the impression the guest was okay.

Alternatively, if you wanted to call attention to your review being negative, you can start it with "NEGATIVE REVIEW" or "NOT RECOMMENDED". Help out future hosts. If the guests left everything filthy, say that in the review. Your fellow hosts want to know. Same if they invited extra guests, if they didn't follow some house rules, or if they checked out an hour late. These are *facts* for the review. You can still give the guest a 5-star review if you'd like. But in the text, be honest. On Airbnb, at the end of the guest review, you can recommend them or not, and the guest won't see this rating.

Remember my bad guest story in the direct booking section? Here was my review. I think you'll agree it is not emotional, just the facts. I checked, and it's still on his profile. Once you bring emotion into the review, it's more likely to get removed.

Guest review for Sean's group of 4 people for 4 nights in Medellín. Overall: ★★★ / Not Recommended I've never met Sean or the other memeber's of his group personally. In their first message they asked for a discount. When I declined, they ended up booking at the stated rate. Sean asked if a ride from the airport is included (it is not), but I told him that I'd send one and pay for it to pick up his group late at night (they arrived to the Airbnb at 1am). I sent the nicest SUV I could find. Sean did not say thank you. They drank $102 worth of beverages I sell in the Airbnb and upon checkout told my cleaner they thought the price was too much. They gave her $12. They used the same drive to the airport upon departure and did not pay him (I ended up paying so my concierge doesn't have to). My concierge told me they thought everything was overpriced. They did eat all of the ice cream I include for free. And they ate some of the snake I also provide for free. My cleaner cooked them special breakfast due to (I believe) them being Jewish. They did not give a tip to the cleaner who is there everyday to cook and clean. They overflowed the hot tub (thankfully not too much) by not turning off the water soon enough. For these, reasons I'm uninteresetd in hosting this group again and am thankful this is the only negative review I've left after 26 reservations. <u>read less</u>

 Daniel, California, United States
Joined in 2013

Minus the typos, you can see I removed all my negative emotional feelings of them out and just wrote the facts of his stay and why I don't want to host them again. Other hosts can decide for themselves based on the facts.

7.4 WHEN SHOULD I SUBMIT A CLAIM FOR GUEST DAMAGE?

Most of the time you should not. Here's my rule: If the damage is less than 10% of the total reservation cost, I consider it a cost of doing business. That's my rule. If I think the guest will reimburse and still not review me negatively (the damage is obvious), then I'll ask right away. Otherwise, I'll wait as long as I can. Because I make a point to ask the guest to tell me of any damage during the check-in, they usually inform me in advance.

I find it interesting how we have regular insurance that we pay for, and we avoid submitting claims. But when we get "free" insurance, we submit more claims. Be sure that the OTAs track this. If you're submitting small claims like for a broken lockbox, you shouldn't. Instead, save it for a real emergency. Side note: don't be a host who doesn't replace things then submits a guest claim when the guest happens to be in the house when something old breaks. Replace/repair amenities before they break.

7.5 SHOULD I APPLY FOR AIRBNB PLUS?

Airbnb Plus is a subset of quality-controlled listings with an application process and an exclusivity clause such that you are only allowed to list on Airbnb. The draw of this program is promised higher rates and occupancy. After viewing the requirements to join, you should only consider the program if your listing is already at that level without you having to do too much extra.

There are some disadvantages to Airbnb Plus, like losing control of how your information is presented. There's also a risk of pickier guests who expect more because it's very obvious they're paying for something extra. In my experience, Airbnb Plus works for about half those who try it. You should have an established baseline of revenue going into it to measure results against in order to better judge if it is worth the continued effort.

7.6 SHOULD I MAKE MY SPACE PET-FRIENDLY?

If you can, yes! This one change has potential to increase your occupancy and rates overnight. That's because there's an undersupply of quality short-term rentals that allow pets. If you want longer reservations, this is a must, as people traveling longer are more likely to bring their pet. If you go this route, you should be providing extra amenities for pet owners like a food and water bowl, indoor pee pads, some toys, poop bags, a comfy place for the pup to sleep, etc. You can rely more on prior reviews to ensure the owner is responsible for their pet. Upon check-in or prior you can ask the guest to sign an additional contract and collect a security deposit. Though you can't collect an additional security deposit on the OTAs, the recommended tool in the Deal Sheet under 'Guest Screening' does provide this service.

7.7 HOW CAN I CONNECT WITH OTHER RENTAL OWNERS IN MY AREA?

Search Facebook groups for "short-term rental/Airbnb/STR [your city]" or the closest big city. The more niche you can go, the more valuable these groups will be for you. Before posting to the group or forum, please perform a search within the group. Maybe your question has already been asked and answered, saving you precious time.

A Google search is always a great place to start, something like 'airbnb host community [your city]'. You could also try popular forums. The most popular that I know of is www.airhostsforum.com. On Airbnb.com, hosts have started hundreds of Facebook groups by location, but you already know that because you follow my YouTube channel (I announced this years ago). If you didn't know, it's going to be located on the menu in your hosting dashboard or you can search something like 'Airbnb Local Host Club' or 'Airbnb connect with hosts near me'. Even the smaller cities have hundreds of members in these official Airbnb groups.

7.8 IS DANNY *JUST* THE BEST?

Why, thank you. I'd like to take this opportunity to personally invite you to leave a review. I genuinely hope I've been able to return 10 times the cost of your time and money in value and future STR success. As it relates to reviews, you already know the importance they have as a host. As an indie author, they might be even more important for me. Every review counts. Even if you don't want to write anything (though written reviews are more heavily weighted in the Amazon search algorithm), you can still select a star rating only, and I would appreciate it deeply. Think about this. The best books on Amazon have tens of thousands of reviews. My last book sold 50,000 copies and it has nearly 800 reviews. **Imagine if my little self-published book got 10,000 reviews.** It would be a dream come true. I know it's not your dream, but I'll shave my head and donate $10,000 to the organization of your choice (I'll send out a poll to those on my email list). Please make my dream come true. You can do that. I'd like you to review the book now. Thank you so much in advance!

Review *Profitable Properties* On Amazon

SCAN ME

7.9 HOW HARD WILL IT BE FOR ME TO RETURN TO A 4.90 IF I HAVE A 4.80 RATING?

That depends on how many reviews you currently have. But it's not going to be easy.

If you have only 10 reviews (nine 5-star and one 3-star), it will take you a further 10 consecutive 5-star reviews. If you have 50 reviews (45 5-star, three 4-star, two 3-star, and one 1-star), it will take you 45 consecutive 5-star reviews to return to a 4.90.

Many hosts are curious if they should just start fresh with a new listing. But the issue might not be with the listing, it might be with the hosting. If you create a new listing, would you return to your unfavorable rating after the same number of reviews? If so, think about first overhauling your hosting strategies and or improving the physical space.

In the bonus items, I have created a Google spreadsheet (tab titled "Airbnb Rating Analysis") where you can enter in your current reviews to find out how many more you need to increase your rating.

7.10 DO I NEED TO COMMUNICATE WITH MY GUEST ON AIRBNB?

Airbnb says that if you communicate with the guest outside of the platform

> **"** you lose the protections of our cancellation and refund policies, Host damage protection, Host liability insurance, Terms of Service, Payments Terms of Service, and other safeguards."[6]

That's pretty clear, right? They also say it's "important that you communicate only through the Airbnb message thread **until you have a confirmed Airbnb reservation.**"[7] [emphasis added] Well, shucks.

To be safe, it's best to communicate on Airbnb. Note, however, that if things go wrong, Airbnb does consider evidence from texts and on messaging apps. Just make sure that the phone number is associated with your account and the same for the guest's phone number.

7.11 SHOULD I BUY ADDITIONAL INSURANCE?

Yes. Specifically, short-term vacation rental insurance. Insurance provided on the OTAs is not actually insurance. In the Deal Sheet, I'll provide my recommended STR insurance provider who offers the correct type of insurance. Here I want to list out some common terms you'll come upon through the process:

Dwelling/Replacement Cost Coverage. This is the cost to rebuild your home in the event of a total loss.

---

[6] https://www.airbnb.com/help/article/209
[7] https://www.airbnb.com/help/article/1121

Other Structures Coverage. This covers features not part of your main home like fences, pools, or a detached garage.

Household Furnishings. The personal property inside the home.

Loss of Use (aka Fair Rental Value). Income protection. This kicks in when the home becomes uninhabitable due to damage.

Per Occurrence Premises. Liability coverage if the guest were to injure themselves while in your home. This will be the highest dollar amount listed on your policy (typically $1 million), but it won't cost much extra due to the low likelihood of occurrence.

Deductible. The amount you will pay prior to your insurance kicking in. The higher the deductible, the lower the monthly premium. If you use insurance like a worst-case scenario coverage, then a higher deductible makes sense. Doing this would mean you'd have to resolve the small issues on your own.

If you're a property manager, you need to be listed as additional insured on the property owner insurance.

7.12 DOES MY HOSTING PROFILE MATTER?

It doesn't until it does. Similar to text, the guests who decide they want to know more about the host are towards the end of their buying journey. Maybe it's down to a few listings, all of which look similar. One of the things the guest can do is view your hosting profile. So how do we *optimize* it? There's nothing overly fancy to do here. Write about your additional expertise as a local. I say how I'm very familiar with the area and ready to help with their itinerary. I also try to make myself seem similar to my FPG. People like people who they feel are similar to them. I list my favorite countries, and they just so happen to be where many of my FPGs are coming from. If you have extra services, you can also say so here. Make it seem like the guest isn't just booking your space, but they also get access to you, your knowledge, your local connections.

It's common that hosts or property managers want to look professional by adding a logo or company name to their profile. I suggest you avoid this. Most likely, it's not giving you any benefit. I'm doubtful any guest is booking your space because of a professional looking logo. After all, on Airbnb, the profile photo isn't even visible on P2. You are raising the guest expectations by presenting yourself as a professional company. And for what? Nothing. Big brands are only valuable because of all the goodwill and meaning they've built up with their product over years with marketing dollars and press. If you're not there yet, your brand or logo isn't doing you any good, but may be hurting you. The profile photo is a cleverly designed trust factor. It's why Airbnb added it, which was genius. Seeing a human face sends a stronger trust signal than a logo. It's why I decided to include my face on the cover of this book.

7.13 SHOULD I CHARGE FOR EXTRA GUESTS?

Maybe. Most hosts only charge for an extra guest after the number of beds you have times two (4 beds x 2 = 8 guests). By charging for extra guests you are making your property more expensive, thus making your listing less flexible. That's not necessarily a bad thing. In an ideal world. we'd rent to as few guests as possible for maximum revenue. If you have a popular listing, you are more able to make your listing less flexible without risk. How much more does it cost you for each additional guest? Are you setting up an extra bed, or is the extra guest going to sleep next to someone else in a bed? Do you want two people per bed? All things to consider. Something else to consider is the cost per guest of your nightly rate and the incremental cost if you add an extra guest fee. If you rent a $200 per night 2-bedroom home with occupancy for two, that's $100 per guest. If you decide to raise your occupancy to four, then your incremental cost (the extra guest charge) should be less than $100 because the value received is not the same as a private bedroom. You could imagine the group could get a 3- or 4-bedroom home for $300 or $400, respectively and might choose that over you.

7.14 WHAT IS THE BEST CANCELLATION POLICY?

While I do believe you're given a slight search rank boost when you choose the most flexible cancellation policy, there are two concepts that come into play here. *The Flexibility Concept* and *One-of-a-Hundred*. *The Flexibility Concept* says that you can choose the strictest policy due to your listing's popularity without any negative effect on your occupancy or rates. *One-of-a-Hundred* says that this one decision is not going to have a meaningful impact on your business; instead, the cumulative effect of the hundred decisions you make to run your business will.

Another reason why I prefer a flexible cancelation policy is that, even if you have a strict one, the guest will often try to get back their money. They'll call you. They'll call Airbnb. Airbnb will call you, sometimes more than once. This is all a waste of time. And if you have a popular listing, those dates will probably get rebooked. At a reduced price, probably. But should you be taking direct bookings, and the guest finds your brand on Google, your online reputation is at risk if you don't return the money. One upset individual can cause a lot of damage. I know. All business owners do.

The reality is that cancellations don't happen often. Some markets do have higher cancellation rates, and they can be extremely frustrating. If you're in this type of market, then it may make sense to have a stricter cancellation policy.

7.15 HOW CAN I GET MORE MEDIUM-TERM BOOKINGS?

There is some confusion regarding this term. In the short-term rental industry, a long-term booking is one month or longer. But, there are also medium-term rentals (MTRs) specifically focusing on multi-month long reservations. For the purposes of this answer, I'm referring to all reservations from about three weeks to three months long. As a monthly Airbnb guest with more than 100 reservations under my belt, I might be the most qualified person in the world to answer this question. And at the end, I'll tell you why you may not *want* medium-term bookings, depending on your motivation.

Medium-term guests value different amenities. Be sure to add in these:

- Office space or desk with comfortable office chair
- Fully-stocked kitchen w/ pots, pans, blender, strainer, Tupperware, can opener, etc.
- An optimal sleeping experience including black out curtains and soft and hard pillows
- Closet space with hangers and drawers
- Large shower head, good water pressure, and shelf in shower
- Large, smart TV
- Pet-, infant-, child-, family-friendly space (optional, but recommended)

A lot of the above is focused on making the guest feel like they're *not* travelling. This is always important, but it becomes essential for medium-term reservations. **Annoyances for short-term stays becomes issues for medium-term reservations**. Examples include a confusing TV remote, noisy sleep environment, uncomfortable chairs, or low-quality/missing common kitchen amenities. These annoyances will lose you reservation extensions and repeat business. Speaking of which, medium-term reservations are more likely to extend so be proactive in offering an extension as soon as you confirm they're a good guest.

These reservations may mean less work, but understand that it's also less revenue, due to customary discounts ranging from 25-50%. Medium-term reservations also create significantly more wear and tear inside your space because these guests are spending more time inside. Your utility costs may also increase.

7.16 HOW THE HELL DO I GET IN TOUCH WITH AIRBNB?

The problem nowadays is not getting in touch with them. You can do that. The problem is getting anything above the bare minimum level of service. Back when I worked there, all employees had to do some customer service so we could empathize with the hosts. Oh, how times have changed!

You can contact Airbnb on Twitter by tagging @AirbnbHelp. Initially you'll get an auto response to send them a private message, and they do respond to those messages with a human.

Of course, you can call them. If you're a Superhost, call from the registered number on your account as there's a dedicated customer support line which usually has minimal wait time. I've found the trick to getting a helpful agent is to call back at different times and on different days until you hear someone that you think works for Airbnb and not an outsourced call center. This doesn't necessarily mean working hours in the USA as I've had luck getting one of the good agents at odd hours. Call center workers are going to be limited in what they can solve for you on the phone.

You can also try the Airbnb Community Center, which is an underutilized tool. Many times, hosts have answered my question better and more quickly than if I had reached out to customer service. There are also Airbnb-employee admins working there who you can sometimes message or tag in your post.

Lastly, and to be used sparingly, you can search LinkedIn for Airbnb employees. Go to the Airbnb company page and click to view the employees who have decided to associate their profile with the company. Don't spam them. Be targeted about which department you're trying to find and send specific persons a message and only when you're in a dire situation.

If it's a really unjust situation, I recommend reaching out to Elliot Advocacy, a consumer advocacy group that does great work and has worked with short-term rental hosts in the past.

7.17 HOW DO I GET MORE RESERVATIONS DURING SLOW SEASON?

Slow season requires advance planning. A successful strategy balances listing flexibility, calendar availability, and price.

First, you need to ensure that your calendar is open for bookings before the competition's calendar is open. Your *next* slow season should always be open. If your busy and slow season are each six months long, at the beginning of busy season your calendar should be open for the next 12 months.

Second, you need to ensure your prices are low enough. During slow season, our goal is occupancy maximization. That means soaking up all the early bookings at rates just slightly lower than our competition. In general, I've noticed that lowering the price is the most effective strategy for most hosts during slow season and not because it's obvious but because hosts tend to not lower it enough. It's likely you'll have a rate 50% of high season, but you'll still earn more than if you were to rent your property on an annual basis.

Third, slow season is time to increase our pool of FPGs by making our listing more flexible (remember *The Flexibility Concept?*). We can do that by relaxing our cancellation policy, lowering the number of minimum nights, increasing discounts for longer reservations, removing our extra guest or pet fees, etc.

If you're currently in slow season and your calendar is totally empty, your best course of action is to lower your price to your minimum for both weekends and weekdays for the next few weeks. Next year, you should keep an eye on future occupancy and plan at least 90 days out.

Here are some additional tips and reminders for slow season:

- Open up your listing on other niche OTAs.
- List on the OTAs of event spaces like Splacer and Peerspace
- Convert more lookers into bookers. Try specifying an additional discount in the title or summary text to encourage the inquiry, like "XTRA 10% OFF Until March"
- Message prior guests reminding them of your space and the 'friends and family' discount

7.18 SHOULD I LIST ON MULTIPLE VACATION RENTAL SITES OR OTAS?

This has become a tough question and can end up being somewhat of a personal preference. In the past, my answer for most hosts was to stick with Airbnb. Today, I think it makes sense for most to consider listing on various OTAs.

If you venture to various platforms, understand that it complicates your life. If you list on three OTAs, that means you need to find tools that integrate with all three platforms so that there are no double-bookings, overlaps, or other mishaps. And that's three times the chance one of those tools encounters a technical glitch. You need to create and manage three (probably mediocre performing) listings.

The argument for listing on a second platform is if your area is niche. If it is a family retreat vacation, a spiritual yoga center, a local destination, or a destination for chefs, etc. then you may consider listing on the vacation rental platform that these subgroups of FPGs use.

In the past I said that you should list on one vacation rental site, probably Airbnb. For some hosts, this is still true. But there's more nuance to this answer today, especially if you decide direct booking is a viable option for you.

If you simply want to list on another big OTA, then I suggest you only open your calendar on the second platform to the next 30 days. You don't need a booking on an alternate platform three months out. Just use it as a sort of extra insurance for available and near-term days that are increasingly less likely to be booked the closer they get.

7.19 HOW MUCH DOES INTERIOR DESIGN MATTER?

This much: a lot. It's the ultimate factor. The listing with nicer interior design will always win. It's the same reason why the most beautiful photos tend to be from famous Instagrammers. In our digital world, the best-looking photos win.

Interior design comes with a cost. It also allows you to charge higher nightly rates. People with money tend to like, and be able to spend money on, nicer things. But it doesn't have to cost a lot. Here are some ideas to get you started.

- Artificial orchids or fake plants can look nice in any rental.
- Change your light fixtures, think of them as illuminated artwork.
- White bedding is the default. It communicates cleanliness.
- Add artwork to your walls. Make sure it is inoffensive. Nature is a good theme. So are (vintage) maps. The bigger the better. HUGE!

- Use super bright white paint with a matte finish on the walls and ceiling. Use the same color for both as this blurs the lines between wall and ceiling making the space feel larger.
- Or, try some wallpaper or paint one wall with a coordinating color.
- Try to incorporate natural materials that have a timeless appeal (marble, stone, wood).
- Add extra pillows on the sofa or beds. The more the merrier. Really.
- Change out the flooring (in one room only if your budget allows).
- Mirrors make all rooms seem bigger, lighter, and more open.
- Put everything you can on a dimmer and use warm light bulbs.
- When outfitting shelf space, no matter which room it's in, the rule is nothing smaller than a cantaloupe.

I'll stop there. Honestly, it's not my specialty. There are two remote interior design firms that I'm aware of but without personal experience. They are www.Havenly.com and www.Decorilla.com. If you try them out, do please let me know of your experience.

7.20 SHOULD I BRAND MY RENTAL?

You should only brand your rental if you accept direct bookings and can be found online under that branding.

If you're neither of these things, delete the brand from your title and text. I often see hosts start their listing title with a cute brand name. This is a mistake because it's not communicating anything to the FPG and, as we already know, the title is for your FPG.

It pains me when I search online for a branded OTA listing, and then it either doesn't exist or something else unrelated already has the name. I kid you not, I just *optimized* a listing, and their unique name is identical to a nursing home in the same city which has claimed the Google My Business listing in search.

If you decide to create an online presence, there are levels to branding. You can create a logo, social media profiles, or a website as we discussed in *Part 6: Direct Bookings*. If you do these things, you should put your brand name in your listing. You can also think about other unique ways to get your brand name in front of your guest with branded slippers, shampoo bottles, business cards, etc. You should start signing your guest messages with the brand name.

7.21 HELP! I CAN'T FIND MY LISTING ON THE OTA.

Most of the time this is user error, and I'll attempt to solve it for you now. First, copy your listing URL, open up an incognito browser window, paste in the URL, and press enter. If you see your listing, then it is public and visible online. This does *not* necessarily confirm it's visible on the OTA search or map.

Now we have to figure out why you're not finding it.

If you recently made a bunch of changes, sometimes your listing goes offline for a period of a few hours while the system processes all of them.

Go into the backend where you manage your listing and ensure that it's active and listed. It's possible you've been suspended, and, even though the listing is visible and public, it's not visible on the map. Maybe you needed to add some tax info or there is a new requirement to fulfill. This is uncommon.

If you're in a market with a maximum number of bookable nights, and you've already reached that yearly cap, you will not be able to find yourself on the OTA map.

Ensure that you're correctly located on the map. Check the address and also the pin location. If this is off, then you would not see your listing where you expect to.

Next step is to go to the OTA and perform a search without dates. If you've been searching with dates, you may not appear because of your minimum night rules, especially if you have various, or existing, reservations.

Zoom the map but not too close. Select maximum number of bedrooms, bathrooms, and guests you allow. If you're still showing hundreds of listings either zoom the map or select additional filters you know are active on your listing. On Airbnb this might be Instant Book, type of place, Superhost, and/or common amenities you've confirmed are selected for your listing.

In my experience, calling Airbnb won't be much help and might take weeks before you get an answer, so it's better to troubleshoot yourself.

7.22 WHAT IS THE NEW LISTING CALENDAR STRATEGY?

This is a strategy I developed for all new listings to increase the likelihood of a strong start. It recognizes that there's a portion of guests who will not book a listing with no reviews. If your calendar is fully open from the start, it hurts your algorithmic stats and lowers your conversion rate. We instead want to dangle a carrot for the algorithm. This strategy was developed for Airbnb but can be applied to any OTA. Here's the strategy:

1. Only open your calendar for the next three weeks
2. Lower your minimum nights to one
3. Set maximum nights at five
4. Reduce price to your minimum or offer a 30% discount, whichever is lower

Even experienced hosts should use this strategy because every new space is different, and you don't yet know if there are things you or your team has overlooked. The guest will know they're getting a great deal, so do not go out of your way to let them know. After all, you don't actually know what your space will rent for once it's a mature listing.

The strategy is designed to get long, positive reviews from our first three reservations. Whether it influences search or guest booking behavior, listings with longer reviews do better. If you know the guest had a good stay, you should reach out to them after a few days soliciting the review as the first ones are super important.

Upon the third, positive review you can open your calendar and raise prices in line with occupancy as we discussed in *Part 5: Pricing.*

Part **8**

HOW TO RANK #1 ON AIRBNB

Welcome to the final section! Below are the top 13 most-important ranking factors on Airbnb, in order of importance. They're based on the following:

- My observed experience interacting with the platform as a guest, host, and property manager
- My interpretation of ongoing platform changes to Airbnb
- Data gathered from consulting data scientists

It need not be mentioned again that on Airbnb, as well as the other major OTAs, search is not static. You are never guaranteed a first-place position for the majority of searches in your area.

1.
Number of Reviews

All else being equal, the listing with more reviews will rank higher. All ranking comes down to whether or not you're making the OTA money. That can show itself positively via actual revenue generated through reservations or negatively via poor guest experiences like cancellations or low-quality homes. From the OTA perspective, you can assume that they want to favor those hosts who are loyal to them. The life of a listing on Airbnb is about a year which factors into this metric. If you're only using one OTA like Airbnb, you probably have more reviews than your competition. A listing with more reviews is also a good indication that the host does not accept money outside the platform.

2.
Review Rating

A listing with 100 reviews and a 4.7 rating could rank higher than a listing with 10 reviews and a 5.0 rating. Another reason why Airbnb prefers number of reviews over ratings is because they know that, by the time the listing with 10 reviews gets to 100, they could have a lower rating, let's say a 4.6. If that's the case, an early guest is really booking a 4.6 home disguised initially as a 5.0 home. This is mismatched expectations. But that 4.7 rated rental with 100 reviews, the guest knows they are booking a 4.7 home, and the expectations are matched. This is why Airbnb prefers more reviews even if the rating is lower. However, the rating is still incredibly important and only second to the number of reviews. A positive 5-star review means the guest is likely to return to Airbnb for a future trip and tell their friends about the service.

I've noticed that listings with longer written reviews tend to rank higher. I haven't been able to confidently attribute the ranking factor to the longer review or if the longer review is simply a consequence of a great listing which tends to rank higher anyway. Or it could be that FPGs place more confidence and, thus, convert higher, on listings with lengthy reviews. Regardless, a focus on my strategies is not only encouraging a review but giving the guest something extra to write about in their long review.

3.
Acceptance Rate

Airbnb values a listing more when it accepts a higher percentage of booking requests, ideally every booking. This is why you're given a search boost for turning on Instant Booking. It doesn't have to do with the Instant Booking as much as your acceptance rate being 100%. Your listing metrics are always compared to your local competition.

4.
Map Location

A lot of your search rank position simply has to do with where your rental is located on the map. Not all guests use the map, but Airbnb always uses the map to rank listings, based on the searched location. Listings in more highly booked neighborhoods will show up higher in search. It's a powerful strategy to move your listings towards these hot spots, but not by too much. Don't be deceptive. Perform a search on your city and your neighborhood to view which areas are being highlighted on the Airbnb map.

5.
Conversion Rate

This is one that you may not have thought about. You'll notice that views are NOT on this list. A lot of hosts focus on views, but this is a waste of time and energy. While views are a ranking factor, Airbnb would rather you get few views because every guest who lands on your listing makes a reservation. Think about it: if you're an average listing you will probably get many views because you have much calendar availability. Airbnb now publishes the conversion rate in their hosting dashboard. In everything you do, focus on converting the FPG.

6.
Returning Guests

Airbnb loves returning guests. I'm sure other platforms do, too. On Airbnb there's even a metric for returning guests on the hosting dashboard. If you have a returning guest book on the platform, that means you are not transacting off the platform after that guest stays with you one time. That means more money for Airbnb which means higher ranking for you. The great news here is that it's low-hanging fruit as the number of returning guests is tiny. You probably need only one per year in most markets to be ahead of the curve.

Sometimes repeat guests prefer to book direct, and that is ok and allowed if the guest suggests it. But, why not take that bonus, positive review. They've already stayed with you, they've probably also positively reviewed you, and you can expect another positive review. They're more likely to review you, pushing up your average review rate which I suspect is also a ranking factor. That bonus, positive review may be worth more to you than saving the commission fee.

7.
Fewest Cancellations

Cancellations are the bane of Airbnb. Hotels don't cancel guest reservations. Vacation rentals do. Airbnb used to offer a 120% bonus to any cancelled guest. So if your reservation was $1,000 and got cancelled, Airbnb would send you $1,200 for the headache and because they know you were likely otherwise to never come back to the platform. Airbnb doesn't do that anymore, but if you're the host cancelling on guests, even once per year, this is very, very bad. The standard here is zero cancellations. I've personally experienced a large dip in ranking with one cancellation, even if it was technically allowed. Other hosts have noticed other oddities like their listings disappearing from search results.

8.
Review Rate

On Airbnb, about 70% of guests submit a review after their stay, but this ranges from around 55% to 80% across markets. Even though Airbnb doesn't publish this statistic, it looks like it is a ranking factor. We've covered many strategies in this book on how to get a higher review rate, but I'll share another with your now. If you do a live check-out, or your cleaner arrives before the guest checks out, you can personally ask the guest to leave a review. Change your check-out time to an hour earlier so that the guest is able to leave a review prior to leaving your property. In my testing, this early check-out time does not affect your booking rate. This also allows you to approve a late check-out request giving you some added goodwill at the time of the review (along with the departure goody bag you offer).

9.
Wishlist Saves

This is one of the few things Airbnb has stated gives you a search rank boost. In Airbnb's words,

> **"** When travelers add your listing to their wishlist, it does indeed help your search ranking!" [8]

---

[8] https://blog.atairbnb.com/search/

Airbnb does want the guest to interact with your listing whether that's a message, an inquiry, or a wishlist save.

10.
Instant Book

❝ You'll also be higher in search results",

says Airbnb, by turning on Instant Book. They're doing this for, you guessed it, more revenue and a more pleasant guest experience. I remember being an employee at Airbnb when they were rolling it out. To be honest, I didn't like it. I was thinking of traditional Airbnb where there's a connection between the host and the guest that makes the experience seem more special and personal. I think this is their competitive advantage. But Instant Book was a natural evolution. The search boost for turning this feature on is much less than you think and even less if you're accepting nearly all booking requests anyways. There are tons of very successful listings without Instant Book activated, including mine. (I sometimes turn it on in line with *The Flexibility Concept*.)

11.
Response Time

Given how ubiquitous automated messages are, this seems to have lost importance in the search rankings, but it's still relevant and easy. The public metric shown on P3 of your listing is a response time of within an hour. However, that is the bare minimum. It's known that quicker responses are more likely to get the confirmed reservation for any single inquiry. You should aim to respond, at least to the first inquiry, within minutes, and you can set this automatically within your chosen PMS.

12.
Flexible Cancellation Policy

Although Airbnb has never officially said that a flexible cancelation policy has a positive effect on your search results, my observation and data correlation says it does for a few reasons. First, Airbnb has stated they

> **❝** encourage more bookings-especially for more flexible listings." [9]

Second, it creates a better guest experience, and Airbnb favors guest experience over host experience (in other words, it's more of a priority to attract guests than hosts). Third, some of the changes that Airbnb makes on the website are suggestive of a preference for listings with flexible cancelation policies. As we're towards the bottom of the ranking factors, this is not likely to have a meaningful effect on your ranking, so only do this if it makes sense for your situation.

13.
Calendar Availability

The more availability you have, the better in terms of search. That's because you are giving the guest more opportunity to interact with your listing (not only book it, but also view it, save it to their wishlist, etc.). Imagine if every listing set its calendar to only be bookable this and next month. Any guest searching for dates three months from now would not have

---

[9] https://blog.atairbnb.com/guest-cancellation/

any options thus making the OTA less competitive. Lost revenue. Of course, that's not the reality. The reality is the opposite. Most hosts have their calendars open for 12 months and 99% of intent-driven searches (searches likely to result in a booking) are for dates within the next five months. This is why calendar availability is last on the list. Over the long-term, you might move the needle slightly in your favor.

Did you notice I didn't include price? If I had, it would be number one. Price has the single biggest impact on your search rank. The thing is, we're not trying to lower our price. To the contrary, we're trying to raise it. While it's a good tool to have as a last resort, competing on price is not a winning strategy.

FINAL NOTES FROM THE AUTHOR

I truly hope that you found immense value in this book. I have a request and an offer. If you want to get in touch with me, you can do so by emailing Danny@OptimizeMyBnb.com. Praise, criticism, typos (I hope not!), introducing yourself—all are welcomed and appreciated. I want to request that you leave me a book review on the platform you used to purchase this book. Just as reviews significantly help your Airbnb listing, they significantly help me. You can also follow me on my travels around the world via my personal Instagram, website blog, or YouTube all under my online persona at dannybooboo.

Daniel V. Rusteen

Be sure to check my website occasionally for all the new and (I hope) exciting stuff I'm up to. As the years go on, I realize more and more that I'm in the STR industry for life. Let's do this together.

Connect with me on:

www.instagram.com/OptimizeMyAirbnb

www.youtube.com/c/OptimizeMyAirbnb

www.twitter.com/OptimizeAirbnb

www.pinterest.com/OptimizeMyBnb

www.linkedin.com/company/OptimizeMyAirbnb

www.facebook.com/OptimizeMyAirbnb

www.OptimizeMyBnb.com

I love and try to respond to all comments!

But please ensure you're asking something that can be appropriately answered via a comment (i.e. it doesn't require a conversation or in-depth explanation). I'm a small team here :)

You can find relevant information as it relates to the book on the dedicated webpage:

www.OptimizeMyBnb.com/Profitable-Properties

If you would like personalized help, you have a few options. You can purchase a consultation call, Super Host Optimization (SHO), Optimized Host, or lifetime access to my course Optimized Business. You can also join my YouTube channel as a paid member for a nominal monthly fee where I host monthly Q&A's. On a case-by-case basis I offer one-on-one paid mentorship for a period of three months or until your third review.

The Profitable Properties "Optimized Business" Course

SCAN ME

More books from the author

Optimize YOUR Bnb:
The Definitive Guide For Ranking #1 In Airbnb Search

Watch the trailer on the book website:
www.OptimizeYOURbnb.com

For Travelers (and Digital Nomads) Not Tourists:
A Guide On How To Connect With a Destination For a More Fulfilling Travel Experience

CPSIA information can be obtained
at www.ICGtesting.com
Printed in the USA
BVHW030509190423
662564BV00003B/358